READERS'

CONSULTANT EDITOR: NICOLAS TREDELL

Published

Carl Plasa	Tony Morrison: *Beloved*
Carl Plasa	Jean Rhys: *Wide Sargasso Sea*
Nicholas Potter	Shakespeare: *Antony and Cleopatra*
Nicholas Potter	Shakespeare: *Othello*
Steven Price	The Plays, Screenplays and Films of David Mamet
Andrew Radford	Victorian Sensation Fiction
Berthold Schoene–Harwood	Mary Shelley: *Frankenstein*
Nick Selby	T. S. Eliot: *The Waste Land*
Nick Selby	Herman Melville: *Moby Dick*
Nick Selby	The Poetry of Walt Whitman
David Smale	Salman Rushdie: *Midnight's Chidren – The Satanic Verses*
Patsy Stoneman	Emily Brontë: *Wuthering Heights*
Susie Thomas	Hanif Kureishi
Nicolas Tredell	F. Scott Fitzgerald: *The Great Gatsby*
Nicolas Tredell	Joseph Conrad: *Heart of Darkness*
Nicolas Tredell	Charles Dickens: *Great Expectations*
Nicolas Tredell	William Faulkner: *The Sound and the Fury – As I Lay Dying*
Nicolas Tredell	Shakespeare: *Macbeth*
Nicolas Tredell	The Fiction of Martin Amis
Matthew Woodcock	Shakespeare: *Henry V*
Angela Wright	Gothic Fiction

Forthcoming

Thomas P. Adler	Tennesse Williams: *A Streetcar named Desire – Cat on a Hot Tin Roof*
Pascale Aebischer	Jacobean Drama
Brian Barker	Science Fiction
Annika Bautz	Jane Austen: *Sense and Sensibility – Pride and Prejudice – Emma*
Matthew Beedham	The Novels of Kazuo Ishiguro
Jodi–Anne George	*Beowulf*
Sarah Haggarty & Jon Mee	Willam Blake: *Songs of Innocence and Experience*
Matthew Jordan	Milton: *Paradise Lost*
Stephen Regan	The Poetry of Philip Larkin
Mardi Stewart	Victorian Women's Poetry
Michael Whitworth	Virginia Woolf: *Mrs Dalloway*
Gina Wisker	The Fiction of Margaret Atwood
Gillian Woods	Shakespeare: *Romeo and Juliet*

Readers' Guides to Essential Criticism
Series Standing Order ISBN 1–4039–0108–2
(outside North America only)

You can receive future titles int his series as they are published by placing a standing order. Please contact your bookseller or, in the case of difficulty, write to us at the address below with your name and address, the title of the series and the ISBN quoted above.

Customer Services Department, Palgrave Macmillan Ltd
Houndmills, Basingstoke, Hampshire RG21 6XS, England

William Wordsworth
The Prelude

TIM MILNES

Consultant editor: Nicolas Tredell

palgrave
macmillan

First published 2009 by
PALGRAVE MACMILLAN

Palgrave Macmillan in the UK is an imprint of Macmillan Publishers Limited,
registered in England, company number 785998, of Houndmills, Basingstoke,
Hampshire RG21 6XS.

Palgrave Macmillan in the US is a division of St Martin's Press LLC,
175 Fifth Avenue, New York, NY 10010.

Palgrave Macmillan is the global academic imprint of the above companies
and has companies and representatives throughout the world.

Palgrave® and Macmillan® are registered trademarks in the United States,
the United Kingdom, Europe and other countries.

ISBN-13: 978–0–230–50082–2 hardback
ISBN-10: 0–230–50082–X hardback
ISBN-13: 978–0–230–50083–9 paperback
ISBN-10: 0–230–50083–8 paperback

This book is printed on paper suitable for recycling and made from fully
managed and sustained forest sources. Logging, pulping and manufacturing
processes are expected to conform to the environmental regulations of the
country of origin.

A catalogue record for this book is available from the British Library.

A catalog record for this book is available from the Library of Congress.

10 9 8 7 6 5 4 3 2 1
18 17 16 15 14 13 12 11 10 09

Printed and bound in China

Aan my vrou, Michelle,
met al my liefde.

Contents

NOTE

Dates of writers, critics, and other significant figures have been given in the Guide whenever possible, but in some cases these are unavailable.

Introduction: The 'Huge and Mighty Forms' of *The Prelude*

The object of this *Guide* is to introduce the reader to key critical readings of the great autobiographical poem by William Wordsworth (1770–1850), *The Prelude*. Commenced in 1798 and periodically expanded and revised until Wordsworth's death in 1850, the work was never published during the poet's lifetime, although the manuscript was known to a small circle of friends and relatives, including his sister Dorothy (1771–1855), his friend and collaborator Samuel Taylor Coleridge (1772–1834), and the essayist Thomas De Quincey (1785–1859). Despite this history (or perhaps because of it), *The Prelude* has come to assume a central place in Wordsworth's literary output. Stated barely, the synopsis of the poem sounds unremarkable: in fourteen books (thirteen in the 1805 version), it charts the poet's intellectual and emotional development from childhood to early adulthood, encompassing his earliest recollections of growing up in the Lake District and his time at school and Cambridge University, his time spent in London and travelling through France, and his first-hand experiences of the immediate aftermath of the French Revolution in the early 1790s.

As anyone already familiar with the poem will testify, however, this summary conveys nothing of the qualities that have caused controversy and debate among readers for over two centuries. For these readers (both supporters and detractors), it is in the intense and lyrical passages of self-reflection, where the poet meditates upon his own consciousness, and upon the relationship between imagination, nature, and society, that the true interest of the poem resides. And yet, for many, the density and opacity of these passages can be as overwhelming as the mountain that rears up – in one of the poem's most celebrated sequences – to pursue the boy Wordsworth across Ullswater:

> ■ a huge cliff,
> As if with voluntary power instinct,
> Upreared its head. I struck, and struck again,
> And, growing still in stature, the huge cliff
> Rose up between me and the stars, and still
> With measured motion like a living thing
> Strode after me.
> [...]

for many days my brain
Worked with a dim and undetermined sense
Of unknown modes of being. In my thoughts
There was a darkness – call it solitude
Or blank desertion – no familiar shapes
Of hourly objects, images of trees,
Of sea or sky, no colours of green fields,
But huge and mighty forms that do not live
Like living men moved slowly through my mind
By day, and were the trouble of my dreams. □

(1805, I, 405–412; 418–426)

Confronted with such lines for the first time, the reader might be forgiven for experiencing his or her own sense of 'darkness' or 'blank desertion'. Certainly, *The Prelude* makes few concessions to its reader. The things to which it ultimately refers, the 'huge and mighty forms that do not live / Like living men', appear shrouded in obscurity, accessible only dimly, through an 'undetermined sense / Of unknown modes of being'. Rather than unpacking itself before the reader, *The Prelude* holds its meanings in reserve, promising riches that somehow lie beyond the immediate significance of the words on the page. The question of how to respond to this aura of an evasive, transcendent meaning in *The Prelude* is one of the central questions behind a long and diverse history of criticism and commentary on the poem, a tradition which – in its myriad attempts to 'understand', 'interpret', 'appreciate', 'psycho-analyse', 'deconstruct', 'gender', 'historicise', and 'green' the poem – is now, with consummate irony, every bit as daunting as the poem itself. Perhaps more than most then, the student of *The Prelude* is a student in need of a guide to criticism of *The Prelude*. Accordingly, the principal aim of this book is to provide the reader with a framework for *Prelude* commentary and scholarship by outlining the theoretical and historical contexts of the 'major' critical trends that have influenced it.

Before proceeding further, I wish to take a leaf out of Wordsworth's book and articulate the scope of this *Guide* negatively. In other words, I want to begin by clarifying what this book is *not*. First, at the risk of stating the obvious, it is not a guide to Wordsworth criticism, but to *Prelude* criticism. With a few notable exceptions, it does not discuss at length studies of Wordsworth that have chosen not to focus their attention on *The Prelude*. Second, the present volume is not and cannot be an *exhaustive* survey of *Prelude* criticism. *The Prelude* is a key text in the canon of English Literature: more than this, as one recent commentator has noted, it is a significant text in the creation of the discipline itself.[1] Since its publication in 1850, a great deal of ink has been spilt on the poem – more, far more, than it is feasible for a companion such as this to survey. In selecting the critical texts to be discussed, I have had to strike a balance between range and depth. What the reader will find below, then, is a guide to '*Essential*' (at least, what this author feels to be 'essential'), but not *all*, *Prelude* criticism. To explore this landscape further, readers are encouraged to consult the reading lists provided at the end of the book.

Although it lay unpublished until 1850, the existence of *The Prelude* was something of an open secret in early nineteenth-century literary circles. As I detail in Chapter 1, however, the existence of (at least four) different versions of the poem was less well known. The only text widely available until 1928 – the fourteen-book *Prelude* – met with a mixed reception. Early reviewers were perplexed by the poem's peculiar fusion of the mundane and the transcendental, the personal and the sublime. In the second section of Chapter 1, I trace how critics such as Leslie Stephen (1832–1904) and Matthew Arnold (1822–88) attempted to wrest *The Prelude* from the grips of the 'Wordsworthians', a group of enthusiasts who, inspired by John Stuart Mill (1806–73), championed the poem as a guide to living a good life. Arnold's argument that Wordsworth is fundamentally a poet of nature was in turn contested by the 'aesthetic', impressionistic reading of the poem proffered by Walter Pater (1839–94).

The debate between Arnold and Stephen as to whether Wordsworth is a nature poet or a moral philosopher writing in verse swiftly becomes a key question for *Prelude* commentary, as does the problematic relationship between the poem's quotidian or 'natural' and transcendental or 'supernatural' aspects. In Chapter 2, I examine the attempt of A.C. Bradley (1851–1935), in his influential *Oxford Lectures on Poetry* (1909), to move beyond these perspectives by stressing the poem's philosophical profundity and its sublime and unparaphrasable qualities. I also discuss the ramifications of two publications from this period: the revelatory biography by Émile Legouis (1861–1937), *La Jeunesse de William Wordsworth* (1896), and the 1928 edition of the 1805 *Prelude* (the first published) by Ernest de Selincourt (1870–1943). These works not only spurred new interest in biographical/psychoanalytical approaches and textual scholarship respectively, they also helped to move *The Prelude* to the centre of Wordsworth studies.

Around mid-century, the study of English literature was increasingly polarized between 'critics', who treated literary works formally, as aesthetic objects, and 'scholars' or intellectual historians, who attempted to understand literature within its historical, cultural, or intellectual contexts. Accordingly, Chapter 3 assesses the impact of the 'New Criticism' upon studies of the style of *The Prelude* by critics such as William Empson (1906–84), Herbert Lindenberger (born 1929), and Christopher Ricks (born 1933), before turning to the rise of the History of Ideas. Within this latter tradition, Morse Peckham and Robert Langbaum (born 1924), building upon earlier work by Arthur Beatty and Newton Stallknecht, argue that *The Prelude* signals a decisive break from the intellectual traditions of eighteenth-century Britain, while M.H. Abrams (born 1912) makes a strong case for reading the poem as the culmination of a late Enlightenment drive 'to naturalize the supernatural and to humanize the divine'. The same drive is also identified by Geoffrey Hartman (born 1929) as the energy behind the poem's Hegelian 'dialectic of consciousness', a concept derived from the German idealist philosopher Georg Wilhelm Friedrich Hegel (1770–1830). Harold Bloom (born 1930) gives this 'dialectic' a distinct twist towards the theories of the founder of psychoanalysis, Sigmund Freud (1856–1939). As one of the most successful and influential attempts to account for the poem's 'natural supernaturalism' and 'poetic philosophy', Hartman's reading of *The Prelude* in his 1964 *Wordsworth's Poetry 1787–1814* stands at a pivotal point in the history of Wordsworth criticism.

The coming of the culture wars of the 1970s, 1980s, and 1990s transformed *Prelude* criticism. During the 1970s, critics influenced by the ideas and methods of feminism, deconstruction, and the psychoanalytic theories of Jacques Lacan (1901–81), rejected many of the assumptions that had underpinned earlier readings of the poem. As I demonstrate in Chapter 4, such commentators no longer saw the 'author' as the focal point of literary criticism. On the contrary, they saw this category as bound up with the very notion of the stable, autonomous 'subject' that they now sought to question. Gradually eroding the conventional interpretative triad of 'author/work/world' with one closer to 'discourse/text/history,' these critical movements came to view *The Prelude* – one of the great reflexive narratives of the self – as a seminal text in the creation of western ideology of the subject. Thus, Paul de Man (1919–83) argues that the poem testifies to a predicament of writing, not consciousness, while Frances Ferguson (born 1947) doubts whether the language of the poem could ever live up to the Romantic totems of 'sincerity' and 'organic form'. Feminist commentators like Mary Jacobus, meanwhile, frequently use the techniques of deconstruction and psychoanalysis to detect in *The Prelude* concealed anxieties about gender and the 'legitimacy' of autobiographical poetry – or, in the cases of Gayatri Chakravorty Spivak (born 1942) and Margaret Homans respectively, to speculate on how the poem appropriates the voice of the 'female' and overcomes the Oedipal complex at its core. Indeed, psychoanalytical readings of the poem, earlier pioneered by critics such as Herbert Read (1893–1968) and F.W. Bateson (1901–78), continue to gain currency in this period. Accordingly, I close this chapter by examining two critics – Richard Oronato and David Ellis (born 1939) – who read the poem as an early example of psychotherapy, a kind of self-analysis in verse.

Like psychoanalysis, the emergence of New Historicism in the 1980s has had a considerable and sustained effect on how modern criticism has come to read *The Prelude*. The defining feature of this family of approaches is its refusal to treat the poem as a purely formal entity. Rather than see it as possessing the completed (or even fragmented) unity of the aesthetic object then, historicists view *The Prelude* as first and foremost a product of historical discourse. Chapter 5 sheds light on the three principal modes of New Historicist commentary on *The Prelude*: the search for a social and historical context (pioneered, among others, by Marilyn Butler [born 1937] and Nicholas Roe); the identification of 'displacement' as the key strategy of the 'Romantic ideology' (central to the work of Jerome McGann [born 1937], James Chandler, David Simpson [born 1951], and Marjorie Levinson [born 1951]); and a final elimination of formalism from literary criticism by the application of the concept of 'historicity' (found in the work of Alan Liu [born 1953] and Clifford Siskin). As becomes clear, each of these modes has very different implications for what a 'historicist' reading of *The Prelude* might look like.

In the final chapter, I make a brief survey of the main developments in *Prelude* criticism over the past fifteen years or so. Despite having had their theoretical foundations attacked over the years, the techniques and methods of deconstruction and New Historicism continue to pervade the field, as is evident in the work of Richard Bourke and Geraldine Friedman. Alternative perspectives, however, have recently emerged in a rapidly changing critical landscape. The first of these is a resurgence in 'formalist' approaches, presented most forcibly in the work of Susan Wolfson (born 1948) and Thomas Pfau (born 1960). Both writers present the case for what I call a 'neoformalist' approach to *The Prelude*, treating the poem not as a finished aesthetic object (as traditional formalists tended to do), but as a work that itself engages with the very problems raised by the agency of form in understanding the construction of subjectivity and history. A second, important critical current to have surfaced in recent years is 'green' criticism, or 'ecocriticism'. This tendency reverses the prioritization of 'history' over 'nature' enforced by New Historicism. The result, as demonstrated in the work of Jonathan Bate (born 1958), Karl Kroeber (born 1926), and James McKusick (born 1956), is that the question of humanity's relationship to the natural environment re-emerges as an urgent and salient (rather then merely displaced) concern of Wordsworth in *The Prelude*. In the closing section of this chapter, I turn to two focal topics of current *Prelude* commentary: the poem's engagement with the question of 'vagrancy' and its relationship to contemporary discourses of space, topography, and geology. Finally, in the book's Conclusion, I consider the possibility that a rising tide of literary criticism, influenced by the French philosopher Gilles

Deleuze (1925–95), may soon lead to the widespread acceptance of a 'nomadic' *Prelude*.

By then, the study of English Literature will probably have moved on, transformed, or even fragmented, into new disciplines. The norms and practices of literary study that *The Prelude* itself helped to create may have disappeared. There can be no guarantees, of course, that *The Prelude* will continue to hold its privileged position within the canon of English Literature – nor, for that matter, is there any certainty that the canon will continue to exist in any recognisable normative or peda-gogical form (though it has proved remarkably durable so far). What is certain, however, is that *The Prelude* has already accumulated a massive body of critical texts, each of which is as revealing about the era in which it was written as it is about Wordsworth. This text is designed to guide the reader of what is arguably Wordsworth's greatest poem around that body.

CHAPTER ONE

In the Cathedral Ruins: *The Prelude* from Conception to Criticism

THE TEXTS OF *THE PRELUDE*

Few of the great works of English literature had a gestation as troubled and complex as that of *The Prelude*. Wordsworth began the poem in 1798, and would continue to work on it until his death in 1850. The fact that it was only published posthumously has meant that modern readers often come to the poem unaware that they are dealing with an unusually unstable text, one whose 'authoritative' state is the subject of ongoing debate.[1] Following the landmark edition of the poem produced by Jonathan Wordsworth, M.H. Abrams, and Stephen Gill for W.W. Norton in 1979, scholars now generally accept that Wordsworth produced at least three main 'versions' of the poem at different stages of his career: following an initial, short poem written in 1799, Wordsworth worked steadily on the project until late 1805, when he produced the first version of the full-length *Prelude* in thirteen books.[2] Extensive revisions to this manuscript in subsequent years meant that the 'official' text published in fourteen books by his executors in 1850 differs in significant respects to the poem as it had been envisaged by the writer at the age of thirty-five. And yet, until Ernest de Selincourt printed the full text of the 1805 version in 1926, the heavily revised 1850 version of *The Prelude* was the only one available to the general reader. It could be argued that the complicated history of the poem's composition reveals a truth hidden in all written compositions presented as complete 'works', namely that the (often arbitrary) decisions made by subsequent editors conceal the radical instability of the writing process. However, even allowing for this argument, *The Prelude* is peculiar, particularly among the canonical works in the language, for having no determinate shape. Students of this poem must first adjust to the awkward reality that they are dealing not with one text, but with three, perhaps four, and arguably more.[3]

The Two-Part *Prelude* (1799)

The *Prelude*'s origins lay in the walking tour of Germany that William took with his sister Dorothy and the poet Samuel Taylor Coleridge in late 1798 and early 1799. One of Wordsworth's objectives in travelling to Germany was to make progress with writing *The Recluse*, an epic poem with social and philosophical themes that he had planned with Coleridge earlier in 1798.[4] *The Recluse* was an ambitious project, conceived as a political and religious statement in verse that would rival *Paradise Lost* (1667), the epic poem by John Milton (1608–74), in scope and grandeur. In 1798, however, work on this poem was not going well – indeed, it was never completed, and only fragments of it survive today. Wordsworth's difficulties in making headway with *The Recluse* in Germany produced a spell of self-doubt and self-examination that eventually drove him to question the precise nature of his own calling as a poet. This in turn led him to search his childhood memories for reasons why he was finding it so difficult to write the poem that he hoped would be his *magnum opus*, his great work. It is his sense of failure with regard to this particular task, then, that produces the opening question of the first version of the poem, usually referred to as the 'Two-Part' or '1799' *Prelude*:

> ■ Was it for this
> That one, the fairest of all rivers, loved
> To blend his murmurs with my nurse's song,
> And from his alder shades and rocky falls,
> And from his fords and shallows, sent a voice
> That flowed along my dreams? □
>
> (1799, I, 1–6)

The word 'this' in the opening line denotes the poet's perceived failure in a task for which he had felt himself to be uniquely equipped by a childhood and youth fostered by the mountains and lakes of Cumberland, and by the river Derwent, the 'fairest of all rivers'. Was this nurturing by nature finally for nothing? Could he have been mistaken all along about his poetic vocation? As Wordsworth peers deeper into his childhood for answers to these questions, he develops the recollections that in turn form Part I of the 1799 *Prelude*. Some of these reminiscences – especially the account of taking a shepherd's boat in Patterdale to row out onto the lake under cover of darkness – have since come to be seen as key passages in the longer versions of the *Prelude*. At this point, however, Wordsworth's objective was not to write a substantial autobiographical work, but simply to answer the question with which he begins the 1799 poem. Accordingly (having by this time returned to England), he sets out to provide an answer in Part II of the poem, composed later that year. Here, having rediscovered the intuitive inner life of his youth, the poet is able to conclude the poem with a confident assertion of the providential power of nature in steering the unformed imaginative activity of youth towards the maturer poetic visions of adulthood:

> ■ if, in this time
> Of dereliction and dismay, I yet
> Despair not of our nature, but retain
> A more than Roman confidence, a faith
> That fails not, in all sorrow my support,
> The blessing of my life, the gift is yours
> Ye mountains, thine O Nature. □

(1799, II, 486–92)

In this way, *The Prelude* of 1799 falls neatly into two parts: Part I, posing the problem of clouded poetic purpose and lost direction, explores the significance of the poet's childhood education at the hands of nature; Part II extends this inquiry by moving into recollections of the writer's adolescence, and concludes with a spiritual and philosophical affirmation of his poetic vocation. In the closing stanza of Part II, Wordsworth includes a farewell passage to Coleridge, praising the other poet as one who, having sought 'The truth in solitude', is also 'The most intense of Nature's worshippers' (II, 506–507). Indeed, Coleridge is an important (albeit silent) presence throughout the 1799 *Prelude*, for it is to him that the poem is addressed. This is significant, for it was largely through the influence and encouragement of Coleridge that Wordsworth had agreed to write *The Recluse*. Coleridge believed that Wordsworth had the potential to become a Milton for the new millennium, a truly philosophical poet for a revolutionary age. Coleridge's expectations of his friend were high, perhaps too high, and it may have been in part the pressure of these great expectations that took its toll on Wordsworth's confidence. Tellingly, Coleridge's response to hearing of progress on the 1799 poem is to see it as part of the larger project: 'I long to see what you have been doing', he writes in October, 'O let it be the tail-piece of "The Recluse"!, for nothing but "The Recluse" can I hear patiently'.[5]

The Five-Book *Prelude* (1804)

Seen through his mentor's eyes then, Wordsworth's work on his autobiographical poem, for all its merits, appeared at worst a distraction and at best a mere 'prelude' to the main event of *The Recluse*. It is for this reason that Wordsworth's widow, knowing all too well of her late husband's ambivalence about the work, suggested the term 'prelude' as an appropriate title for the first published version of the poem in 1850. Wordsworth himself, determined that such an egocentric exercise ('it seems a frightful deal to say about one's self', he frets in a letter of the time[6]) should never see the light of day separated from *The Recluse*, never gave the poem a title, instead preferring to think of it as an extended poem to Coleridge. Indeed, when Wordsworth returned to the poem at the beginning of 1804, his main impetus was again to write something for his friend, who was at that time preparing to leave for what would become a two-year sojourn in Malta (Dorothy Wordsworth reports in a letter dated 13 February, William 'is chearfully engaged in composition, and goes on with great rapidity. He is writing the Poem on his own early life which is to be an appendix to the Recluse'[7]). The immediate result of this progress was a new version of *The Prelude* in five books. In the process of completing the five-book poem, Wordsworth wrote to Thomas De Quincey (then an eighteen year-old aspiring writer), outlining the work's place in his oeuvre:

■ This Poem will not be published these many years, and never during my lifetime, till I have finished a larger and more important work to which it is tributary. Of this larger work [*The Recluse*] I have written one Book and several scattered fragments: it is a moral and Philosophical Poem; the subject whatever I find most interesting in nature, Man, Society, most adapted to Poetic illustration. To this work I mean to devote the Prime of my life and the chief force of my mind. I have also arranged the plan of a narrative Poem [*The Excursion*]. And if I live to finish these three principal works I shall be content. That on my own life, the least important of the three, is better [than] half complete [...].[8] □

Little faircopy text remains of the 1804 five-book *Prelude*, in which the poet traces his life up to his days as a student at Cambridge University. Following the critic Jonathan Wordsworth's suggestion that the 1804 poem could be constructed from existing manuscripts, the scholar Duncan Wu published his edition of the five-book *Prelude* in 1997.[9] Despite this, the five-book *Prelude* is less discussed today than its younger and older siblings, despite the fact that it includes most of the important sequences that would appear in later forms of the poem, such as the episode of the 'Drowned Man', and the 'Ascent of Snowdon' passage with which all subsequent versions of the poem would close.

The Thirteen-Book *Prelude* (1805)

Another reason why the 1804 version is now largely forgotten may be that the flurry of activity of that spring was itself quickly overshadowed by what followed: within months of completing the five-book *Prelude* Wordsworth sat down to enlarge it once again, the result being the massive thirteen-book *Prelude* that was completed in 1805. Nonetheless, Wordsworth was sufficiently satisfied with the first three books of the 1804 text to leave them unchanged in the huge expansion of the poem that was to follow (Book IV of the 1804 poem was adapted to form Books IV and V of the 1805 *Prelude*, while Book V was broken up into the fragments that became the last two-thirds of Book XI and the first third of Book XIII [the 'Ascent of Snowdon']). By late 1805 then, *The Prelude* comprised the following Books:

■   I. 'Introduction: Childhood and School-time'
     II. 'School-time (Continued)'
    III. 'Residence at Cambridge'
     IV. 'Summer Vacation'
      V. 'Books'
     VI. 'Cambridge and the Alps'
    VII. 'Residence in London'
   VIII. 'Retrospect: Love of Nature Leading to Love of Mankind'
     IX. 'Residence in France'
      X. 'Residence in France and French Revolution'
     XI. 'Imagination, How Impaired and Restored'
    XII. 'Same Subject (Continued)'
   XIII. 'Conclusion'[10] □

And yet, as a contemporary letter reveals, far from convincing him of its independent merits, finishing the thirteen-book *Prelude* seems only to have made Wordsworth even more uneasy about the value of the autobiographical work that he had already described to De Quincey as 'the least important' of three main projects of his poetic career:

■ I have the pleasure to say that I finished my Poem about a fortnight ago. I had looked forward to the day as a most happy one [...] but it was not a happy day for me – I was dejected on many accounts; when I looked back upon the performance it seemed to have a dead weight about it, the reality so far short of the expectation; it was the first long labour that I had finished, and the doubt about whether I should ever live to write the Recluse, and the sense which I had of this Poem being so far below what I seemed capable of executing, depressed me much [...]. This work may be considered as a sort of portico to the Recluse, part of the same building, which I hope to be able erelong to begin with, in earnest; and if I am permitted to bring it to conclusion, and to write, further, a narrative Poem of the Epic kind, I shall consider the *task* of my life as over.[11] □

Foremost among the 'many accounts' for Wordsworth's dejection around this time was the death at sea of his brother, John (1772–1804), in February. The news halted work on *The Prelude* for over two months. Nonetheless, by June of that year the work was ready, and soon after Dorothy diligently set about preparing a fair and final manuscript. Finally, having dealt with the 'portico', Wordsworth felt ready to make progress with the main building: *The Recluse*.

Having been put aside to await the publication of its larger companion piece, the 1805 *Prelude* remained a private poem, shown only to close friends. Fittingly, it is the poem's dedicatee, Coleridge, who, having heard Wordsworth read all thirteen books in January 1807, provides us with a first critical assessment in his ode 'To William Wordsworth: Lines Composed, for the Greater Part on the Night, on which He Finished the Recitation of his Poem (in Thirteen Books) Concerning the Growth and History of His Own Mind'. The opening of this poem reveals the excitement with which Coleridge received the poem:

■ Friend! O Teacher! God's great Gift to me!
Into my heart have I receiv'd that Lay
More than historic, that prophetic Lay,
Wherein (high theme by Thee first sung aright)
Of the Foundations and the Building-up
Of thy own Spirit, thou hast lov'd to tell
What may be told to th' understanding mind
Revealable; and what within the mind
May rise enkindled. Theme as hard as high! □

(1–9)

'Hard' and 'high' as the theme of the 'Building-up' of the poet's spirit may have been, however, Coleridge continued to see *The Prelude* as essentially the foundation-stone of a grander work that would confirm Wordsworth's position 'in the Choir / Of ever-enduring Men' (42–43) and heir to Milton. It is by foreshadowing *The Recluse* that *The Prelude* is '[m]ore than historic', and a 'prophetic Lay'. However, not only was this particular prophecy left unfulfilled, but the manuscript as Wordsworth left it in 1805 was to remain unprinted until 1926. In other words, the version of the poem that today is the most widely read by students of Wordsworth was all but forgotten in the 120 years following its completion. To understand why this occurred, we need to examine how the role played by *The Prelude* in Wordsworth's vision of his poetic legacy, together with its relations with his other major works, changed as an ageing poet adapted to a century in which 'Romantic' enthusiasms were gradually being exchanged for 'Victorian' pieties.

The Fourteen-Book *Prelude* (1850)

Considering the fate of *The Prelude* between 1805 and the way it first appeared only weeks after Wordsworth's death almost half a century later involves, among other things, tracing its relationship with Wordsworth's other 'long' poems. Of these, the most significant are: *Home at Grasmere*, *The Excursion*, and (of course) *The Recluse*. The first of these, *Home at Grasmere*, which Wordsworth had begun around 1800 and completed in the summer of 1806, was originally intended to be the first Book of *The Recluse*. Essentially a celebration of the landscape and people of Grasmere, however, this poem was ill suited to carry the weighty philosophical themes envisaged for the *magnum opus*. Consequently, though as late as the 1830s Wordsworth would return to the manuscript of *Home at Grasmere* in his repeated attempts to breathe new life into *The Recluse*, invariably his efforts brought him, finally, back to *The Prelude*.

In 1808 Wordsworth attempted to address the philosophical themes of *The Recluse* directly in the poem *Tuft of Primroses*, but with little success. Instead, the most significant progress he made on *The Recluse* in the two decades following the completion of the thirteen-book Prelude was with *The Excursion*, itself a poem adapted from an earlier, shorter work, *The Ruined Cottage* (1797–98). Published in 1814, *The Excursion* is the only substantial part of the *Recluse* project to appear in print during Wordsworth's lifetime. As a result, it was *The Excursion* rather than *The Prelude* that formed the basis upon which Wordsworth's reputation as a writer of sustained narrative verse was judged for much of the nineteenth century. Nonetheless, in his Preface to the 1814 poem, Wordsworth was at pains to connect the two works, linking both in turn to the project of *The Recluse*:

■ It may be proper to state whence the Poem, of which The Excursion is a part, derives its Title of THE RECLUSE – Several years ago, when the Author retired to his native Mountains, with the hope of being enabled to construct a literary Work that might live, it was a reasonable thing that he should take a review of his own Mind, and examine how far Nature and Education had qualified him for such an employment. As subsidiary to this preparation, he undertook to record, in Verse, the origin and progress of his own powers, as far as he was acquainted with them. That Work, addressed to a dear Friend [...] has been long finished; and the result of the investigation which gave rise to it was a determination to compose a philosophical Poem, containing views of Man, Nature, and Society; and to be entitled, The Recluse; as having for its principal subject the sensations and opinions of a Poet living in retirement. – The preparatory Poem is biographical, and conducts the history of the Author's mind to the point when he was emboldened to hope that his faculties were sufficiently matured for entering upon the arduous labour which he had proposed to himself; and the two Works have the same kind of relation to each other, if he may so express himself, as the Antichapel [*sic*] has to the body of a gothic church.[12] □

At this point, however, the 'gothic church' existed largely on the drawing board. Estrangement from Coleridge (upon whom he had relied in the past for guidance on intellectual matters) in the years since 1805 had further retarded Wordsworth's progress with the main philosophical section of *The Recluse*. Nonetheless, his ambitions for the latter were underscored by the fact that, along with *The Excursion*, he printed a verse 'Prospectus' to *The Recluse*. And as Stephen Gill notes, in writing the 'Preface' to *The Excursion*, Wordsworth had other objectives in mind:

■ In this incaculably important Preface Wordsworth was doing many things. He was keeping faith both with himself and Coleridge as they were at Alfoxden, when *The Recluse* was first conceived, and with the sense of blessedness he had celebrated in *Home at Grasmere* [...]. He was declaring that the 'Poet living in retirement' was not in retreat from the world but engaged with it at the profoundest level. He was affirming that all his published work [...] was part of an edifice whose significance was only now coming into view. It was a poet's manifesto and a prophet's utterance, the most important revelation of himself that Wordsworth was ever to publish. But it, and the volumes it introduced, failed in the short term to achieve any of his aims.[13] □

Indeed, much to Wordsworth's irritation, even sympathetic critics were puzzled by *The Excursion*. William Hazlitt (1778–1830), for one, noted that '[a]ll accidental varieties and individual contrasts are lost in an endless continuity of feeling, like drops of water in the ocean stream. An intense intellectual egotism swallows up everything.'[14] Hostile critics, meanwhile, were scathing. Francis Jeffrey (1773–1850), in particular, wrote in the *Edinburgh Review*: 'This will never do [...]. The case of Mr Wordsworth, we perceive, is now manifestly hopeless; and we give him up as altogether incurable, and beyond the power of criticism.'[15] *The Excursion*'s mixed reception had two important consequences: first, the fact that the poem drew charges of egocentricity despite its varied use of narrative personae (the recluse, the pastor, and the pedlar) made Wordsworth even more anxious about the monovocal *Prelude*; second, the accusation levelled by Jeffrey and others that the poet's 'peculiar system' was both overbearing and unintelligible shook his already weakened confidence in being able to develop a coherent theoretical framework for *The Recluse*.

Work continued sporadically over subsequent years on the major poem, but letters written by William and Dorothy during this period often report that Wordsworth is either buried in reading or turning back to earlier poems such as *Home at Grasmere* (written 1800–06) and *The Prelude*. Eventually, around the mid-1830s, Wordsworth seems to have accepted that his 'Antichapel' of *The Prelude* abutted a gothic church in ruins. His dream of writing a great philosophical poem for the age had produced no more than fragments: indeed, like the over-grown ruins that inspired 'Tintern Abbey' (1798), the poems *Home at Grasmere*, *The Excursion* (1814), The 'Prospectus' to *The Recluse* (written 1800), and (to a lesser extent) *Tuft of Primroses* (written 1808) could only suggest the presence of the superstructure they were meant to sup-port. Tellingly, for the first time in 1836 *The Excursion* was reprinted without the extended title bearing the words: 'Being a portion of THE RECLUSE'. Two years later, the sixty-eight year-old Wordsworth admits to an American visitor that the master-project of his life's work had in the end proved to be 'something beyond his powers to accomplish'.[16] Soon after, as a close friend reports, he began to prepare *The Prelude* for posthumous publication, effectively acknowledging that this work would become his major epic poem:

> ■ Our journey was postponed for a week, that the beloved old poet might accomplish the work that he had in hand, the revising of his grand auto-biographical poem, and leaving it in a state fit for publication. At this he has been labouring for the past month, seldom less than six or seven hours in the day, or rather one ought to say the whole day, for it seemed always in his mind – quite a possession; and much, I believe, he has done to it, expand-ing it in some parts, retrenching it in others, and perfecting it in all.[17] □

The rewriting of *The Prelude* in 1838–39, together with revisions made in 1816/19 and 1832, determine the major differences between the 1805 *Prelude* and the 'official' posthumous version of 1850. This process was so thorough, indeed, that upon arriving at Rydal Mount soon after the poet's death, Christopher Wordsworth, Jr. (William's nephew) is able to report that little editorial work on the manuscript is required, 'for it was left ready for the Press by the Author'.[18]

How, then, does the 'official' *Prelude* that the wider reading public encounters for the first time in 1850 compare with the text of 1805? The most obvious difference is that the later work has grown another book, although this is largely the result of earlier material being restruc-tured rather than a whole book's worth of new material having been added (principally by the division of Book Ten, 'Residence in France and French Revolution' into two shorter books: 'Residence in France – Continued' and 'France – Concluded', which, in turn, becomes Book Eleven). In overall length the two works are not greatly different. Indeed, even before he began his final revisions, Wordsworth had already decided to hive off the closing section (almost 400 lines) of Book Nine into a separate poem, which was published as *Vaudracour and Julia* in 1820. Other changes are suggestive. Book Twelve (previously Book Eleven) signals the ageing writer's modified priorities with the addition of a new key term, appearing in 1850 as 'Imagination *and Taste*, How Impaired and Restored' (my emphasis).

THE VICTORIAN *PRELUDE*

Initial Reaction among the Reviewers

On publication in 1850, *The Prelude* received a polite, if lukewarm, critical reception. The heavyweight periodicals – the *Quarterly Review* and *Edinburgh Review* – ignored it, while others paid more attention to the *Memoirs of William Wordsworth*, written by his brother, Christopher (1807–85), and published the following year. There were a number of reasons for the tepid reaction. To begin with, the poem was largely overshadowed by the publication in the same year of *In Memoriam*, an ethical-religious meditation to rival *The Prelude* in scale and ambition written by Alfred Tennyson (1809–92), the poet who would succeed Wordsworth as Laureate. There were, however, deeper reasons for Victorian ambivalence towards the poem. In a sense, *The Prelude* in 1850 was a poem both behind and ahead of its time. On one hand, readers knew what to expect from Wordsworth, who was by now a familiar, even dated, figure. Unglamorous and disengaged from metropolitan society, the austerity and naturalism of Wordsworth's verse now looked bleak and passé. John Keats (1795–1821) and Percy Bysshe Shelley (1792–1822), not the Lakers, had become the models for mid-nineteenth-century poetry, and compared to the sumptuous colours of Tennyson and the Pre-Raphaelites (for example, the poet and painter Dante Gabriel Rossetti [1828–82]), Wordsworth's earthy browns and greys seemed to belong to another era. Similarly, *The Prelude*'s visionary passages could easily appear jejune to a society adjusting to industrialization in ways unanticipated by the younger Wordsworth. Finally, despite the revisionary efforts of his later years, Wordsworth continued to be associated in the public mind with Jacobinism and pantheism, two lost causes from the Age of Revolution.

However, as many modern critics (discussed in the chapters below) note, it could be argued that the true significance of Wordsworth's vision, in particular his intense focus on memory and the quotidian, was lost on the Victorians, who recoiled, as Jeffrey had years earlier, from what they perceived to be his obfuscatory 'metaphysics' and embarrassing obsession with the commonplace. The exploration of this important dimension of Wordsworth's poetry would be left to later generations of critics: for the Victorians, meanwhile – and especially for the first reviewers – *The Prelude* presented a poetic curiosity, the value of which lay for the most part in its antiquarian interest. Accordingly, at first the poem was commonly read, first, as 'background' to Wordsworth's 'major' poems – particularly *The Excursion*, for which it was (mis-takenly) seen as a dry run – and, second (thanks to its rapid posthumous release and the publication of Christopher Wordsworth's *Memoirs*), as Wordsworth's dying words: part epitaph, part obituary.

Nonetheless, even the unearthing of what the *Eclectic Review* dubbed as a 'fossil relic' caused a stir in the literary world. The appearance of *The Prelude* had been long anticipated, particularly since Thomas De Quincey's allusion in 1839 to 'a great philosophic poem of Wordsworth's, which is still in MS., and will remain in MS. until after his death'.[19] Like many of the 1850 reviews, the *Eclectic Review*'s coverage highlights the poem's novelty as 'the first *regular versified* autobiography we remem-ber in our language' while treading warily around the metaphysics of Wordsworth's 'great soliloquy':

■ For well nigh thirty-four years the public curiosity has been excited by the knowledge that there existed in MS. an unfinished poem, of very high pretensions, and extraordinary magnitude, from the pen of the late [...] poet-laureate of Britain. [...] All of it that is publishable, or shall ever be published, now lies before us; and we approach it with curiously-mingled emotions – mingled, because although a fragment, it is so vast, and in parts so finished, and because it may be regarded as at once an early production of his genius, and its latest legacy to the world. It seems a large fossil relic – imperfect and magnificent – newly dug up, and with the fresh earth and the old dim subsoil meeting and mingling around it.

The 'Prelude' is the first *regular versified* autobiography we remember in our language. [...] We grant, then, to Wordsworth's detractors, that his eye was introverted, that he studied himself more profoundly than aught else but nature – that his genius was neither epic, nor lyric, nor dramatic – that he did not 'look abroad into universality' – that he is monotonous – and that to sympathize fully with his strains, requires a certain share both of his powers and of their peculiar training. But all this we look at as only a needful statement of his limitations; and we pity those who produce it for any other purpose. Future ages will be thankful that a formation so peculiar, has been so carefully preserved. The 'moods' of such a mind will be ranked with the dramas, lyrics, and epics of inferior poets. His monotony will be compared to that of the ocean surges, which break now on the shore to the same tune as they did the eve before the deluge. His obscurities will appear jet black ornaments. His fragments will be valued as if they were bits of the ark. [...]

In reading the 'Prelude,' we should never forget that his object is not to weave an artful and amusing story, but sternly and elaborately to trace the 'growth of a poet's mind'. This is a metaphysical more than a biographical purpose. He leads us accordingly, not so much from incident to incident, as from thought to thought, along the salient points of his mental history. [...] The chapters in this poem might have been very properly entitled, 'Moods in Boyhood,' 'Moods in Cambridge,' 'Moods among my Books,' 'Moods among the Alps,' 'Moods in France,' &c. Characters, indeed, rush occasionally across these moods. [...] but they come like shadows, and like shadows depart, nor does their presence prevail for more than a moment to burst the web of the great soliloquy. Indeed, whether with them or without them, among mountains or men, with his faithful terrier, and talking to himself by the wayside, or pacing the Palais Royale, Wordsworth is equally and always alone.[20] □

As Wordsworth had feared, many readers felt uncomfortable with the poet's attempt to journey into his own mind without what the reviewer of *Tait's Edinburgh Magazine* called the 'legitimate aids of poetic art'. Specifically, it was the ascetic quality of Wordsworth's introspective moods, the perceived lack of dash and colour, that readers, who were by now accustomed to the high–tempo narratives and exotic sets of the poetry of Lord Byron (1788–1824), found hard to accept. Accordingly, *Tait's* registers disappointment, though no surprise, at what it sees as the poem's artlessness and lack of variety and incident:

■ As 'The Prelude' is not, nor pretends to be, a tale of stirring interest, and as it is also of very considerable length, it necessarily requires all legitimate aids of poetic art to sustain the continued attention of the reader. Unfortunately, Wordsworth never attributed to these their just importance [...]. The walk which Wordsworth selected was very limited, though by no means unworthy. He is the poet of the external phases of Nature, but only in her milder moods. He cannot make, as Byron did, 'the live thunder leap from crag to crag', but he serenely gazes with artless joy on the sun sinking behind the dark outline of a Cumbrian fell, and his soul hovers in rapture over the silvery mist that fills the vale at daybreak [...]. The texture of his composition is in general eminently artless. From multiplicity he shrinks as from confusion; and in no instance does he summon thoughts and feelings from various regions to converge like troops in a campaign, and to bear with irresistible effect on a point long since predetermined. His is the ripple of the brook, and not the collective might of waters slowly gathering to break in one huge billow on the shore.[21] □

And yet, running through many early reviews of the poem is an uneasy sense that Wordsworth's poetry is important *because of*, not despite, its opacity and difficulty. Thus, while the *Gentleman's Magazine*, notes, with a mild tone of regret, Wordsworth's lack of sensuousness, it acknowledges Wordsworth's importance to the revolution that took place half

a century earlier, turning poetry from a mere pastime or 'amusement'
meant to beguile the hours, into an activity fit for serious, inquiring,
and intellectually energetic minds:

■ The sensuous element was omitted in his composition. His sympathies
are absorbed by the magnificence and the mystery of external nature, or by
the vigour and freshness of the human soul when under immediate contact
with nature's elemental forces and influences. Neither was there ever any
poet of his degree less dramatic than Wordsworth. All the life in his ballads,
in his narrative poems, in his Excursion, is the reflex of his own being. The
actors in his scenes are severe, aloof, stately, and uniform; grand in their
isolation, dignified in their sorrows. [...] The lyrical ballads [1798, 1800], the
critical prefaces, and the renown of Wordsworth, have wrought one of the
greatest literary revolutions the world has ever seen [...]. Men had already
asked themselves the question, shall we continue to obey phantasms, or
shall we search for realities; and poets were also beginning to say, at least in
Germany and England, is our vocation for the apparent only, or for the true?
Verse was regarded no longer as an elegant accomplishment, or the poet
merely as one who could *amuse* a vacant hour, but not instruct a thoughtful
one. Childish things were put away; and poetry resumed the dignity, and
almost the stature, of its first manhood.[22] □

Indeed, the fact that that some reviewers preferred to treat *The Prelude*
primarily as a work of philosophy says a lot about just how divided
opinion remained about the legacy of the literary revolution that
Wordsworth had helped to bring about. In Philadelphia, for example,
Graham's Magazine finds the poem to be excellent as 'metaphysics', elevating Wordsworth above the Scottish philosopher David Hume (1711–76)
and the German philosopher Immanuel Kant (1724–1804) in conveying 'real available knowledge of the facts and laws of man's internal
constitution'. As poetry, however, the reviewer considers it inferior to
much of his other work, including 'The White Doe', a poem that has
long since lost its place at the heart of the Wordsworthian corpus:

■ It must be admitted, however, that 'The Prelude', with all its merits, does
not add to the author's great fame, however much it may add to our knowledge of his inner life. As a poem it cannot be placed by the side of The
White Doe, or The Excursion, or the Ode on Childhood, or the Ode on
the Power of Sound; and the reason is to be found in its strictly didactic
and personal character, necessitating a more constant use of analysis and
reflection, and a greater substitution of the metaphysical for the poetic process, than poetry is willing to admit. [...]
   If 'The Prelude' has thus fewer 'trances of thought and mountings of the
mind' than 'The Excursion', it still bears the marks of the lofty and thoughtful
genius of the author, and increases our respect for his personal character.

[...] We believe that few metaphysicians ever scanned their consciousness with more intensity of vision, than Wordsworth was wont to direct upon his; and in the present poem he has subtly noted, and firmly expressed, many new psychological laws and processes. The whole subject of the development of the mind's creative faculties, and the vital laws of mental growth and production, has been but little touched by professional metaphysicians; and we believe 'The Prelude' conveys more real available knowledge of the facts and laws of man's internal constitution, than can be found in Hume or Kant.[23] □

The Prelude was certainly proving difficult to classify. Indeed, as one reads the 1850 reviews, it is hard to avoid the conclusion that many reviewers struggled to find the kind of poetic analogues that would enable them to conduct an adequate evaluation of *The Prelude*'s significance and merits. Some did not even try: indeed, in those reviews less inclined than the Philadelphia *Gentleman's Magazine* to applaud Wordsworth's 'metaphysical' poetry, one can detect the faint echo of the accusation, made by Francis Jeffrey decades earlier, that Wordsworth was scarcely a proper poet, merely a spinner of his own 'peculiar system'. Others, however, endeavoured to get to grips with the poem by drawing comparisons with contemporary works: thus, while the *Eclectic Review* intimates that *The Prelude* is a poetic equivalent to *Sartor Resartus* ('The Tailor Re-patched' [1833–34], a prose work by Thomas Carlyle [1795–1881]), the *British Quarterly Review* compares the poet with Johann Wolfgang von Goethe (1749–1832), the poster-boy of mid-Victorian autobiography, albeit much to the disadvantage of the former:

■ Regarding the work before us, we have first to say that it is not so much a complete autobiography of the poet up to his thirtieth year, as a theoretic retrospect of what the poet himself considered significant in that portion of his life. [...] And here again, keeping up the instructive contrast between Goethe and Wordsworth, one sees the difference between the two poets. Goethe, the larger and more complex nature, writes an autobiography full of facts, incidents, sketches, episodes; advancing, openly at least, no theory in the course of his genius, but artistically evoking out of his past life the most beautiful and sweet of its multitudinous recollections. Wordsworth, a poet too, but of a mind more meagre and didactic, first stretches as it were a line of bare autobiographic theory along the period he means to traverse, and then hangs upon it a few reminiscences that shall be ornamental and illustrative. [...]

'The Prelude', we will venture to say, ought, like the 'Dichtung und Wahrheit', ['Poetry and Truth' (1811–31)] to have been written in prose. [...] That Wordsworth should have made such an attempt in verse at all, is to be regarded as a consequence of his peculiar theory of poetic diction, and as a proof how thoroughly he believed in that theory. According to that theory, large portions of the poem which, from another point of view, would appear decidedly cold and prosaic, are strictly and sufficiently poetical. Still even Wordsworth himself, with all his faith in the title of verse to be made a vehicle even for the most ordinary circumstances and statements, might have seen that, by preferring the element of prose, he could have been more anecdotic, interesting, and communicative.[24] □

The *Dublin University Magazine* is more forgiving, but like many commentators from this period it professes no little bemusement over Wordsworth's interest in the more quotidian aspects of experience:

■ [The reader] will also find more of the eccentricities of this great author than his own later judgement would probably have approved. There are many heavy and prosaic passages, and some matters of familiar, and not very important, narrative are given a solemnity which cannot but provoke a smile. But these are but casual clouds floating in the pure Wordsworthian sky. Ever and anon, he springs from level talk or ponderous triviality into the most glorious heights of poetry [...].[25] □

Overall, however, the responses of the 1850 reviewers initially suggested that Wordsworth's concerns over how the public would receive a poem like *The Prelude* had been well founded. It was commonly felt that *The Prelude* magnified the least attractive facets of Wordsworth's poetry – which is to say, the least attractive facets of the poet Wordsworth: his egotism; his lack of sympathy with other human beings; his lack of sensuousness; his subordination of the 'poetic' principle (however that was construed) to a metaphysical hobbyhorse. The judgement of *The Examiner* is worth recording here, finally, because it touches on all of these issues:

■ The great defect of Wordsworth, in our judgement, was want of sympathy with, and knowledge of, men. From his birth till his entry at college, he lived in a region where he met with none whose minds might awaken his sympathies, and where life was altogether uneventful. On the other hand, that region abounded with the inert, striking, and most impressive objects of natural scenery. The elementary grandeur and beauty of external nature came thus to fill up his mind to the exclusion of human interests. To such a result his individual constitution powerfully contributed. The sensuous element was singularly deficient in his nature. He never seems to have passed through that erotic period out of which some poets have never emerged. A soaring, speculative imagination, and an impetuous, resistless self-will, were his distinguishing characteristics. From first to last he concentrated himself within himself [...]. There is intense reality in his pictures of external nature. But though his human characters are presented with great skill of metaphysical analysis, they have rarely life or animation. He is always the prominent, often the exclusive, object of his own song.[26] □

Poetry versus Philosophy

The later stages of the nineteenth century saw four significant develop-ments in critical attitudes to Wordsworth's poetry in general. First, the strangeness of Wordsworth's poetry intensified the debate over whether he was, first and foremost, a 'poet' or a 'philosopher', as commenta-tors developed evermore subtle and elaborate arguments to defend their claims. Second, largely through the influence of Matthew Arnold, the late nineteenth century witnessed the elevation of Wordsworth's repu-tation into that of the pantheon of great English-language poets, com-parable to that of William Shakespeare (1564–1616) and John Milton. A third development saw the emergence a new critical framework, based upon a distinctly aesthetic and sensuous paradigm, that enabled critics – notably Walter Pater – to offer a principled alternative to the moral-philosophical and didactic approaches to the poet's work that had dominated the debate for much of the nineteenth century. Finally, and most crucially for the present purpose, the debate over the position of *The Prelude* in the Wordsworthian corpus raged on without any signs of a consensus. Thus, while Arnold maintained that *The Prelude* formed a large part of the 'baggage' of Wordsworth's weaker work that must be discarded if his reputation was to be saved, A.C. Bradley considered the widespread neglect of this poem to be one of the great failings of nineteenth-century criticism.

One way of grouping at least some of these changes together is to see them all as bound up with a general drift away from the didactic inclinations of early nineteenth-century criticism, much of which – encouraged by John Stuart Mill's account in his *Autobiography* (1873) of how he had been rescued from youthful depression by finding in Wordsworth's verse 'a source of inward joy, of sympathetic and imaginative pleasure, which could be shared in by all human beings' – had looked to the venerable Laker for spiritual edification in the age of the machine.[27] As the reviews cited above suggest, the early Victorians tended to see Wordsworth as the poet of reflective morality rather than of the senses, or indeed (as Wordsworth himself would have preferred to be read) of the visionary union of thought, feeling, and language. Increasingly, this image of the poet coalesced into the picture of a 'Wordsworthian' moral system, a philosophical antidote to the ills of modernity. Instrumental in the promulgation of this picture were the 'Wordsworthians' themselves, a group of enthusiasts who were keen to promote Mill's idea that Wordsworth's poetry was *edifying* by unpacking its 'lessons' for the modern age. As F.W. Bateson points out, this had some unfortunate consequences for Wordsworth's early legacy:

■ The potential danger in the relationship between Wordsworth and the Wordsworthians was that it might turn into that of a spiritual healer ministering to a congregation of sick souls [...]. Long before the man's death [...] the poet had tended to become dissociated from him, and throughout the nineteenth century the poet Wordsworth was regarded primarily as a healer.[28] □

Well-intentioned works by Wordsworth enthusiasts reduced the complexity of the poet's output by concentrating on his early poems and underscoring (often rather artificially) their didactic features. As a result, *The Prelude* continued to baffle Victorian readers, many of whom found it difficult to square the poem's content with its supposed 'doctrine', its quotidian subject matter with its philosophising. With the advent of the 1870s, however, this picture begins to change. A number of commentators began to read Wordsworth's poetry in ways that endeavoured to escape what earlier readers had found to be the paradox of transcendence found in the commonplace. Richard Holt Hutton (1826–97), writing in 1871, was one of these critics:

■ The commonplace modern criticism on Wordsworth is that he is too transcendental. On the other hand, the criticism with which he was first assailed [...] was that he was ridiculously simple, that he made an unintelligible fuss about common feelings and common things. The reconciliation of these opposite criticisms is not very difficult. He drew uncommon delights from very common things. [...] The same sort of power which scientific men have of studiously fixing their minds on natural phenomena, till they make these phenomena yield lessons and laws of which no understanding, destitute of this capacity for detaching itself entirely from the commonplace train of intellectual associations, would have dreamt, Wordsworth had in relation to the objects of the imagination. He could detach his mind from the commonplace series of impressions which are generated by commonplace objects or events, resist and often reverse the current of emotion to which ordinary minds are liable, and triumphantly justify the strain of rapture with which he celebrated what excites either no feeling, or painful feeling, in the mass of unreflecting men. Two distinct peculiarities, and rare peculiarities of character, chiefly assisted him in this – his keen spiritual courage, and his stern spiritual frugality. □

Significantly, Hutton turns to *The Prelude* as an example, arguing that, with these two qualities – 'volition and self-government' on one hand, and, on the other, 'spiritual frugality' (namely, a reluctance, unlike Shelley and Byron, 'to trench upon the spiritual capital at his disposal') – Wordsworth is able to transform his subject matter in a way unlike no other poet: 'He does not discern and revivify the *natural* life which is in it; he creates a new thing altogether, namely, the life of thought which it has the power to generate in his own brooding imagination.' In this way, Hutton turns what was once puzzling and discouraging about much of Wordsworth's poetry, and *The Prelude* in particular, into something precious and unique: the transformation of the quotidian into imagination. In this respect, 'his works are the most completely outside the sphere of Shakespeare's universal genius. In solitude only could they have originated, and in solitude only can they be perfectly enjoyed.' But they are no less important or valuable for that. Moreover, Hutton reverses the judgement of the *Quarterly*'s reviewer by comparing Wordsworth and Goethe in a way that is more flattering to the former:

■ Natural rays of feeling are refracted the moment they enter Wordsworth's imagination. It is not the theme acting on the man that you see, but the man acting on the theme. [...] It is in this that he differs so completely in manner from other self-conscious poets – Goethe, for instance, who in like manner always left the shadow of himself on the field of his vision. But with Goethe it is a shadow of self in quite a different sense. Goethe watches himself drifting along the tide of feeling, and keeps an eye open outside his heart. But though he overhears himself, he does not interfere with himself; he listens breathlessly, and notes it down. Wordsworth, on the other hand, refuses to listen to this natural self at all. He knows another world of pure and buoyant meditation; and he knows that all which is transplanted into it bears there a new and nobler fruit.[29] □

If Hutton's depiction of Wordsworth is couched in the discourse of capitalism – that of the parsimonious poet who hordes and carefully invests his spiritual capital, resulting in a form of literary production in which basic emotional materials are transformed into the value-added creations of imagination – Walter Pater's essay, published three years later in the *Fortnightly Review* (April 1874) and later included in his book *Appreciations* (1889), detaches the poet entirely from the machinery of modern economic life:

■ An intimate consciousness of the expression of natural things, which weighs, listens, penetrates, where the earlier mind passed roughly by, is a large element in the complexion of modern poetry. It has been remarked as a fact in mental history again and again. It reveals itself in many forms; but is strongest and most attractive in what is strongest and most attractive in modern literature. [...] Of this new sense, the writings of Wordsworth are the central and elementary expression: he is more simply and more entirely occupied with them than any other poet [...]. There was in his own

character a certain contentment, a sort of inborn religious placidity, seldom found united with a sensibility so mobile as his, which was favourable to the quiet, habitual observation of inanimate, or imperfectly animate, existence. [...]
He has a power likewise of realising, and conveying to the consciousness of the reader, abstract and elementary impressions – silence, darkness, absolute motionlessness: or, again, the whole complex sentiment of a particular place, the abstract expression of desolation in the long white road, of peacefulness in a particular folding of the hills. □

For Pater, the great strength of Wordsworth's poetry lies in his ability to fuse form and content, word and idea, into a singular impression of consciousness. Challenging the consensus of the early reviewers that the 'sensuous element was singularly deficient' in Wordsworth, he argues that the animism of *The Prelude* itself becomes a form of sensuousness:

■ In the early ages, this belief [in animism], delightful as its effects on poetry often are, was but the result of a crude intelligence. But, in Wordsworth, such power of seeing life, such perception of a soul, in inanimate things, came of an exceptional susceptibility to the impressions of eye and ear, and was, in its essence, a kind of sensuousness. At least, it is only in a temperament exceptionally susceptible on the sensuous side, that this sense of the expressiveness of outward things comes to be so large a part of life. That he awakened 'a sort of thought in sense', is Shelley's just estimate of this element in Wordsworth's poetry. □

Such sensuousness, Pater maintains, saves *The Prelude* from the charges of dogmatism and system-spinning, since in Wordsworth, even the most profound philosophical ideas are subordinated to form and expression:

■ And so he has something, also, for those who feel the fascination of bold speculative ideas, who are really capable of rising upon them to conditions of poetical thought. He uses them, indeed, always with a very fine apprehension of the limits within which alone philosophical imaginings have any place in true poetry; and using them only for poetical purposes, is not too careful even to make them consistent with each other. To him, theories which for other men bring a world of technical diction, brought perfect form and expression, as in those two lofty books of *The Prelude*, which describe the decay and the restoration of Imagination and Taste.[30] □

   Pater's approach to Wordsworth is the product of his aestheticism, whereby moral and cognitive questions are subsumed by a concern with the pulsating life of sensations and impressions that, he believed, fundamentally constitute human experience. Influential as his reading of Wordsworth was, however, his attempt both to neutralize the debate over Wordsworth's 'philosophy' and to establish *The Prelude* as a central poem in the poet's corpus settled neither question decisively, as two important studies produced at the end of the 1870s attest. In the first of these, the philosopher and intellectual historian Leslie Stephen gives a detailed and scholarly account of Wordsworth's 'system' as moral philosophy, an approach that is swiftly countered by Matthew Arnold, who argues that rescuing Wordsworth's poetic reputation involves rejecting the idea that his work contains a 'philosophy of life', together with the notion that *The Prelude* is an important work within the poet's oeuvre.

Stephen's principal aim is to place Wordsworth's poetry in the context of broader philosophical inquiry:

■ The great aim of moral philosophy is to unite the disjointed element, to end the divorce between reason and experience, and to escape from the alternative of dealing with empty but symmetrical formulae or concrete and chaotic facts. No hint can be given here as to the direction in which a final solution must be sought. Whatever the true method, Wordsworth's mode of conceiving the problem shows how powerfully he grasped the questions at issue. If his doctrines are not systematically expounded, they all have a direct bearing upon the real difficulties involved. □

Stephen's approach differs from earlier attempts to outline Wordsworth's 'philosophy' in two key respects: first, although he takes Wordsworth seriously as a thinker, he does not find in his writings the presence of a doctrine 'systematically expounded' – instead, he envisages the poet working at the interface between logic and intuition; second, while early Wordsworth enthusiasts turned to his work much as a student would to a teacher (or even, as Pater complained, as a novice would to a priest), Stephen's approach to the poet is made first and foremost in his capacities as an academic and an intellectual historian. The age was past in which Wordsworth's nature mysticism seemed to impart an urgent message to humanity:

■ [T]he great problem of life, that is, as he conceives it, is to secure a continuity between the period at which we are guided by half-conscious instincts, and that in which a man is able to supply the place of these primitive impulses by reasoned convictions. This is the thought which comes over and over again in his deepest poems, and round which all his teaching centred.[31] □

Despite Stephen's high estimation of Wordsworth, it is only with Matthew Arnold's introduction to *Poems of Wordsworth* (1879) that we find the first gathering of a wave of critical appreciation that will ultimately lead to *The Prelude* being recognized as one of the major works of nineteenth-century English literature. And yet, Arnold himself considered *The Prelude* a second-rate work. In his Introduction, he sets out his general case in unequivocal terms:

■ Wordsworth has been in his grave for some thirty years, and certainly his lovers and admirers cannot flatter themselves that this great and steady light of glory as yet shines over him. He is not fully recognized at home; he is not recognized at all abroad. Yet I firmly believe that the poetical performance of Wordsworth is, after that of Shakespeare and Milton, of which the world now recognizes the worth, undoubtedly the most considerable in our language from the Elizabethan age to the present time.[32] □

For Arnold, Wordsworth's poetic achievement has been obscured in the three decades following his death by the dense overgrowth of 'inferior' work that the poet produced, largely outside the period 1798–1808 – a decade, Arnold believes, in which Wordsworth was working at the height of his powers. As a result, giving Wordsworth his due as a poet involves dispensing with the 'baggage' of the weaker poetry so often applauded by the Wordsworthians. It soon becomes clear that by 'weaker', Arnold means 'philosophical': ultimately, recognizing Wordsworth's high merits as a poet means acknowledging the mediocrity of a poem like *The Prelude*:

■ *The Excursion* and *The Prelude*, his poems of greatest bulk, are by no means Wordsworth's best work. His best work is in his shorter pieces, and many indeed there are of these which are of first-rate excellence. [...] Wordsworth composed verses during a space of some sixty years; and it is no exaggeration to say that within one single decade of those years, between 1798 and 1808, almost all of his really first-rate work was produced. A mass of inferior work remains, work done before and after this golden prime, imbedding the first-rate work and clogging it, obstructing our approach to it, chilling, not unfrequently, the high-wrought mood with which we leave it. To be recognized far and wide as a great poet, to be possible and receivable as a classic, Wordsworth needs to be relieved of a great deal of poetical baggage which now encumbers him.[33] □

Arnold's dispute with the Wordsworthians (with whom he loosely groups Stephen) boils down to two claims: first, at his best, Wordsworth does not have a *philosophy* of life that he illustrates poetically; instead, he applies beautiful ideas to life by communicating to us 'the joy offered to us in nature'. Second, even if Wordsworth *did* have a philosophy, such a possession would make him a worse, not a better poet. Poetry, Arnold insists, is itself a criticism of life, not a system for living: indeed, he ventures to add, 'poetry is the reality, philosophy the illusion':

■ It is important, therefore, to hold fast to this: that poetry is at bottom a criticism of life; that the greatness of a poet lies in his powerful and beautiful application of ideas to life, – to the question: How to live. Morals are often treated in a narrow and false fashion, they are bound up with systems of thought and belief which have had their day, they are fallen into the hands of pedants and professional dealers, they grow tiresome to some of us. [...] A poetry of revolt against moral ideas is a poetry of revolt against *life*; a poetry of indifference toward moral ideas is a poetry of indifference towards *life*.

[...]

Where, then, is Wordsworth's superiority? It is here; he deals with more of *life* than they do; he deals with *life*, as a whole, more powerfully.

No Wordsworthian will doubt this. Nay, the fervent Wordsworthian will add, as Mr Leslie Stephen does, that Wordsworth's poetry is precious because his philosophy is sound; that his 'ethical system is as distinctive and capable of exposition as Bishop Butler's' [Joseph Butler (1697–1752), theologian, best known for *Analogy of Religion* (1736)]; that his poetry is informed by ideas which 'fall spontaneously into a scientific system of thought'. But we must be on our guard against the Wordsworthians, if we want to secure for Wordsworth his due rank as a poet. The Wordsworthians are apt to praise him for the wrong things, and to lay far too much stress upon what they call his philosophy. His poetry is the reality, his philosophy [...] is the illusion. Perhaps we shall one day learn to make this proposition general, and to say: Poetry is the reality, philosophy the illusion. But in Wordsworth's case, at any rate, we cannot do him justice until we dismiss his formal philosophy.

[...]

Wordsworth's poetry is great because of the extraordinary power with which Wordsworth feels the joy offered to us in nature, the joy offered to us in the simple primary affections and duties; and because of the extraordinary power with which, in case after case, he shows us this joy, and renders it so as to make us share it.[34] □

In this way, despite the efforts of admirers such as Pater, critical perception of the 1850 *Prelude* by the end of the century was, largely thanks to Arnold, that of a work that added very little, if anything, to the poet's gathering reputation. Unsettling the assumptions underlying this perception would involve rethinking the value and purpose of poetry generally. It is to this reappraisal, initiated at the dawn of the twentieth century, that I turn in the next chapter.

CHAPTER TWO

Revaluations: The Early Twentieth Century

THE CHALLENGE OF THE TWENTIETH CENTURY

Despite the decline of the 'Wordsworthians', late-Victorian approaches to Wordsworth continued to be framed, overall, within questions of taste, propriety, insight, and personality. These were linked to an index of literary value that owed much to ideas originally developed in Wordsworth's own time. Thus, for the aesthete Pater, Wordsworth was a poet who captured the quickness of life through his sensory impressions; for the philosopher and intellectual historian Stephen, he was an unsystematic moral philosopher who explored reality through intuition; for the cultural guardian Arnold, he was the critic of 'life', whose finest moments appeared in his shorter, lyrical poems. With the advent of the twentieth century, however, important changes occurred to the contexts in which Wordsworth's poetry was treated. All of these were related, in one way or another, to the single most important reorientation in Wordsworth studies to emerge in the early twentieth century: the 'rediscovery' of *The Prelude*.

The Prelude among the Professors

The first development, and the one with by far the greatest long-term repercussions, was the creation and spread of English Literature as a 'discipline' within the institutions of higher education. This in turn led to what might be called the 'professionalisation' of English Literature. Of course, Wordsworth had long since ceased to speak to his readers with the voice of a contemporary. Now, however, he became enshrined within a literary canon whose custodians were not (or not only) journalists and cultural commentators, but professors of literature: historians, biographers, and archivists. Consequently, as the general debate regarding the qualities of Wordsworth's poetry continued, a new debate was emerging as to what kind of *academic* questions it raised. Increasingly, this new breed of reader emphasized the *understanding* of poetry over its enjoyment or 'mere' appreciation. Wordsworth was no longer a poet just to be read; he was a poet to be *studied*.

At the forefront of this transformation is A.C. Bradley, whose *Oxford Lectures on Poetry* were first published in 1909. Here, we witness a major shift in the critical debate, one which Bradley instigates, like so many innovators, not so much by settling the old questions, as by raising a new one: what is the essence of Wordsworth's poetry? The answer, he finds, is twofold: it is at once *sublime* and *mystical*. The implications of Bradley's strategy in his Oxford lectures for the reception of Wordsworth's longer poems can hardly be overstated, for while Arnold had elevated Wordsworth's reputation only on the condition that these works were marginalized, Bradley is the first to argue authoritatively for Wordsworth's pre-eminent position in the canon, *based on* the value (the sublimity and mysticism) of poems such as *The Excursion* and *The Prelude*:

■ [N]ot a little of Wordsworth's poetry either approaches or actually enters the province of the sublime. His strongest natural inclination tended there. He himself speaks of his temperament as 'stern', and tells us that

> to the very going out of youth
> [He] too exclusively esteemed *that* love,
> And sought *that* beauty, which, as Milton says,
> Hath terror in it.

[Prelude XIV, 243–246]

This disposition is easily traced in the imaginative impressions of his child-hood as he describes them in *The Prelude*. His fixed habit of looking

> with feelings of fraternal love
> Upon the unassuming things that hold
> A silent station in this beauteous world,

was only formed, it would seem, under his sister's influence, after his recovery from the crisis that followed the run of his towering hopes in the French Revolution. It was part of his endeavour to find something of the distant ideal in life's familiar face. And though this attitude of sympathy and humility did become habitual, the first bent towards grandeur, austerity, sublimity, retained its force.

[...]

We may put the matter, secondly, thus. However much Wordsworth was the poet of small and humble things, and the poet who saw his ideal realized, not in Utopia, but here and now before his eyes, he was, quite as much, what some would call a mystic. He saw everything in the light of 'the visionary power'. He was, for himself

> The transitory being that beheld
> This Vision.

He apprehended all things, natural or human, as the expression of something which, while manifested in them, immeasurably transcends them.[1] □

Against Arnold, then, Bradley maintains that one cannot cherry-pick Wordsworth's verse: its sublime and mystical facets must be accepted, he argues, if the real merit of Wordsworth's poetry is to be appreciated:

■ Now we may prefer the Wordsworth of the daffodils to the Wordsworth of the yew-trees, and we may even believe the poet's mysticism to be moonshine; but it is certain that to neglect or throw into the shade this aspect of his poetry is neither to take Wordsworth as he really was nor to judge his poetry truly, since this aspect appears in much of it that we cannot deny to be first rate.[2] □

Arnold, Bradley complains, was handicapped in his reading of *The Prelude* partly because, 'having himself but little turn for philosophy, he was disposed to regard it as illusory; and further because, even in the poetic sphere, he was somewhat deficient in that kind of imagination which is allied to metaphysical thought'.[3] Thus,

■ he either ignores or depreciates that aspect of the poetry with which we are just now concerned. It is not true, we must bluntly say, that the cause of the greatness of this poetry 'is simple and may be told quite simply'. It is true, and it is admirably said, that this poetry 'is great because of the extraordinary power with which Wordsworth feels the joy offered to us in nature, the joy offered to us in the simple primary affections and duties'. But this is only half the truth.[4] □

Wordsworth then, is neither a philosopher in verse (as Stephen had suggested), nor simply a poet affirming the joys of nature (as Arnold had insisted): his intuitions have a philosophical character, which corresponds to ideas propounded by the German thinkers Kant, Hegel, Friedrich Wilhelm Joseph von Schelling (1775–1854), and Arthur Schopenhauer (1788–1860), but they resist systematization:

■ My main object was to insist that the 'mystic', 'visionary', 'sublime', aspect of Wordsworth's poetry must not be slighted. [...] His poetic experiences, his intuitions, his single thoughts, even his large views, correspond in a striking way, with ideas methodically developed by Kant, Schelling, Hegel, Schopenhauer. They remain admirable material for philosophy; and a philosophy which found itself driven to treat them as moonshine would probably be a very poor affair. But they are like the experience and the utterances of men of religious genius; great truths are enshrined in them, but generally the shrine would have to be broken to liberate these truths in a form which would satisfy the desire to understand.[5] □

Bradley's hugely influential discussion changes the terms in which *The Prelude* will be discussed for much of the twentieth century. He does this in two ways: first, by underscoring the sublimity and mysticism in *all* the poetry, he insists that Wordsworth be taken seriously as a thinker and visionary as well as a poetic craftsman – indeed, that these roles are inseparable. Second, he constructs a hermeneutic 'shrine' around *The Prelude*. Bradley maintains that Wordsworth's poetry is unique in the manner in which it fuses metaphorical and literal meaning. As a result, the meaning of the poem, though pregnant with truth, is resistant to interpretation through ordinary language. This in turn opens up, as it were, a space for criticism outside both poetry and philosophy. It is with this space, conceived as profound but ineffable, that later twentieth-century criticism will be occupied.

Bradley's insistence on the unparaphrasable nature of Wordsworth's language influenced a second critical current, which also emerged from the academy: textual scholarship. Thus, while Victorian readers had, for the most part, encountered Wordsworth's poems – including occasional excerpts from *The Prelude* – in anthologies, one finds in the textual criticism of Ernest de Selincourt and Helen Darbishire (1881–1961) the first concerted attempt to represent the curve of Wordsworth's poetic development through careful editorial oversight. De Selincourt's publication, for the first time, of parallel texts of the 1805 and 1850 versions of *The Prelude* is the most significant instance of this new scrupulousness. Darbishire was the first to submit the variant texts of the poem to a thorough critical analysis. In her essay, 'Wordsworth's *Prelude*', published close on the heels of De Selincourt's parallel edition, she initially notes the most obvious differences between the two poems: the 'bald simplicity' of the earlier text giving place 'to a more decorative, more obviously literary form', while 'revolutionary politics [are] checked', to make room for a 'more orthodox pattern' of moral and religious conceptions.[6] However, she continues:

■ [T]he most vital changes lie deeper still; they touch what we should now call the psychology of the poem. The inspiration of Wordsworth's poetry had its vitalising source in the power with which he realised a particular experience. The experience begins in sensation and ends in thought. It begins in such an adventure of the senses as that of his boyish birds-nesting:

> Oh! when I have hung
> Above the raven's nest, by knots of grass
> And half-inch fissures in the slippery rock
> But ill sustained, and almost (so it seemed)
> Suspended by the blast that blew amain,
> Shouldering the naked crag, oh, at that time
> While on the perilous ridge I hung alone,

> With what strange utterance did the loud dry wind
> Blow through my ear! the sky seemed to me not a sky
> Of earth – and with what motion moved the clouds! –

(a passage whose power and significance is inexplicable; for what can we say of those last bare words except that they 'carry alive into the heart' something we have all heard with our ears and seen with our eyes, yet never felt with so strange a thrill?)

[...]

The core of the experience was an intense consciousness of Nature passing through his senses to his mind; and the growth of that consciousness, its action and reaction upon his inner life, is the central theme of *The Prelude*. The experience was peculiar simply in its intensity. So pure and strong was the life his senses led that it passed, on a tide of feeling, into the life of his spirit. Here lies the mystery which he calls, in a significant phrase, the 'incumbent mystery of sense and soul'. What matters to us is not so much to understand the experience as to realise it, not so much to solve the mystery as to see where it lies. This is what the early *Prelude* helps us to do. In it Wordsworth told the inner workings of his mind as nakedly and truthfully as he could; and the changes most to be deplored in the later text are those which overlay or obscure the naïve immediate expression. They generally mar the poetry; they always disguise the truth.[7] □

One can detect more than a faint echo of Bradley in Darbishire's claim that the power and significance of *The Prelude* is 'inexplicable', and in her assertion that '[w]hat matters to us is not so much to understand the experience as to realise it'. Moreover, in her deprecation of what she sees as the bland pieties and orthodoxy of the 1850 poem, and celebration of the simplicity, intensity, and honesty of the 1805 version, she reflects the changing literary values of her own era.

The Private Life of *The Prelude*

A third major development in this period that radically altered attitudes to Wordsworth's poetry was a heightened interest in his personal life. This also refocused interest in *The Prelude*, not least by making Wordsworth's biography a focal point in debates about his work. The origins of this trend lie with the appearance of what is effectively the first full-length study of *The Prelude*: Emile Legouis' *La Jeunesse de William Wordsworth*, which was published in 1896. Legouis highlighted Wordsworth's stay in France in the early 1790s and his connections with the French Revolution. He also drew attention to the love affair that the poet had during this period with Annette Vallon, and the birth of their daughter, Caroline, in 1792. While Legouis's study is circumspect in drawing inferences about Wordsworth's poetry from his life, however, Herbert Read's *Wordsworth* (1930) goes further, arguing that Wordsworth's 'decline' following his 'great decade' was largely the result of an abiding and crippling sense of guilt over the affair and his abandonment of Annette and Caroline. The notion that Wordsworth's work weakened following a 'magical' decade of productivity between 1798 and 1808 was hardly new – it had already been trailed by Arnold – but it had new life breathed into it by De Selincourt's and Darbishire's acclaim for the 1805 *Prelude*. Read's contribution to this debate is to offer a biographical explanation for the poet's failing voice, arguing, with Legouis, that the main interest of *The Prelude* lies not in its 'biographical veracity', but in the 'delicate relations' it reveals 'between poetry and the poet's experience'. As Read explains in his Introduction, his argument falls into two parts:

■ I have two general intentions. The first is strictly biographical, and concerns the development of Wordsworth's personality. That has too often and too exclusively been treated as an intellectual development. I wish to treat it as equally an emotional development. Wordsworth himself set a certain fashion by writing *The Prelude*, which was conceived as an account of the growth of a poet's *mind*. This was quite specifically the intention of the author of that remarkable poem. But what is the mind of the poet? Is it conceived as independent of the body? [...] The *Prelude* is a great poem; upon its greatness we base the claim of Wordsworth to be considered as one of our major poets; but its greatness does not consist in its biographical veracity. It is not a true poem in that sense. Rather it is a deliberate mask. It is an idealization of the poet's life, not the reality. To show what that reality was – that is my first purpose.

My second purpose is critical [...]. I believe that Wordsworth in his life and literary activities reveals more clearly than any other poet in our literature the delicate relations that exist between poetry and the poet's experience. [...] The division between his good poetry and his bad poetry is clear and unmistakable. The good poetry is almost entirely confined to a definite period. What correlations can we make between the physical, psychological and economic factors in Wordsworth's life, and the nature of his verse?[8] □

Following this biographical method, Read is unable to agree with Arnold that Wordsworth's qualities as a poet only emerge once one ignores his philosophy, since 'in practice it is impossible to say where the philosophy ends and the poetry begins [...]. His poetry is his philosophy and neither can be distinguished from his private belief.'[9] The key to understanding all of these, he argues, is the poetic epiphany the poet experienced following his return from his second visit to France:

■ It came as an aftermath, as an issue from the emotional storm that descended upon him in France. As that storm subsided, the outraged feelings sought compensation in memories; and then, at first slowly, then riotously, the treasury of his unconscious mind, so richly stored in child-hood, was opened and given forth in the poetry of one wonderful decade.

Such is the main theme of this book. Wordsworth was a poet, and supreme poet, for a limited period of about ten years. This period does not emerge gradually out of his youth or adolescence. It begins almost sud-denly at the age of twenty-seven; it comes to an end, just as suddenly, at the age of thirty-seven.[10] □

While Read subscribes wholly to Arnold's notion of Wordsworth's 'miraculous decade', he maintains that the work produced in this period, especially the 1805 *Prelude*, cannot fully be appreciated without a biographical account of the emotional backwash that followed the poet's intense affair with Annette Vallon:

■ Above all, I want to emphasize the interdependence of emotional and intellectual development. We grow to hate the object of a dead passion, but we do not acknowledge this to ourselves; we transfer that hatred to things associated with the dead passion. In this manner, Wordsworth gradually renounced the cause of humanity. That was one process of emotional com-pensation. Another existed in the poetic sublimation of his feelings.[11] □

This poetic 'sublimation' fuels Wordsworth's considerable poetic out-put between 1798 and 1808. However, Read argues, once the poet had exhausted this supply of unprocessed emotional material, he found no other reserves with which he could fire his imagination. This situ-ation was not helped by his increasingly complacent personality or his increasingly comfortable lifestyle. Wordsworth's growing conserva-tism, his avoidance of emotional excitement and intellectual challenge, and above all his preference for the tranquilizing life of middle–class country retirement and a passionless marriage to Mary Hutcheson, ultimately suffocated his poetic voice:

■ 'Feeling comes in aid of feeling' – that continues to be the basis of Wordsworth's poetic activity. But a poet who has hurtfully segregated and isolated his being, both externally by divorcing himself from a critical mas-culine society, and internally by denying his instinctive love and making merely a placid convention of marriage – such a poet is killing his feelings at the root. Composition becomes more and more difficult – more and more an enervating experience.[12] □

Whatever one makes of Read's argument, it is significant for two rea-sons: first, it confirms the newly assumed place of *The Prelude* as per-haps *the* central text in the Wordsworthian corpus; second, by refusing to take the meaning of the life experiences the poem describes at face

value – by reading, as it were, against the grain – it sets an important precedent for how the poem will be approached by future critics.
Read, for example, interprets the elision of the 'Vaudracour and Julia'
episode (a story, like that of William and Annette, of frustrated love) in
Book IX from versions of the MS after 1820 as the editorial intervention of an older writer who was already well advanced in the unhappy
process of 'killing his feelings at the root'.

With his keen interest in the hinterlands of Wordsworth's psychological life, Read has more than one occasion to note the 'abnormal
affection that existed between brother and sister'.[13] This 'abnormal' relationship between William and Dorothy in turn becomes a major theme
of F.W. Bateson's 1954 study, *Wordsworth: A Reinterpretation*. Bateson's
book builds its argument around a highly speculative account of the
poet's sublimated emotional life, an approach which raised a few eye-
brows when the book was first published. In his Preface to the second
edition, Bateson defends his interpretation of the relationship between
William and Dorothy, arguing that such an approach is unavoidable
when dealing with Romantic poets: 'There is an omnipresent difference in kind between the best Romantic poetry and that written before
and after it,' he argues: '*the reader's continuous awareness in it of the poet
himself*'.[14] Moreover, he adds, a new critical paradigm is required if
Wordsworth's reputation is to survive in the twentieth century:

■ If we are to go on wanting Wordsworth's poetry, that too must be capable
of providing some kind of intellectual satisfaction. The sentimental satisfac-
tions that it gave the Wordsworthians and the Arnoldians have not survived
two world wars, a world slump and the atomic bombs. In the mid-twentieth
century, to put it crudely, the poems must *make sense*; and to make sense
of them the modern reader must be able to relate them significantly to the
emotional undercurrents of Wordsworth's life and personality. □

Significantly, it is in *The Prelude*, Bateson argues, that 'Wordsworth
has given us a model of how to guess intelligently, if not always quite
frankly, about both the man himself and his extraordinary powers'.[15]
In particular, Bateson finds the peculiar character of the poet's relationship with nature to be symptomatic of underlying psychological
disturbances:

■ In his self-analysis in *The Prelude* Wordsworth lays particular stress on
the contribution of fear to his natural piety. In an interesting passage in
Book I, for example, a distinction is drawn between the 'gentlest visitations'
with which nature may educate a specially 'favor'd Being' (he seems to
have had Dorothy in mind here) and the 'Severer interventions' employed
in his own case. He was disciplined, he says, by 'pain and fear'. Nature's

instructions were sometimes milder, but that was 'rarely in my boyish boys'. Generally speaking his initiation into the religion of nature was painful and alarming.

There was certainly a neurotic element in Wordsworth's attitude to nature. His ecstatic, terrified absorption in natural scenery is worlds away from the healthy delight of [Geoffrey] Chaucer [c.1343/4–1400] and Shakespeare in the processes of vegetable and mineral growth. Wordsworth's nature – 'rocks and stones and trees,' rivers and mists, winds, stars and rainbows – is curiously uncreative and dead. Was it perhaps primarily a mirror in which his subconscious mind could reflect itself? Things can often be said in terms of 'nature', through the intervention of a symbol, that cannot be said, or even thought, directly and objectively.[16] □

For Bateson, the main interest of *The Prelude* lies in its therapeutic value for Wordsworth. Faced by things 'that cannot be said' – chiefly, his incestuous love for Dorothy – Wordsworth forsakes direct engagement with the world (social commentary and philosophical speculation) in favour of an exploration of his own mind and memory, a strategy that Bateson dubs the 'egotistical sublime'. This strategy, however, comes at a price:

■ The author of the Lucy poems, 'Intimations of Immortality' and *The Prelude* [...] could only solve his personal crisis – the tragic discovery that he and his sister were passionately in love with each other – by eliminating every other being except himself from his emotional life. This process was largely, though not, I think, wholly, an unconscious one, and a casual inter-course was, of course, maintained with friends and acquaintances, including Dorothy. He even got married and had a family. But nobody seems to have been able during those difficult years to make any real contact with the deeper levels of his personality. The intensity with which as a school-boy and an undergraduate he had looked out onto the physical world and the profound emotional hunger which he had felt for primitive human nature in his second phase were now diverted into recollection in tranquil-ity, a process as selective as it was concentrated. Dorothy, for example, the innocent cause of the crisis, was excluded from Wordsworth's mem-ories of the past. It is significant that she plays no part in the account of the Cockermouth years in *The Prelude* [...]. [T]here was no place for her in the organs of Wordsworth's poetic imagination, and she was cut out like so much decayed tissue. The uncompromising ruthlessness of it is awe-inspiring, an act of necessary cruelty, inevitable but heart-breaking – to himself (there can be no doubt of it) even more than to Dorothy. So Agamemnon sacrificed Iphigenia [see the tragedy *Agamemnon* by the ancient Greek dramatist Aeschylus (525/4–456 BC)]. In the last analysis it is, I think, the absoluteness of this inner integrity above all that compels our reluctant admiration.[17] □

Finally then, the importance of *The Prelude* lies in what it betrays, in its elisions, lacunae, and internal pressure points, about the tragedy of Wordsworth's emotional life.

Bateson's symptomatological approach reflects growing interest in psychoanalytic methods in literary criticism, a tendency that gained considerable ground in the 1950s and early 1960s. It is no coincidence that another notable piece of psychoanalytic commentary on *The Prelude* dates from the same decade: Jonathan Bishop's influential 1959 essay, 'Wordsworth and the "Spots of Time".' Rather than use Wordsworth's autobiography to construct a general argument about the poet's career, however, Bishop brings recent psychological studies of memory to bear on the more local question of the role played by the 'spots of time' that punctuate the poem:

> ■ *The Prelude* is at the center of our experience of Wordsworth; at the center of our experience of *The Prelude* are those 'spots of time' where Wordsworth is endeavouring to express key moments in the history of his imagination. [...] Using the phrase in a looser sense, the 'spots of time' must include the descriptions of [...] such single events as the famous Stolen Boat episode, the Dedication to poetry, the Discharged Soldier, the Dream of the Arab-Quixote, the memory of the Winander Boy, the Drowned Man, Entering London, the father and the Child and the Blind Beggar, Simplon Pass, The Night in Paris, Robespierre's Death, and Snowdon. [...] How do we get into them? What sense does these crucial experiences make as we go over them in our minds? What do they appear to be *about*?[18] □

As Bishop examines these passages more closely, he establishes uncanny similarities between them: figural duplications, thematic echoes, and the recurrence of certain emotional rhythms and registers. This discovery leads him to conclude that behind these outwardly different reminiscences lies the same basic psychical exercise, rehearsed by the poet over and over again in an attempt to express buried and barely accessible emotional content:

> ■ We may even claim that *The Prelude* constitutes the record, half-concealed in a commonplace autobiographical structure, of a process which, in these days, we would call a self-analysis; the precipitate of an interior battle, a sequence of maneuvers against the incomprehensible, fought out in the public domain of verse.[19] □

Studies like Bateson's and Bishop's mark a new departure in *Prelude* criticism. First, by treating the poem as a 'case study' of psychological conflict and displacement, they reaffirm the poem's central (now almost pre-eminent) position in the Wordsworthian corpus. Second, and in a sense, more importantly, their estimations of *The Prelude*'s 'importance' do not rest upon 'literary' evaluations, traditionally conceived. One can detect in these commentators a desire to make literary criticism more rigorous, more 'serious', less based on aesthetic preference and moral judgement. This is clearly Bateson's intention. In his Preface to the first edition of *Wordsworth: A Reinterpretation*, he surveys the state of Wordsworth criticism at mid-century and finds little to celebrate. While 'Arnoldians' such as Darbishire have done little more than repeat 'what Arnold himself said in 1879', he claims, the New Criticism 'has contributed curiously little to our understanding of Wordsworth' beyond producing 'disappointingly perfunctory or marginal' essays. Worse, Bateson observes, 'there has been nothing in book-form, as far as I know, that can be said to have been written from a specifically twentieth-century point of view' (Read's book is an exception, Bateson admits, but even its habit 'of finding Annette lurking behind every rock, stone and tree becomes monotonous and irritating').[20]

Reassessing Tradition

One of the essays that Bateson found to be 'disappointingly perfunctory' was by F.R. Leavis in his study of Wordsworth in his 1936 book *Revaluation*. It is certainly true that unlike Bateson, Leavis has no theory to push. His principal aim is to rescue Wordsworth from the Victorians, especially Arnold, who had transmuted the poet into a simple nature worshipper and celebrator of 'life'. Against this, Leavis argues that Wordsworth's poetry represents 'a continuous development out of the eighteenth century', extending the Augustan tradition of Mark Akenside (1721–70), James Thomson (1700–48), and Thomas Gray (1716–71).[21] This debate aside, Leavis's essay is mainly occupied with correcting what he perceives to be the exaggerations or misapprehensions of other critics. Thus, against Read and other readers tempted to speculate on the lack of sensuality or eroticism in *The Prelude*, he maintains that there are 'no signs of morbid repression anywhere in Wordsworth's poetry'.[22] Similarly, against Bradley's insistence on the poet's mysticism he emphasizes the sobriety of Wordsworth's style and 'his essential sanity and normality'.[23] Finally, he offers a nuanced assessment of the perennial problem of Wordsworth's 'philosophy':

■ For Wordsworth's 'philosophy' certainly appears, as such, to invite discussion, and there is a general belief that we all know, or could know by re-reading *The Prelude*, what his doctrines concerning the growth of the mind and relation of Man to Nature are. His philosophic verse has a convincingly expository tone and manner, and it is difficult not to believe, after reading, say, Book II of *The Prelude*, that one has been reading a paraphrasable argument – difficult not to believe, though the paraphrase, if resolutely attempted, would turn out to be impossible. [...] This, at any rate, describes fairly the working of Wordsworth's philosophic verse. His triumph is to command the kind of attention he requires and to permit no other.[24] □

In this way, Leavis praises Wordsworth's philosophy as the achievement of an accomplished style – a rhetorical feat whereby the poet educes a certain kind of concentration from the reader – rather than the triumph of high argument. And yet, detecting the sleight of hand whereby *The Prelude* sways its reader does not lead Leavis to dismiss the power of Wordsworth's thought:

■ By an innocently insidious trick Wordsworth, in this calm ruminative progression, will appear to be preoccupied with a scrupulous nicety of statement, with a judicial weighing of alternative possibilities, while actually making it more difficult to check the argument from which he will emerge, as it were inevitably, with a far from inevitable conclusion. [...] Yet the burden of *The Prelude* is, nevertheless, not essentially ambiguous, and Wordsworth's didactic offer was not mere empty self-delusion. [...] He had, if not a philosophy, a wisdom to communicate.'[25] □

On the nature of this 'wisdom', however, and its relation to the purely philosophical, Leavis does not expand. It was not the purpose of *Revaluation*, nor was it Leavis's forte, to probe the philosophical implications of a poetry whose 'wisdom' outran any philosophy. Other critics of this period, however, were ready to undertake this task, and it is to these that we must turn now.

MIND AND NATURE

I mentioned at the beginning of this chapter that a number of developments in the first half of the twentieth century came together to effect a radical change in the way Wordsworth's poetry – and the place of *The Prelude* within it – was perceived. I have already discussed three of these: the rise of 'academic' criticism; the development of textual scholarship; and the growth of psychoanalytic interest in the relationship between Wordsworth's great autobiographical poem and his own life. A fourth change that occurred was a major reorientation in the way critics approached the 'philosophical' dimension of *The Prelude*. In a sense, this development was initiated as early as the first decade of the twentieth century by Bradley's identification of a tension in Wordsworth's poems between transcendentalism and naturalism. As critics and scholars began reassessing Wordsworth's thought in the wake of two world wars, however, they were less inclined than their Victorian forebears to cast the poet as the purveyor of quietistic wisdom and the wholesome philosophy of a life lived in defiance of urban modernity. Bateson's demand that Wordsworth be made relevant to the age of the atom bomb is typical of this new mindset, but not all readers felt that the former's psychoanalytical methods offered the most promising route to understanding *The Prelude*. Instead, they began to ask more searching questions about the character of Wordsworth's thought: could it be taken seriously as, say, a critique of scientific rationality? did it offer a coherent view of life, or was it essentially 'mystical' as Bradley had maintained? which streams of European thought had exercised the greatest influence over it? did it present a unified statement, or an awkward suspension of irreconcilable perspectives?

The Critique of Science

It is the first of these questions that the philosopher A.N. Whitehead (1861–1947) addresses in his discussion of *The Prelude* in his 1826 work, *Science and the Modern World*. Whitehead spent much of his career attacking the traditional division of nature into the realm of appearances (what we perceive through the senses) and that of causation (the colourless, silent world that gives rise to our experience). The job of science, he argues, was not to go in search of hidden 'causes', but to explore the content of perception. In *The Prelude*, Whitehead finds a powerful critique of the scientism of modernity, exhibiting a heightened awareness of the fundamental unity of mind and nature, what he describes as the relationship between the 'prehensive' (intuitive) unities of thought and the 'modal' (formal) connections between them:

■ Wordsworth's greatest poem is, by far, the first book of *The Prelude*. It is pervaded by this sense of the haunting presences of nature. A series of magnificent passages, too long for quotation, express this idea. Of course, Wordsworth is a poet writing a poem, and is not concerned with dry philosophical statements. But it would hardly be possible to express more clearly a feeling for nature, as exhibiting entwined prehensive unities, each suffused with modal presences of others:

> Ye presences of Nature in the sky
> And on the earth! Ye visions of the hills!
> And Soul of lonely places! can I think
> A vulgar hope was yours when ye employed
> Such ministry, when ye through many a year
> Haunting me thus among my boyish sports,
> On caves and trees, upon the woods and hills,

Impressed upon all forms the characters
Of danger or desire; and thus did make
The surface of the universal earth
With triumph and delight, with hope and fear,
Work like a sea? ...

In thus citing Wordsworth, the point which I wish to make is that we forget how strained and paradoxical is the view of nature which modern science imposes on our thoughts. Wordsworth, to the height of genius, expresses the concrete facts of our apprehension, facts which are distorted in the scientific analysis. Is it not possible that the standardized concepts of science are only valid within narrow limitations, perhaps too narrow for science itself?[26] □

Whitehead enlists the poet in his own attack on abstract systems of rationality that place too much emphasis on the analytical power at the expense of the synthetical. For Whitehead, the fact that Wordsworth 'is a poet writing a poem, and is not concerned with dry philosophical statements' actually makes him more, not less interesting from the perspective of philosophy, for it is precisely the poet's view of nature as always already imbued with *value* that modern science, with its 'standardized concepts', has neglected. What Wordsworth recognizes – and *The Prelude* expresses – is that philosophy can never become objective by detaching itself entirely from human values:

■ I hold that philosophy is the critic of abstractions. [...] Both Shelley and Wordsworth emphatically bear witness that nature cannot be divorced from its aesthetic values; and that these values arise from the cumulation, in some sense, of the brooding presence of the whole onto its various parts.[27] □

To see what is at stake in Whitehead's reading of *The Prelude*, we need only turn to D.G. James's counterargument in *Poetry and Scepticism*, published a decade later in 1936. Where Whitehead casts Wordsworth as the scourge of scientism and the calculating intellect, James depicts him as a writer whose work was handicapped by a basic misunderstanding regarding the role that science plays (or, more precisely, does *not* play) in human life. This failing in itself James finds lamentable, but it is worsened considerably in his eyes by the fact that Wordsworth's own experience, he believes, should have counselled him against such a fundamental error. In *The Prelude*, he argues,

■ Wordsworth writes in resentment of the life of intellectual inquiry. But why? Wordsworth should surely have seen that there is as urgent a practical and moral necessity to exercise the intelligence to the full extent of its powers as to the exercise the powers of the imagination. And later, we find the following –

> Science then
> Shall be a precious visitant; and then,
> And only then, be worthy of her name:
> For then her heart shall kindle; her dull eye,
> Dull and inanimate, no more shall hang
> Chained to its object in brute slavery ...

nor –

> Shall it forget that its most noble use,
> Its most illustrious province, must be found
> In furnishing clear guidance, a support
> Not treacherous, to the mind's *excursive* power.

This is the height of nonsense. Such a condescending attitude to science is merely silly [...]. It is monstrous to seek to justify science and philosophy by any other than intellectual values; it is still more monstrous that Wordsworth should thus ignore all that his experience had most clearly taught him. Had he reflected a little more he would have seen, what indeed he should have seen from his own experience, that science is simply irrelevant to the problems of life. [...] The fact is that science can no more offer clear guidance or reliable support to the imagination than it can offer false guidance or doubtful support to the imagination; and there was a time in Wordsworth's life when he saw this, compelled on him as it was by the very anguish of his experience.[28] □

Of course, the 'science' of which Whitehead and James write in the early twentieth century is quite a different entity from that with which Wordsworth would have been familiar. The 'scientific analysis' of the world that Whitehead criticizes had long since been professionalized and separated into disciplines, each of which deployed a discourse inaccessible to those who had not gone through a lengthy and rigorous process of education and training. The 'science' of which Wordsworth writes, however, is, at base, a form of natural philosophy, the terms of which could still generally be understood by those with the intelligence, inclination, and leisure to pursue them. Whitehead's claim, however, is that, those differences notwithstanding, *The Prelude* offers a challenge to a certain outlook or set of attitudes common to any rigidly 'scientific' conception of the world, and that this challenge has lost neither its urgency or its acuity with the advent of the twentieth century.

The Rise of Intellectual History

As mentioned above, a further question that increasingly occupied readers of *The Prelude* in the early twentieth century concerned

Wordsworth's philosophical antecedents, and his relationship to different traditions of thought in Europe. The pioneering work in this subject was undertaken by American scholars such as Arthur Beatty and Newton Stallknecht. Beatty's 1922 study, *William Wordsworth: His Doctrine and Art in their Historical Relations*, offers a distinctive reading of the poet by placing him squarely within a long and distinguished tradition of British empirical thought. As he puts it, '[b]y connecting Wordsworth with English philosophy we may the more clearly see why he approached his theories by way of associationism, and discussed them in such terms as nature, emotion, imagination, fancy, activity, power, reason and so on'.[29] Like many commentators from this period, Beatty bases his readings of *The Prelude* upon the 1850 version, a practice he continues in the second edition of his book – printed in 1927, a year after De Selincourt's publication of the 1805 text – on the grounds that his primary concern with the poem is philosophical rather than stylistic. On this point Beatty's argument is unequivocal:

■ [W]e must note at once that the method by which he [i.e. Wordsworth] explains the union of the mind of man with this goodly universe is essentially in line with the general tradition of English philosophy. There can be no manner of doubt that he approaches the whole problem of mind from the angle of Locke, basing his whole theory on the assumption that thought originates in experience, and that out of the products of sensation, or experience, ideas and the more complex forms of mentality are developed.[30] □

Beatty is keen to represent Wordsworth as a poet who extends the empirical and materialist tradition in Anglophone philosophy. According to Beatty, the poet does this in two ways. First, his poetry assimilates the key precept of the empiricist philosopher John Locke (1632–1704), namely, that all human knowledge is based upon experience; second, it builds on the doctrine of the association of ideas expounded by David Hartley (1705–57). Hartley's theories were an important early influence upon Wordsworth and Coleridge. At their core is the materialist argument that sensation and perception are the products of the vibration of minute particles (the association of ideas) in the brain. Beatty argues that *The Prelude* incorporates associationist theory, and in particular, the Hartleian thesis that human emotions are secondary to sensation, and derived from feeling through a process of association:

■ A most important aspect of Hartley's treatment of these two faculties of the affections and understanding is their mutual relations. [...] Hartley plainly makes the affections derivative from ideas [...]. This makes emotion, or feeling, secondary to the intellectual processes. [...] The secondary and 'factitious' nature of emotion is explicitly maintained by Wordsworth in many passages, and is always assumed. In a notable passage of *The Prelude*, he says that he 'has been sedulous to trace how Nature by extrinsic (*i.e.* "factitious") passion first peoples the mind with forms sublime or fair'; and goes on to develop this idea. As a child he felt 'gleams like the flashings of a shield', and,

> the earth
> And common face of Nature spake to me
> Rememberable things; sometimes, 'tis true,
> By chance collisions and quaint accidents
> (Like those ill-sorted unions, work supposed)
> Of evil-minded fairies), yet not vain
> Nor profitless, if haply they impressed
> Collateral objects and appearances,
> Albeit lifeless then, and doomed to sleep
> Until maturer seasons called them forth
> To impregnate and to elevate the mind,
> – And if the vulgar joy by its own weight
> Wearied itself out of the memory,
> The scenes which were a witness of that joy
> Remained in their substantial lineaments
> Depicted on the brain, and to the eye
> Were visible a daily sight; and thus
> By the impressive discipline of fear,
>
> By pleasure and repeated happiness,
> So frequently repeated, and by force
> Of obscure feelings representative
> Of things forgotten, these same scenes so bright,
> So beautiful, so majestic in themselves,
> Though yet the day was distant, did become
> Habitually dear, and all their forms
> And changeful colours by invisible links
> Were fastened to the affections.

This is pure associationism, both in the doctrine of the extrinsic nature of feeling and in the quite definite naming of the particular passions of *fear* and *pleasure* as the leading forces in this association and transmutation of feeling.[31] □

Beatty's argument that *The Prelude* is 'pure associationism' implies that, on a thematic level, the poem engages with the issue of how human psychology is formed by the association of ideas. But it goes further than that. For Beatty, *The Prelude* is an associationist poem both thematically and *methodologically*: in other words, association determines not just the subject matter of the poem, but also the *manner* in which it was composed and formed by the poet. This is why, he claims, the influence of Locke and the empirical tradition must always be fore-grounded in any interpretation of Wordsworth's poetry:

> ■ [I]f we remember that Wordsworth's poetry is fundamentally influenced by Locke and associationism we can easily understand why he adopts the psychological, autobiographical method so generally used in his poetry. [...] From his associationistic connections come his methods of conducting *The Prelude*. It is biographical in a sense, but not purely or mainly so: it is a psychological, or philosophical, poem, which gives a sketch of the chief factors in the development of a mind from childhood to maturity.[32] □

For some commentators, however, this picture of Wordsworth's philo-sophical affiliations was one-dimensional. Almost two decades later, Newton Stallknecht's study, *Strange Seas of Thought* (1945), attempted to steer the debate towards a more distinctly non-empirical picture of the poet, one that stressed the influence of continental theology of the seventeenth century rather than the Enlightenment rationalism of the eighteenth. As he puts it in his opening chapter, 'my purpose in this study is to examine the content and the origin of the major concepts by means of which Wordsworth presents his view of life. These concepts constitute the rational aspect of a philosophy that is not itself primar-ily rationalist.'[33] For Stallknecht, far more significant than Locke in this 'rational [...] philosophy that is not itself primarily rationalist' is the theologian Jakob Boehme (1575–1624). Boehme's works argue for the possibility of an immediate spiritual contemplation of the divine through the 'language' of nature by defending an ontology in which God and nature are one. As Stallknecht points out, however, Boehme's mysticism clashed with the discourse of empirical objectivity that Wordsworth had inherited from British eighteenth-century philoso-phy. As a result, he argues, we find in a poem like *The Prelude* a 'strug-gle' between a rationalist/empirical tradition (represented by Locke, the Encyclopaedists of the French Enlightenment, and the political thinker and novelist William Godwin [1756–1836]), and a mystical/intuitive one (represented by Boehme, the founder of the Society of Friends [Quakers] George Fox (1624–91), and the religious writer William Law [1686–1761]):

> ■ The latter books of *The Prelude* record a prolonged struggle between two ways of thought: mystical intuition, on one hand, and, on the other, 'scientific' reason supported only by the evidence of sensuous observation. The rational 'enlightenment' of the *philosophe*, deliberately and methodic-ally produced, is opposed to the insight of the poet and mystic which comes upon him often uninvited and never deliberately planned. Historically, we may say that in Wordsworth's thought of 1795 two traditions conflict: that of

Locke, the Encyclopaedists, and Godwin against that of Boehme, Fox, and Law: on the one hand the political theory of the French Revolution, on the other the faith of the mystical enthusiast.[34] □

While Stallknecht's conclusions about Wordsworth are in many respects the opposite of Beatty's, however, his method of exposition and analysis is remarkably similar. Like Beatty, he draws parallels between Wordsworth and a purportedly influential earlier writer by directly comparing passages selected from *The Prelude* with extracts from the work of the latter. Thus, when he comes to discuss Wordsworth's treatment of the senses in *The Prelude*, for example, he cites Boehme's work *A Treatise of Christ's Testament* (1624):

■ For both Wordsworth and Boehme, the senses are not to be scorned by the mystic and the nature-lover. The senses link the human mind to the world around it, and it is in large measure through the senses that the activity and power of things come home to the mind. [...] But more striking still are the echoes of Boehme which appear in *The Prelude*. Let us first consider a famous passage from Book VI (ll. 525 ff.). We must consider both versions, that of 1805 and that of 1850.

> Imagination – here the Power so called
> Through sad incompetence of human speech,
> That awful Power rose from the mind's abyss
> Like an unfathered vapour that enwraps,
> At once, some lonely traveller. I was lost;
> Halted without an effort to break through;
> But to my conscious soul I now can say –
> 'I recognise thy glory:' in such strength
> Of usurpation, when the light of sense
> Goes out, but with a flash that has revealed
> The invisible world, doth greatness make abode,
> There harbours; whether we be young or old,
> Our destiny, our being's heart and home,
> Is with infinitude, and only there;
> With hope it is, hope that can never die,
> Effort, and expectation, and desire.
> And something evermore about to be. [...]

The figure of *imagination* arising from the *abyss* and the mention of *desire* and of *something evermore about to be*, linked as they are with the notion of infinitude, must be considered with reference to the following passages (*A Treatise of Christ's Testament*, Chapter I):

3. For if there be a Formability to a Figure, then there must also have been a Cause from whence the Form were arisen, and God were not one only God, who were without Ground, Time, and Place; for all that hath a

Beginning hath a Ground; but that which hath no Beginning, is without Ground and Form.[35] □

Here, as elsewhere, no small part of the weight of Stallknecht's argument rests upon a fairly straightforward juxtapositioning of materials, often without further comment. Yet, though he finds *The Prelude* to be a poem rich in intellectual drama, caught between contrary legacies, he retains an ambivalence about its contribution to modernity. In particular, he bemoans 'Wordsworth's failure to integrate the philosophy of *The Prelude* with a theory of duty', a failure which 'constitutes a real loss to our modern culture'.[36] Finally, Stallknecht concludes, *The Prelude* fails to answer the questions: 'How are we to describe the interplay of conscience and ethical imagination without surrendering one wholly to the domination of the other? In other words, what is the inner check, and how is it related to imagination?'[37]

Wordsworthian Ambivalence

Questions like these helped to fuel the rise of a new kind of critical approach to *The Prelude*, exemplified by Beatty and Stallknecht, which sought to place the poem within a coherent narrative of intellectual history. This in turn influenced literary critics who retained an interest in more 'formal' questions, in particular those relating to Wordsworth's style and his attitude towards, and uses of, language. In particular, two studies from the 1950s reflect this influence by redirecting critical emphasis towards two key themes: language and temporality.

The first of these is *The Egotistical Sublime* by John Jones (born 1924), published in 1954. Unlike Beatty and Stallknecht, Jones has no general thesis to peddle about *The Prelude*. Instead, he is interested in the way in which Wordsworth rejects the eighteenth-century notion of language as the 'dress of thought' through his counterargument that language *embodies* thought:

■ Born into time, Wordsworth said that language is the incarnation of thought. Thought incarnate is not thought expressed, or there would be no need to distinguish the word and the mathematical symbol; but when he refuses to allow that thoughts are clothed in words, he fears not so much a direct confusion with mathematics as the reducing of language to a conceptual instrument, external to those who use it. Language must have a corresponding inwardness in order to enact the reciprocity of nature.[38] □

However, according to Jones, Wordsworth remained ambivalent about the implications of the notion of language as the 'incarnation' rather than the ornament of thought. On one hand, encouragingly, language no longer appeared to be arbitrary, the mere 'dress' of the intellect and imagination: instead, it was the living form, the manifestation of thought. On the other hand – rather less hearteningly – viewing language as unified with mind in this way threatened to incarcerate thought and experience within the prison-house of language. This in turn creates a peculiar contortion within Wordsworth's poetry: a simultaneous striving to embrace, and to escape, the agency of the letter. Thus, Jones identifies the 'murmured succession, the fearful patter, the prolonged striving' that he detects in Wordsworth's style as 'different kinds of escape almost from language itself, to experience worlds outside language'. Alongside this, however, there is the constant tendency of Wordsworth's language to turn in on itself: it is as if, realizing that there is no positive experience outside language, *The Prelude* endeavours to escape language by negating its presence:

■ Wordsworth carries his delight in negatives to the point of tiresome mannerism: there are too many double negatives, such as 'not unnoticed'; too much rhetorical piling of adjective on adjective – 'unchastened, unsubdued, unawed, unraised' – and pointless circumlocution – 'not seldom' and 'nor seldom' appear five times in the final text of *The Prelude*. But the roots of this practice run very deep; the balance of positive and negative is a mode of reciprocity, like echo and reflection in his landscape. It also shows the unmathematical nature of language. If two minuses make a plus, it is a special kind of plus: the negative form can be on its own account heart-piercing.[39] □

Here, Jones makes an important suggestion. By comparing the 'unmathematical' negativity of Wordsworth's language to the exchanges of 'echo and reflection' in his encounters with landscape, Jones intimates that at the heart of the poem is a phenomenological process in which the relationship between mind and world is always *mediated*. According to this account – and contrary to traditional readings of *The Prelude* – the poem does not trace the way the poet's consciousness *transcends* nature, but explores the dynamic give–and–take (what Jones calls the 'mode of reciprocity') wherein mind constitutes nature and nature constitutes mind: an activity better described as *dialectical*. It is this dialectic of consciousness and world that is expressed by the negativity of Wordsworth's language.

Where Jones sees negativity as a product of Wordsworth's ambivalence over language, David Ferry identifies a more fundamental ambivalence at the heart of Wordsworth's poetry, and *The Prelude* in particular. In the Preface to his 1959 book *The Limits of Mortality*, Ferry clearly positions his own discussion 'against the "Arnoldian" tendency to take Wordsworth's vocabulary of feeling at face value' and 'against attempts,

like that of Sir Leslie Stephen, to endow Wordsworth with a coherent morality or ethic'. He aligns himself with those critics who 'have
tended to see his language not as an exercise in "simplicity" and "nat-
uralness" but as a symbolic system'.[40] Ferry believes that the function
of the critic is to discover in the poet 'ideas and feelings which can in
some way be related to our own deepest feelings and ideas, and which
are able to make their appeal ultimately outside the limits of their own
time'.[41] It is here that Wordsworth's ambivalence comes into play, for
the 'ideas and feelings in Wordsworth's most important poems', Ferry
argues, 'are lovingly hostile to the humane world'. This ambivalence
or loving enmity is especially apparent in Wordsworth's view of 'man's
relations to nature with respect to his mortality':

■ For it is the limits of mortality that define man as what he is, individual,
idiosyncratic, circumscribed; and it is against the mortal limitations of man
that Wordsworth, in my view of him, conceived such a hatred.[42] □

For Ferry, then, *The Prelude* is a text in conflict with itself. On one
hand, it pushes towards an antihumanistic view of reality – what Ferry
calls 'sacramentalist' – as the poet portrays nature as a symbol of man's
fundamentally *infinite* nature:

■ *The Prelude* is our summary example of how a symbolic or sacramentalist view of the world tends to derogate or at least limit the variety of
'ordinary' human emotions and involvements, those defined by limitation in
time and space. For a poet like Wordsworth, the world is not so much the
scene of such involvements as it is a kind of cipher or hieroglyph, symbol-
izing man's fundamental and unchanging relation to order. Those things in
man which must be defined as distinctively human can only be regarded as
intrusions into, even perversions of, that fundamental relation.[43] □

This vision is antithetical to everyday humanity: as such, it precludes
quotidian or commonplace experience, because such experience connotes finitude, and thus death. And yet, Wordsworth's antihumanism
could never entirely vanquish his awareness of temporality, the inevitable intrusion of contingency and human personality into the mind's
relationship with nature. As a result, the poet's consciousness that these
'limits of mortality' will always be the ruin of his eternal, symbolic, or
'sacramental' view of nature produces a poetry that is, for Ferry, fundamentally *tragic*:

■ The natural scene can be the equivalent of the eternal, but man, because
he has personality, is doomed to his temporal limitation:

Should the whole frame of earth by inward throes
Be wrenched, or fire come down from far to scorch

Her pleasant habitations, and dry up
Old Ocean, in his bed left singed and bare,
Yet would the living Presence still subsist
Victorious, and composure would ensue,
And kindlings like the morning – presage sure
Of day returning and of life revived.
But all the meditations of mankind,
Yea, all the adamantine holds of truth
By reason built, or passion, which itself
Is highest reason in a soul sublime;
The consecrated works of Bard and Sage,
Sensuous or intellectual, wrought by men,
Twin labourers and heirs of the same hopes;
Where would they be?

(Bk. V, ll. 30–45)

Because of this limitation, which makes one despair of even the greatest human achievements (indeed *especially* of them), man's sacramental imagination is necessarily a failure, and the poet harkens desperately back to the lost childhood, which had exhibited a 'mystical' relation to eternity and which needed no intercessors. The poem never seeks to assert, it is true, that this mysticism can be regained. But the effects of its nostalgia are apparent everywhere, at worst in the unresolved ambiguity of the concluding books, straining as they do at a tone of triumph which is constantly being undercut, and at best in such a passage as the dream of the stone and the shell in Book V (ll. 50–140). There the poet recognizes most clearly the fundamental pessimism of his attitude toward human experience and toward poetry, and there, because of this recognition, his vision is genuinely tragic.[44] □

The detection of a fundamental ambivalence or equivocation in *The Prelude* marks a turning point in Wordsworth criticism at mid-century. In the 1950s, critics such as Jones and Ferry are, on the whole, content to observe these tensions and move on to analyse and evaluate Wordsworth's poetry following traditional methods of interpretation, invoking notions of authorial intention and poetic form that Wordsworth himself would not have found especially surprising or challenging. Later commentators, however, would find in Wordsworthian ambivalence symptoms of a more troubling condition, one which undermined the very concepts of 'author' and 'meaning'.

CHAPTER THREE

Style, Philosophy, and Phenomenology

By the 1960s, a number of new trends are evident in the critical reception of *The Prelude*. First, critics were eager to locate Wordsworth within a tradition of visionary, prophetic, and apocalyptic writing, one which resonated nicely with the political upheavals in Europe and America in the 1960s and 1970s. At the same time, many commentators were ready to view the complexities of the mind/nature relation in Wordsworth in terms of dialectic rather than paradox. More fundamental still, however, were the transformations that were taking place in the ways in which English literature was studied and taught, changes which, in turn, raised new sets of problems.

Chief among these transformations was the erosion of the empirical basis of traditional scholarship and historicism. Many critics were now prepared to challenge the image of criticism as the interpretation and evaluation of a given text (an object) by an 'impartial' reader (a subject). At the forefront of this dissent were the critical movements inspired by the expanding theoretical fields of psychoanalysis (which, following Sigmund Freud, tended to treat texts in terms of the psychopathology of creativity), structuralism (which, following the linguist Ferdinand de Saussure [1857–1913], sought to understand the text purely as a system of signs), and above all, phenomenology (which, following the philosophers Edmund Husserl [1859–1938] and Martin Heidegger [1889–1976], explores texts for the disclosure of being through consciousness).

Ultimately, these readings were in turn to be questioned by the changing theoretical, historical, and methodological assumptions of the succeeding decades. Moreover, even as these currents were brought to bear upon criticism and commentary on *The Prelude*, traditional lines of inquiry about the poem continued to be extended and revised. Thus, in this period, which saw Geoffrey Hartman's groundbreaking phenomenological study and Harold Bloom's influential reading of Wordsworth's poetry, we also find significant work by William Empson and Christopher Ricks on the style of *The Prelude*, as well as

M.H. Abrams' landmark reassessment of the poet's philosophical outlook and background. It is to the question of style that I shall turn
first.

STYLE AND THE NEW CRITICISM

Some of the finest studies of the style and rhetoric of *The Prelude*
appeared between the 1950s and 1970s. Written at a time when the
influence of New Criticism was at its peak in English Literature
departments in North America and the United Kingdom, they
incorporate the hallmarks of that family of methods: chiefly, a belief
in the autonomy of the literary text and a disregard for 'external' –
historical, biographical, or social – factors in interpretation, as well
as an opposition to paraphrase and a dedication to dealing with texts
directly through 'close reading', involving a detailed attention to matters of irony, metaphor, symbol, paradox, verbal nuance, and thematic
structure. Leavis's demonstration (discussed in the section on The
Challenge of the Twentieth Century in Chapter 2) of the rhetorical
sleight of hand, or 'innocently insidious trick', whereby Wordsworth
manoeuvres his reader into accepting a highly contentious metaphysical argument, is a good example of this kind of approach. Broadly
within the same tradition is William Empson's account of *The Prelude*'s
vocabulary in his 1951 book *The Structure of Complex Words*. Other
studies must be cited here: Herbert Lindenberger's seminal 1963
monograph, *On Wordsworth's* Prelude, and Christopher Ricks' widely
anthologized 1971 essay, 'Wordsworth: "A Pure Organic Pleasure
from the Lines".' Although there are vital differences between these
works (Empson, for example, is no enemy of paraphrase in criticism), all generally eschew the more speculative turns of theory and
the broad philosophical generalizations of the history of ideas in
order to concentrate upon the formal and stylistic characteristics of
Wordsworth's poem.

A frontrunner for such approaches is William Empson's *The
Structure of Complex Words*, which, though not (as the title indicates) on
Wordsworth alone, brings close attention to bear upon the resonances
and ambiguities of key terms in his poetry. One such term upon which
Empson fastens is 'sense'. He is initially intrigued by the fact that in
roughly three-quarters of the instances where this word occurs in *The
Prelude*, it does so at the very *end* of a line, as in the 'Stolen Boat' episode, where the poet recounts how his brain 'Worked with a dim
and undetermined sense / Of unknown modes of being' (I, 418–420).
The effect of this in most cases, he observes, is that the term is held
'slightly apart from the stock phrase it comes in, so that some wider

meaning for it can be suggested'.[1] It is this wider meaning that interests Empson, for here the word 'sense' denotes neither sensation (as in
the 'five senses') nor judgement (as in 'common sense'), but something
altogether more elusive, namely, an awareness that is vague, intuitive,
and instinctive.

As Empson observes, this particular sense of the term 'sense' was
still quite new to the English language at the time that Wordsworth
was writing. Its ambiguous role in *The Prelude* is thus partly explained
by the fact that its connotations remained unsecure: Wordsworth's use
of the word in the poem, Empson claims, is marked by a hesitancy
that betrays his anxiety that 'sense' might morph into other, undesired
cognates: simple 'sensation'; scientific 'good sense'; sentimental 'sensibility'; or (worse yet) voluptuous 'sensuality'. In this respect, 'sense'
is no ordinary word, for it reflects an ambiguity at the very heart of
Wordsworth's writing. For while it is clearly vital for Wordsworth's
conception of mind and meaning that his use of 'sense' 'left room
for the alternative reading', the instability of this particular word has
broader implications about the relationship between meaning and
belief: in short, how do we make sense of the world and of others
when we are unclear about what *sense* the word 'sense' has?[2] This raises
philosophical problems in which neither Wordsworth nor Empson
care to become embroiled. Indeed, according to Empson, Wordsworth
did not have a *theory* about the term, 'but a manipulative feeling, of
what he could make it do; a thing more familiar perhaps to poets than
critics'.[3] The problem of how Wordsworth articulates 'sense' in *The
Prelude* is for Empson, then, a problem fundamentally of *style*, not of
theory.

One consequence of this ambiguity within the meaning of the word
'sense' is a drawing together of the rhetorics of sensation and imagination in *The Prelude*. Wherever 'the sense of' something is invoked,
the poet is enabled by the vagueness of the central term to flit between
what is asserted as fact and what is imagined:

■ The effect is that, though Sensation and Imagination appear as the two
extreme ends of the scale in view, so that one might expect them to be
opposites, the word is so placed that it might equally well apply to either.
And the middle of the scale, the idea of ordinary common sense, is cut from
these uses no less firmly than the idea of sensuality.[4] □

Empson believes that it is Wordsworth's stylistic exploitation of the
ambiguity of 'sense', rather than any theory of knowledge, that enables
'"Sensation and Imagination [to] interlock"' in *The Prelude*.[5] The
ambiguous relationship between the two faculties produces, in turn,
some curious effects. The most striking of these is the way in which

the poem appears both to denigrate and to exalt sense(–perception). To illustrate this, Empson turns to the 'Simplon Pass' passage in Book VI. Here, he notes how sense is figured as both a pathway and a barrier to insight:

■ On being told that he had crossed the Alps, he says, 'Imagination' –

That awful Power rose from the mind's abyss
Like an unfathered vapour that enwraps,
At once, some lonely traveller. I was lost;
Halted without an effort to break through;
But to my conscious soul I now can say
'I recognise thy glory'; in such strength
Of usurpation ...

[VI, 594–600]

– and 'the light of sense goes out.' [...] The next paragraph [...] calmly begins by saying that what this news caused at the time was 'a melancholy slackening'. But they hurry on down the gorge and see

The immeasurable height
Of woods decaying, never to be decayed ...
Winds thwarting winds, bewildered and forlorn ...
The rocks that muttered close upon our ears,
Black drizzling crags that spake by the way-side
As if a voice were in them; the sick sight
And giddy prospect of the raving stream ...

Nature is a ghastly threat in this fine description; he might well as in his childhood, have clasped a tree to see if it was real. But what all this is *like*, when the long sentence arrives at its peroration, is 'workings of one mind' (presumably God's or Nature's, so it is not merely *like*),

Characters of the great Apocalypse,
The types and symbols of Eternity,
Of first, and last, and midst, and without end.

The actual horror and the eventual exultation are quite blankly identified by this form of grammar.[6] □

Empson is struck by the way in which the horror of the immediate 'sense' (sensation) of the scene before Wordsworth merges almost imperceptibly with the exultation that accompanies its broader 'sense' (meaning, significance). This ambivalence is brilliantly captured, he claims, in the phrase 'the light of sense goes out', which simultaneously suggests a light extinguished *and* a light projected, illuminating the world. The only problem with this strategy, he further contends, is that what tends to get lost amid all the easy traffic between sensation and imagination is the presence of a mediating, *common* sense:

> ■ The word, I maintain, means both the process of sensing and the supreme act of imagination, and unites them by a jump; the same kind of jump as that in the sentence about crossing the Alps, which identifies the horror caused by the immediate sensations with the exultation that developed from them. And in both cases, one might complain, what is jumped over is 'good sense'; when Wordsworth has got his singing robes on he will not allow any mediating process to have occurred.[7] □

Of course, Wordsworth does not always have his 'singing robes' on, and on those occasions he is more prepared to acknowledge the mediating agencies of sensation and reflection. However, the ambiguity of 'sense' in *The Prelude* means that the poem remains ambivalent about the relationship between 'sense'-perception and 'the sense of' something provided by the visionary imagination. This ambivalence will later be explored in phenomenological terms by Geoffrey Hartman, and as a feature of Wordsworth's denial of history by Alan Liu. Empson, however, confines himself to noting that the 'jump' from one sense of 'sense' to the other comes, in his view, at the price of 'good sense'.

I mentioned above that critics of Empson's stripe can roughly be characterized by what might be described as a resistance to theory. Of the commentators discussed here, Herbert Lindenberger takes the greatest pains to stress that he has no *general* argument to peddle on *The Prelude*. As he insists in the 'Foreword: "Ways of Looking"': 'This study does not seek to propound a thesis, nor does it work toward any one conclusion. It is, rather, an attempt to illuminate a single major literary work from a number of points of view. I might well have called it "Thirteen Ways of Looking at *The Prelude*" [...].' That Lindenberger feels that *The Prelude* merits a book–length study of its own indicates the extent to which the poem has risen in the canon of English Literature in the hundred and thirteen years since it was first published. Indeed, as Lindenberger notes, *The Prelude* is now 'looked upon with greater respect than at any time since its publication little more than a century ago; indeed, it holds a more elevated place than any long poem in English since *Paradise Lost*'. And yet, in its steady promotion the poem has not been immune to the curse of monumentalization that often besets 'canonical' works. Consequently, Lindenberger laments the fact that Wordsworth's greatest work has 'been relegated (or elevated) to the role of Sunday reading in the modern secular world'.[8] Accordingly, one of the primary aims of *On Wordsworth*'s Prelude is to rescue the poem from its place in the ranks of worthy but unread works of Great Literature.

It is for this reason, among others, that Lindenberger himself is wary of making a 'case' about Wordsworth's poetry. The last thing he wants to do is give the impression that he is merely delivering yet another Sunday sermon on *The Prelude*. Instead, he attempts, by adopting a range of different perspectives, to bring out the multifaceted brilliance of the poem. This is not to say that he does not foreground certain ideas or thematize aspects of Wordsworth's rhetoric that he finds to be striking or conspicuous. In particular, in the early chapters of the book, Lindenberger concentrates on what he calls 'Wordsworth's "rhetoric of interaction"'. This form of rhetoric in Wordsworth is difficult to study, he claims, first because the poem wavers between 'two areas of reference [...] the poem as personal history and as prophetic utterance', and, second, because much of the success of the poem is 'due to the manner in which Wordsworth was able to find a mode of language and organization to encompass both areas at once'.[9]

Like Ferry and Jones before him, Lindenberger is intrigued by a hesitancy or ambivalence in the rhetoric of *The Prelude*: here, this ambivalence is construed as residing between the poet's 'private' and 'public' voices. He adopts the distinction made by the poet and critic T.S. Eliot (1888–1965) between three poetic voices: 'the first voice is that of "the poet talking to himself – or to nobody", the second that of "the poet addressing an audience", the third, "the poet when he attempts to create a dramatic character"'. Lindenberger uses this schema to argue that, in *The Prelude*, 'the second voice is constantly trying to emerge out of the first'. In this way, the poem hovers between private rumination and public address:

■ To put it another way, what goes on in the poem is a constant flight from the subjectivity of private experience to the assertion of publicly communicable and valid truths. The pattern from private to public is evident in the closing phase of most of the visionary moments within the poem.[10] □

Yet another way of thinking about this phenomenon is in terms of a tension between the subjective and objective rhetorical postures produced by Wordsworth's 'effort to create an external reality for his private, transcendental world'. Indeed, this strain that Lindenberger identifies is manifest in the very idea of *The Prelude*, which was, after all, originally conceived as a poem of personal reflection and growth that is at the same time *addressed* to Coleridge. As Lindenberger puts it:

■ The fact that the poem is addressed throughout to Coleridge is, as it were, a guarantee of its movement from the first to the second voice, from revery and personal vision to public statement. Thus, in that visionary moment in Book IV where he depicts his walk home after the dance he addresses Coleridge just at the point when he is about to interpret the meaning of his experience:

> Magnificent
> The morning was, a memorable pomp,
> More glorious than I ever had beheld.
> The Sea was laughing at a distance; all
> The solid Mountains were as bright as clouds,
> Grain-tinctured, drench'd in empyrean light;
> And, in the meadows and the lower grounds,
> Was all the sweetness of a common dawn,
> Dews, vapours, and the melody of birds,
> And Labourers going forth into the fields.
> —*Ah! need I say, dear Friend, that to the brim*
> *My heart was full*; I made no vows, but vows
> Were then made for me; bond unknown to me
> Was given, that I should be, else sinning greatly,
> A dedicated spirit.

(IV, 330–344; italics mine)

The epistolary convention becomes a means of achieving the sense of an audience – if only an audience of one – and thus of giving a public definition to a state of mind which might otherwise have remained meaningful to the poet alone.[11] □

There is, however, a further dimension to Lindenberger's argument. *The Prelude*, he contends, should be viewed as occupying a pivotal moment in literary history, insofar as it stands 'at a sort of meeting-point between two views of literary form: the modern view that the form of a work results from the demands and rhythms of personal vision, and the traditional view of objectively existing writing styles and structures to which the writer accommodates his personal interests'.[12]

Lindenberger's own approach to Wordsworth's rhetoric in *The Prelude* is two-pronged: first, he considers it as a *performance* or 'reenactment' of the dialogue between self and nature; second, he examines it in terms of the images of 'interaction' that it contains. Thus, Wordsworth's

■ habit of interchanging qualities of the animate and inanimate, of the mind and external nature, is central to *The Prelude* [...] as it is to no other part of his work. It is the natural method with which he communicates his early spiritual experiences and accounts in poetic terms for his mental and emotional development; above all, it is his way of recapturing poetically that sense of the unity of all existence which he had felt on so intuitive a level in early childhood. In *The Prelude* [...] he does not merely portray the interworkings of discernible objects, but creates a lively interplay of what we would normally call abstract concepts. Thus, in the phrase 'The

Power which ... Nature thus / Thrusts forth upon the senses' (XIII, 84–86) the abstractions are brought to life through the highly charged physical activity suggested by the verb. In this passage:

> Thus the pride of strength,
> And the vain-glory of superior skill
> Were interfus'd with objects which subdu'd
> And temper'd them, and gradually produc'd
> A quiet independence of the heart,

(II, 69–73)

the word 'heart' is the closest we get to any tangible object. Yet he creates a brief but intense drama centred about the assertiveness of the human ego, which, in the process of 'interfusion', loses the upper hand to the unnamed objects of external nature, which in turn – after the suggestions of bold but controlled activity in the verbs 'subdu'd' and 'temper'd' – succeed in bringing the conflict to a peaceful conclusion.[13] □

Christopher Ricks' essay, 'Wordsworth: "A Pure Organic Pleasure from the Lines"' combines the stylistic analysis of Empson and Lindenberger with a sharp attention to how the spatial disposition of verse can affect the meaning of a poem. Like Lindenberger, Ricks initially turns to T.S. Eliot for guidance, citing the latter's partial definition of verse as '"a system of *punctuation*"' in support of his founding argument that the peculiar punctuation of poetry or verse is 'the white space' that appears after the end of each line. At the same time, like Empson, Ricks is interested in how the 'sense' (in both 'senses' of the word 'sense', i.e., 'feeling' and 'meaning') of an *ending* determines the work of language, and poetry in particular. The white space at the end of a line of poetry presents the reader with an ambiguous form of ending: it 'constitutes some kind of pause; but there need not be any pause of formal punctuation, and so there may be only equivocally a pause at all'.[14]

This is significant, Ricks argues, since form can echo content. As he puts it, 'the use of line-endings can be a type or symbol or emblem of what the poet values, as well as the instrument by which his values are expressed'. In Wordsworth's case, these values appear, first, as a twin commitment to unity and individuality (thus, the 'separate line of verse must not be too simply separate, and yet it must have its individuality respected'[15]), and, second, as a concern that none of the five senses should 'tyrannize over the others [...]. The eye and ear (and not only those two senses) must be reconciled neither lording it over the other'.[16] It was of vital importance to Wordsworth that his poetry embodied these values of organic unity and sensory balance, not just in its spirit, but in its *form*. And it is for this reason, Ricks claims, that the poet fixed upon blank verse as the appropriate verse form for *The Prelude*.

This is interesting in itself, but Ricks notices something further in Wordsworth's poetry, namely an awareness of the power of the verse *line* (with its 'sense' of an ending) to shape the experience of poet and reader alike. This grants to poems like *The Prelude* a reflexivity regarding their own construction that is peculiarly Wordsworthian. Indeed, Ricks argues, given the preoccupations mentioned above, this should not be surprising: 'Since the verse is to epitomize such harmony and balance, it is natural that the word *line* or *lines* should figure so often in Wordsworth's lines, sometimes with a covert metaphorical application to the verse-lines themselves.' With this heightened sensibility of the effect that the boundary caused by the white space at the end of each line has upon the reader's consciousness, 'Wordsworth evokes both the line and the line-ending' in *Home at Grasmere* (originally conceived as the first part of *The Prelude*'s pendant poem, *The Recluse*):

> ■ Dreamlike the blending of the whole
> Harmonious landscape; all along the shore
> The boundary lost, the line invisible
> That parts the image from reality;
>
> (*Home at Grasmere*, 574–7)

> The boundary is also that which we cross when we pass from one 'line' to another; the 'line invisible' is also that which separates one line from another, 'invisible' because it is emblematized on the page by the white space. Invisible, but not non-existent; there is no thing solidly there, no formal punctuation, but there is nevertheless the parting – by means of a significant space, a significant vacancy – of one thing from another.[17] □

The boundary of white space at the end of each line is in Wordsworth's verse both a 'parting' and a medium, an absence that is also a presence, full of meaning. In the *Prelude*, Ricks argues, Wordsworth reveals the poetic and metaphysical significance of traversing this line – although he believes that the 1850 version of the poem is less effective in transmitting this concern than the earlier manuscript of 1805:

> ■ Consider too the self-referring effect created in the skating episode by invoking 'The rapid line of motion'. And there is the disconcerting mixture of gains and losses – as so often – in the two versions of *The Prelude*, Book I, 588–93:
>
> *1805:*
>
> > even then,
> > A Child, I held unconscious intercourse
> > With the eternal Beauty, drinking in
> > A pure organic pleasure from the lines

Of curling mist, or from the level plain
Of waters colour'd by the steady clouds.

1850:

> even then,
> I held unconscious intercourse with beauty
> Old as creation, drinking in a pure
> Organic pleasure from the silver wreaths
> Of curling mist, or from the level plain
> Of waters coloured by impending clouds.

1850 has the richly proleptic suggestion of 'impending', and it retains the critical inaugurations of the last two lines, both *Of*. But it weakens the force of the other prepositions, removing *With* from the head of the line and *in* from the end of the line, thereby abolishing the engrossing energy of the enjambment: 'drinking in / A pure organic pleasure.' (The *1850* line-break at 'drinking in a pure / Organic pleasure' is altogether ineffectual.) But the superiority of *1805* is clearest in the change from 'the lines / Of curling mist' to 'the silver wreaths / Of curling mist.' On the one hand, the austerity of *lines* has been sacrificed to prettiness; on the other, a suggestiveness too has been sacrificed. For the word *lines* unobtrusively related Wordsworth's delight in 'the eternal Beauty' to his own beautiful lines which are here speaking; we were given a sense of what the 'pure organic pleasure' was, by experiencing its literary counterpart, a 'pure organic pleasure' of a literary kind, drinking it in from these very *lines*. It is a bad bargain which trades away both austerity and suggestiveness. Just for a handful of silver wreaths.[18] □

Not for the first time, a twentieth-century critic finds that the 'prettiness' and mainly ornamental accomplishment of the 'Victorian' *Prelude* has been bought at too high a price in terms of the raw and 'austere' beauty of the earlier versions, especially that of 1805. For, Ricks, however, a further loss has been incurred, namely, the way in which the poem's reflexive delight in the turn of its own 'lines' dovetails with the 'pure organic pleasure' Wordsworth felt in nature.

PHILOSOPHY AND THE HISTORY OF IDEAS

Although the 1960s and early 1970s saw the emergence of a number of landmark studies of *The Prelude*'s style, it is, perhaps, the impact of the new discipline of the history of ideas upon Wordsworth criticism that most distinguishes the period as a whole. The notion of the History of Ideas was conceived by the American philosopher A.O. Lovejoy (1873–1962) and colleagues at Johns Hopkins University, eventually leading to the founding of a journal, the *Journal of the History of Ideas*, in 1940.

Stated simply, the history of ideas is an interdisciplinary approach to intellectual history. In its Lovejovian mould, it seeks historically to locate and trace certain 'unit-ideas' through a range of different cultural, artistic, political, and intellectual fields (Lovejoy's own work, *The Great Chain of Being: A Study in the History of an Idea*, published in 1936, did precisely this for the ideas of plenitude, continuity, and gradation). However, a broader effect of Lovejoy's innovations was the reinvigoration of the field of intellectual history in general, and by the 1960s their reverberations were being registered within Wordsworth criticism, and *Prelude* scholarship in particular.

This in turn led many critics to revisit earlier debates over Wordsworth's philosophical debts and affiliations. Thus, the 'empiricist'/'mystic' dichotomy that had defined these issues for Arthur Beatty and Newton Stallknecht decades earlier was re-examined in the 1960s by critics such as Morse Peckham and Robert Langbaum. Significantly, neither finds Beatty's contention that *The Prelude* is best understood in the context of an eighteenth-century British tradition of empiricism and associationism to be very convincing. Peckham, indeed, argues the reverse: the philosopher who most resembles Wordsworth, he contends, is not the arch-empiricist Locke, but the transcendental idealist Kant. Wordsworth, Peckham maintains, is too often cast simply as

■ a nature poet; but that is an error, and particularly unfortunate one, for so to categorize him is to identify him with the nature poets of the eighteenth century, who selected from the natural world in order to confirm their conviction that by the activity of the imagination man derives value from nature through the imaginative perception of the meaningful order of the world. □

For Wordsworth, on the contrary, nature presented 'a source of emotional disturbance' as well as calmness, and this was because he believed that the mind 'was not merely reflective and imitative; it was not a mere mirror; it was a lamp'. The health and strength of the human imagination thus assumes an importance in Wordsworth's poetry that is unprecedented in eighteenth-century nature poetry, indeed, in English literature in general. As Peckham observes, not for no reason is the climax of *The Prelude* entitled 'The Imagination and Taste, How Impaired and Restored': 'Clearly, the old meaning of "imagination" has been discarded for a new one.'[19]

It is this new conception of imagination that Peckham finds to be fundamentally Kantian in character. On the face of it, this would appear to be an unpromising line of argument, not least because Wordsworth read no Kant himself (deriving most of what little knowledge he had of the philosopher from conversations with Coleridge, who quickly became a disciple). The fundamental argument of Kant's most influential work, the *Critique of Pure Reason* (1781) is that experience is not organized merely according to the contingent, empirical connections made by the association of ideas (as Hume had argued), but by *a priori* forms of cognition generated by the mind itself. Although this meant that the philosopher, like the younger poet, stressed the fundamental creativity of the human mind in shaping its own experience, one struggles to find in Wordsworth a poetic equivalent to Kant's theory that the possession of certain *a priori* concepts is the precondition for experience itself.

For Peckham, however, there were two key elements in his intellectual background that Wordsworth shared with the German philosopher. The first of these was a deep scepticism about what Peckham calls 'the marvelous fantasies of the late Enlightenment', the 'schemes of human regeneration, of social perfection' that had fed the rationalistic ideology and enthusiasm (including the young Wordsworth's) of the French Revolution. As the Revolution slid into Terror and ultimately war, however, Wordsworth came to doubt the basic tenets of the philosophy that had underwritten its ideals. As Peckham writes, the aftermath of Revolution 'shattered his faith that a solution to moral difficulties could be found in the study of the empirical world' – a faith that Kant had already undermined by arguing in the *Critique of Pure Reason* that reason, in the absence of sensation and imagination, was incapable of making sense of human experience.

This brings us to the second link that Peckham claims to find between Wordsworth and Kant. Peckham notes that when the poet, revolted by political events, fled London for the tranquillity of life with his sister on a farm in southern England, 'he did a most interesting thing. For a year and a half he studied mathematics':

■ Like Kant he found that only in mathematics could be found a perfect self-consistent order. That order was in the mind, not in reality. But whereas Kant, with his devotion to the technicalities of academic philosophy, buried deep and almost completely suppressed the emotional drives, in Wordsworth they were right at the surface. □

According to Peckham, this turn to mathematics was the first step taken by the poet into the resources of his own consciousness, his own mind, 'in order to regain orientative equilibrium'.[20] After this, it was entirely natural for Wordsworth to turn further inwards, away from society and the measures of empirical reality, and towards the tranquil but powerful forces contained within his own memory. It is this turn that ultimately leads to the writing of *The Prelude*, in which, Peckham argues, by tracing the growth of an 'active', formative mind that shapes its own reality even as it is shaped by external circumstances, Wordsworth expresses a vision of human consciousness that is the poetic analogue of Kant's transcendentalism:

- 'There are,' he said, 'in our existence spots of time',

       passages of life in which
  We have had deepest feeling that the mind
  Is lord and master, and that outward sense
  Is but the obedient servant of her will.

  Innumerable passages in this poem enable us to comprehend and experience the emotional vitality and force that must have lain behind the academic and abstract style of Kant. Yet because Wordsworth was an amateur philosopher and more interested in emotional vitality than correctness and impregnability of reasoning, Wordsworth said things that Kant would never have said. The mind, he was convinced, was exquisitely adapted to the outer world, and that world was equally adapted to the mind. Of the union of the two he speaks as of a wedding and a consummation, the offspring of which is creation. Yet in comparison to the mind, the world is passive, although a wise passiveness is necessary to prepare the mind for a consummation. That passiveness is necessary to free the mind from its superficial drives toward rational comprehension. [...] We see intuitively, through subconscious powers, into the structure of order of which the visible universe is a symbol. Really it is not too far distant a position from Kant's notion that the structural power of the mind is a guarantee that the world has a structure, even though the mind cannot create a structure which corresponds to the structure of the world.[21] □

In pursuing his comparison then, Peckham intimates that Wordsworth goes even further than Kant, insofar as the former's prizing of intuitive insight enables him to suppose that the mind can at least experience the union of the 'inner' (subjective) and 'outer' (objective) worlds. Moreover, the roots of Wordsworth's epistemological boldness lie in his medium: poetry can access the mysteries of human existence in ways that philosophy cannot. In this way, in *The Prelude*, '[t]he hypothetical organicism of Kant has been metamorphosed into an experienced reality':

-    Not Chaos, not
  The darkest pit of lowest Erebus,
  Nor aught of blinder vacancy, scooped out
  By help of dreams – can breed such fear and awe
  As fall upon us often when we look
  Into our Minds, into the Mind of man –
  My haunt, and the main region of my song.

It is the imagination that redeems the world; in the deepest recesses of the self is the source of value. In opening ourselves to beauty and to terror we release its power.[22] □

While Peckham makes the positive case for Wordsworth as quasi-transcendentalist, another critic, Robert Langbaum, portrays Wordsworth's quest in *The Prelude* negatively, as a response to – and largely a reaction against – Lockean empiricism. Opening his 1967 *PMLA* article, 'The Evolution of Soul in Wordsworth's Poetry', Langbaum compares the challenge posed to eighteenth-century conceptions of the 'human' by Locke's philosophy to that posed by the development of artificial intelligence in the late twentieth century. As he frames it, '[t]he best analogy to the challenge raised by Locke is the challenge raised in our time by computers. For Lockean man is like a computer in that everything inside him comes from outside, through sensation; so that Lockean man gives back only what has been "programmed" into him.'[23] It is Langbaum's contention that Wordsworth's *Prelude* is tantamount to a poetic rebuttal of this reductive account of consciousness and experience. The basic problem Wordsworth has with Locke's 'computer' account of intelligence, Langbaum maintains, is that it can too easily eliminate the activity of 'soul':

■ Now in *The Prelude* Wordsworth was trying to answer some such question as this regarding Lockean man. If we consider that the human psyche is built up of sensations, then at what point do sensations add up to soul, or how do we jump from sensations to soul? We can understand Wordsworth's answer to Locke if we imagine him answering the question in regard to computers. His answer would be that computers will never be human until they are born and grow up. □

Sensations, for Wordsworth, pulsate with singularity, in a way that defeats the calculating, purely aggregative reach of Locke's computational model of mind. No passive, comprehensively programmable system of intelligence could cope with such singularity; an active, creative mind, however, could. It is this latter model of mind, Langbaum claims, that Wordsworth trails in *The Prelude*. If sensations are to be transmuted into 'soul', then this can only be, as Langbaum puts it, 'because the sensations reach an ever-changing mind that transforms them as a merely passive receiver, the sort of mind Locke likens to blank paper could not'.[24]

Langbaum, it should be remembered, is writing in the 1960s, when computer technology was still very much in its infancy. Nonetheless, he is alert enough to the possibilities presented by artificial intelligence to attempt to forestall an objection that might be raised against his argument, namely that it relies upon an oversimplified and limited conception of what computers might be capable of, even if only in principle. Langbaum's response to this counterargument centres upon Wordsworth's idea of 'joy' and its irreducible role in the relationship between mind and nature:

> ■ It may be argued that computers, too, as they learn, offer a changing receiver to external data. This brings us to the second important point in Wordsworth's answer to Locke. Wordsworth portrays the mind as itself part of the nature it perceives; and it is this connection, sensed through what Wordsworth calls *joy*, that gives us confidence in the reality of ourselves and the external world. Dare one predict that no computer is likely to have this organic connection or to sense it through *joy*?
>
> In *The Prelude*, Wordsworth tells us that his life began to the sound of the Derwent River that 'loved / To blend his murmurs with my nurse's song' and 'sent a voice / That flowed along my dreams', making
>
>> ceaseless music that composed my thoughts
>> To more than infant softness, giving me
>> Amid the fretful dwellings of mankind
>> A foretaste, a dim earnest, of the calm
>> That Nature breathes among the hills and groves.
>>
>> (I, 270–281; 1850)
>
> There, in the best Lockean fashion, Wordsworth traces all his mature thoughts back to the sound of the river. But unlike Locke, Wordsworth presents the mind as an active principle. [...] The blending and interchange turn sensation into experience, an experience of joy that will in future years spread around the mature man's thoughts an affective tone – a tone objectified in 'the calm / That Nature breathes'. This tone, this atmosphere of the mind, sensed as at once inside and outside the mind, is what the mature man will call *soul*.[25] □

For the Lockean intelligence model of 'data–input–process' then, Wordsworth's *Prelude* substitutes a conception of 'nature–joy–soul'. Unlike Peckham, however, Langbaum's reading of Wordsworth does not lead him to consider whether a Kantian, transcendental framework might present a more useful philosophical framework through which to explore the poem. Instead, he revisits an old debate about the relationship between Wordsworth's writing and the theory, originating from the Greek philosopher Plato (428–348 BC), that the mind accesses spiritual truths not through *empirical* experience (i.e., experience mediated via the five senses) of the natural world, but through an intuitive apprehension of the *ideal* essence, or 'form' of reality:

> ■ Much ink has been spilled over the question whether Wordsworth believed that his apprehension of spirit came from outside or inside, whether he was

a Lockean empiricist or a Platonic believer in innate ideas. The answer is that Wordsworth, when he is writing his best poetry, uses both doctrines as possibilities, blending them in such a way as to evoke the mystery he is talking about – the mystery of life, vitality, organic connection. The case should teach us something about the proper relation of ideas to poetry. □

Wordsworth, it turns out, was a philosophical magpie, using a bit of Locke here and a pinch of Plato there, depending on what suited his purpose at a given time. And yet, while some might view this strategy as a dangerous courting of incoherence, Langbaum defends it as a positive virtue: the 'case' of Wordsworth 'should teach us something about the proper relation of ideas to poetry', he maintains, precisely because it demonstrates that the meaning of a poem such as *The Prelude* cannot be cashed out merely in terms of its philosophical ideas. Instead, we should approach it with the same sense of 'mystery [...] vitality, organic connection' in which Wordsworth retained such faith.

Finally, Langbaum argues, there is a lesson to be drawn from the impossibility of encapsulating *The Prelude* 'philosophically'. This is that Wordsworth triumphed as a poet even as he failed to produce the great anti-Lockean *philosophical* poem that Coleridge was urging him to write:

■ The case also suggests why *The Prelude* [...] is so much more successful than what we have of that long philosophical poem, *The Recluse*, of which *The Excursion* is Part Two. *The Prelude* is successful, and successful as an appropriately modern poem of ideas, just because Wordsworth did not consider that he was at that point writing a philosophical poem. [...] Aside from the fact that *The Prelude* portrays a mind in evolution not in repose, we precisely do not find there the doctrinaire anti-Lockean stand described by Coleridge.[26] □

In contrast to the studies of Peckham and Langbaum, M.H. Abrams' landmark study *Natural Supernaturalism* (1971) does not focus solely or even primarily upon Wordsworth's philosophical pedigree. It certainly seeks to understand Wordsworth's work through a narrative of intellectual history, and in this sense, at least, it falls into a distinguished tradition of twentieth-century studies written under the banner of the history of ideas. However, while Peckham and Langbaum, to varying degrees, seek to insert the poet within one or other philosophical tradition, Abrams is more interested in the lessons that can be drawn from the poetry – including *The Prelude* – regarding the transformation of romantic, and indeed, modern consciousness following the 'late' Enlightenment. Moreover, he brings to his discussion a sharper appreciation of the reflexivity between poetic 'form' and philosophical 'content'.

As Abrams states in his Preface, a central concern of *Natural Supernaturalism* is to trace the Romantic 'secularization of inherited theological ideas' in England and Germany. In this way, the Romantics 'save traditional concepts [...] which had been based on the relation of the Creator to his creature and creation, but [...] reformulate them within the prevailing two-term system of subject and object, ego and non-ego'.[27] The Romantic 'High Argument,' then, typically involves the invocation of a discourse through which 'characteristic concepts and patterns of Romantic philosophy and literature' constitute 'a displaced and reconstituted theology, or else a secularized form of devotional experience'.[28] Hence the title of Abrams' book: the phrase 'Natural Supernaturalism' (which he borrows from the Victorian essayist and historian Thomas Carlyle) encapsulates the Romantics' general tendency 'to naturalize the supernatural and to humanize the divine'.[29]

Wordsworth's *Prelude* echoes this tendency, Abrams continues, in that it presents the reader with a secularized spiritual odyssey, a visionary quest narrative with no theological telos or end. Indeed, the fact that *The Prelude* has neither a clear beginning nor an ending, Abrams avers, reveals one of the quintessentially Romantic qualities of the poem: its circularity. This 'radically achronological' construction is a symptom of the 'crisis' of autobiography in an age when spiritual revelation was increasingly rendered as a privileged form of apperception, or self-knowledge. With no external religious theme to pursue, the Romantic writer turns inwards to seek revelatory truth within himself/herself, only to find that this in turn provokes a curious kind of reflexivity: bereft of a theological argument, the mind must reflect upon its own becoming, a process which encompasses the very act of *writing* itself. Thus, in *The Prelude*,

■ Wordsworth does not tell his life as a simple narrative in past time but as the present remembrance of things past, in which forms and sensations 'throw back our life' (I, 660–1) and evoke the former self, which coexists with the altered present self in multiple awareness that Wordsworth calls 'two consciousnesses'. There is a wide 'vacancy' between the I now and the I then,

> Which yet have such self-presence in my mind
> That, sometimes, when I think of them, I seem
> Two consciousness, conscious of myself
> And of some other Being. □

(II, 27–33)[30]

Key to understanding *The Prelude*, Abrams insists, is the manner in which the impossibility of disentangling the 'two consciousnesses' (past and present selves, or the self that is written about, and the self that does the writing) reappears as a determining feature of the *form* of Wordsworth's verse. As a result, the poem develops an identifiable rhythm of gain, loss, and recovery:

■ *The Prelude*, correspondingly, is ordered in three stages. There is a process of unified mental development which although at times suspended, remains a continuum; this process is shattered by a crisis of apathy and despair; but the mind then recovers an integrity which, despite admitted losses, is represented as a level higher than the initial unity, in that the mature mind possesses powers, together with an added range, depth, and sensitivity of awareness, which are the products of the critical experiences it has undergone.[31] □

Rather than a vicious circle, then, the thought-pattern of *The Prelude* is, for Abrams, an ascending spiral staircase of self-exploration and illumination, a spiral that must include its own act of composition:

■ *The Prelude*, then, is an involuted poem which is about its own genesis – a prelude to itself. Its structural end is its own beginning; and its temporal beginning [...] is Wordsworth's entrance upon the stage of his life at which it ends.[32] □

It is at this point that Abrams identifies a parallel between Wordsworth's poetry and the work of the German idealist philosopher Georg Wilhelm Friedrich Hegel, insofar as both see the dialectical growth of mind as a 'circuitous journey'. Thus, in the 'Ascent of Snowdon' passage in the final book of *The Prelude*, what the poet finally discovers is not just the sublimity of nature or the deepest truth of his own consciousness, but the relationship of interdependence between the two:

■ The last book of *The Prelude*, in symmetry with its first book, also opens with a literal walk which translates itself into a metaphor for the climactic stage both for the journey of life and of the imaginative journey which is the poem itself. [...] As in Hegel's contemporary *Phenomenology* [1807] the spirit, at the close of its educational journey, recognizes itself in its other, so Wordsworth's mind, confronting nature, discovers itself in its own reflected powers:

A meditation rose in me that night
Upon the lonely Mountain...
                    and it appear'd to me
The perfect image of a mighty Mind. □

Ultimately, for Abrams, it is by secularizing and internalizing the idea of the traditional religious–philosophical quest narrative that *The Prelude* acquires a 'circular organization'. Crucially, however, '[t]his circularity of its form, we now see, reflects the circularity of its subject matter'.[33]

THE DIALECTIC OF CONSCIOUSNESS

Abrams' reinvigorating take on the history of ideas reflects how, by the mid-1960s, a new theoretical energy was evident in Wordsworth criticism. Above all, Geoffrey Hartman's seminal *Wordsworth's Poetry 1787–1814* (1964) (followed in 1987 by a collection of essays, *The Unremarkable Wordsworth*) helped to shift the set of assumptions against which the 'philosophy' behind Wordsworth's poetry was interpreted and evaluated. Just as importantly, however, it transformed the critical debate over what precisely is at *stake* in Wordsworth's engagement with the development of his own mind and its relationship with nature. For Hartman, like Abrams, phenomenology, or the study of how being is disclosed through experience, is fundamental to understanding *The Prelude*. Influenced by Hegel and Heidegger, Hartman sees the phenomenological patterns and rhythms of the poem as structured by a give-and-take between mind and nature. He connects these rhythms in *The Prelude* to a dialectic of consciousness that mediates between two (for Wordsworth) unpalatable extremes: on one hand, a pantheistic subjugation or 'binding' of the mind to nature, and, on the other, an 'apocalypse' of the imagination in which the visionary consciousness transcends the merely natural.

Accordingly, in *Wordsworth's Poetry*, Hartman notes that with a few exceptions, critics of Wordsworth have traditionally divided into two camps: on one hand, the majority, who see the poet as (to put it crudely) a worshipper of nature, and on the other, a minority of dissenters who argue that the poet's conception of imagination 'may be *intrinsically* opposed to nature'. The purpose of Hartman's intervention is to advance an argument that cuts across these perspectives by offering a third alternative, namely that Wordsworth pursued a course of nature-worship that led him *away* from nature:

■ It can be shown, via several important episodes of *The Prelude*, that Wordsworth thought nature itself led him beyond nature; and, since this movement of transcendence, related to what mystics have called the negative way, is inherent in life and achieved without violent or ascetic discipline, one can think of it as the progress of a soul which is *naturaliter negativa*.[34] □

Hartman's depiction of the growth of the poet's mind as a '*via naturaliter negativa*' brings us back to the Hegelian structure that both he and Abrams identify as the governing framework of *The Prelude*. In the *Phenomenology of Mind*, Hegel argued that the objective world is fundamentally relational, that is, that it depends upon an 'other', namely, a subject. Since all that exists is mind, objects have no independent existence. The mind, however, must go through a process of overcoming the illusion that there is an objective world that exists separately from it. This process Hegel describes in triadic or dialectical terms: the mind is first estranged from itself, and then returns to itself. Consciousness, in other words, must first *negate* itself before it can realize itself and achieve its full positivity. As a consequence, the emergence of the self can be characterized as a struggle of the mind to achieve transcendence over the otherness of objectivity (an objectivity that is ultimately recognized in its true form as the negation of subjectivity). Yet since the self's *involvement* in relations of otherness is a precondition of its very identity, the mind's complete transcendence of the world is impossible.

What this means for Wordsworth, Hartman claims, is that although the poet's mind realizes itself fully only by way of alienating itself through the objectivity of nature, the self can never be entirely free from nature. Only through nature can the poet learn that the destiny of mind is to surpass nature. As a result of this logic in Wordsworth, Hartman argues, the poet vacillates between love of nature (pantheism) and a desire for complete freedom from nature (what Hartman terms 'apocalypse'). It is this dialectic of consciousness, or *via naturaliter negativa*, that Hartman detects throughout *The Prelude*, even in its opening lines:

■ In the exultant first lines of *The Prelude*, Wordsworth had foreseen the spirit's power to become self-creative. Though fostered by nature it eventually outgrows its dependence, sings and storms at will (I, 33–8). The poet's anticipation of autonomy is probably less a matter of pride than of necessity: he will steal the initiative from nature so as to freely serve or sustain the natural world should its hold on the affections slacken. His poetic power, though admittedly in nature's gift, must perpetuate, like consecration, vital if transitory feelings. Without poetry the supreme moment is nothing.

> Dear Liberty! Yet what should it avail
> But for a gift that consecrates the joy?

> (I, 31–32)

But he is taught that the desire for immediate consecrations is a wrong form of worship. The world demands a devotion less external and willful, a wise passiveness which the creative will may profane. The tempest 'vexing its own creation' is replaced by a 'mellowing sun, that shed / Mild influence.' Nature keeps the initiative. The mind at its most free is still part of a deep mood of weathers.[35] □

The paradoxical lesson that the mind must learn is that of the necessity for its own growth of constraint and correction:

> ■ Wordsworth's first experience is symptomatic of his creative difficulties. One impulse vexes the creative spirit into self-dependence, the other exhibits nature as that spirit's highest object. The poet is driven at the same time from and toward the external world. [...] The poet's account of his creative difficulties (I, 146–269) documents in full his vacillation between a natural and a more than natural theme [...]. Is this indeterminacy the end at which nature aims, this curious and never fully clarified restlessness the ultimate confession of his poetry?[36] □

Hartman's answer to this question, in short, is yes. Accordingly, he reads the first part of Book I as Wordsworth's exploration of his own failure to write *The Recluse*, a visionary epic poem in the tradition of Milton. This failure in turn must be understood in terms of the Hegelian cast of the Wordsworthian consciousness, which cannot jettison its awareness of its own dialectical dependence upon nature. Imagination seeks to transcend nature, but in doing so merely attests to the fact that it cannot work in the absence of nature. As Hartman observes:

> ■ An unresolved opposition between Imagination and Nature prevents him from becoming a visionary poet. It is a paradox, though not an unfruitful one, that he should scrupulously record nature's workmanship, which prepares the soul for its independence from sense-experience, yet refrain to use that independence out of respect for nature. His greatest verse *still takes its origin* in the memory of given experiences to which he is often pedantically faithful. He adheres, apparently against nature, to natural fact. □

The poet's 'shrinking from visionary subjects' raises a further question: 'Is Wordsworth afraid of his own imagination?'[37] To answer this, Hartman turns to the passage in *The Prelude* where the poet–narrator comes face to face with his own imagination: the Crossing of the Alps. In this celebrated passage in Book 6, Wordsworth recalls how he and a friend crossed the Alps during a walking tour of France and Switzerland in the summer of 1790 (a period in which the poet still felt that the recent events of the French Revolution were a cause for celebration and optimism). At the time, the event was a disappointment: as Wordsworth recalls, he and his companion crossed the Alps – coming through Simplon Pass – without even realizing it. There was no great moment of revelation before nature, no sublime epiphany – in other words, no natural experience that could come up to the expectations that he had prepared in his own mind. And yet, what Hartman finds to be revealing in this passage is the fact that a visionary moment *is* experienced by the poet: not in crossing the Alps, but in reflecting upon the journey many years later:

■ Not until the moment of composition, some fourteen years after the event, does the real reason behind his upward climb and subsequent melancholy slackening strike home; and it strikes so hard that he gives to the power in him, revealed by the extinction of the immediate external motive (his desire to cross the Alps) and by the abyss of intervening years, the explicit name Imagination:

> Imagination – here the Power so called
> Through sad incompetence of human speech,
> That awful Power rose from the mind's abyss
> Like an unfathered vapour that enwraps,
> At once, some lonely traveller. I was lost;
> Halted without an effort to break through;
> But to my conscious soul I now can say –
> 'I recognise thy glory.'

(VI, 592–9)

Thus Wordsworth's failure vis-à-vis nature (or its failure vis-à-vis him) is doubly redeemed. After descending, and passing through a gloomy strait (621 ff.), he encounters a magnificent view. And crossing, one might say, the gloomy gulf of time, his disappointment becomes retrospectively a prophetic instance of that blindness to the external world which is the tragic, pervasive, and necessary condition of the mature poet. His failure of 1790 taught him gently what now (1804) literally *blinds* him: the independence of imagination from nature.

I cannot miss my way, the poet exults in the opening verses of *The Prelude*. And he cannot, as long as he respects the guidance of nature, which leads him along a gradual via negativa to make his soul more than 'a mere pensioner / On outward forms' (VI, 737 f.).[38] □

Just as the mind comes to appreciate its dependence upon nature, so it follows 'that nature, for Wordsworth, is not an "object" but a presence and a power; a motion and a spirit; not something to be worshipped and consumed, but always a guide leading beyond itself. This guidance starts in earliest childhood.'[39] Without such guidance, the Wordsworthian 'I' always stands upon the brink of a 'precarious self-consciousness', that is, the condition of a mind, trapped in in its adolescent state, in which the craving for complete independence and an unmediated vision of absolute reality (what Hartman terms 'apocalyptic') threatens to produce its own kind of blindness and paralysis. Hartman compares Wordsworth to the medieval Italian poet Francesco Petrarch (1304–74) and to the theologian and author of the *Confessions*,

St. Augustine of Hippo (350–430):

■ Wordsworth's experience, like Petrarch's or Augustine's, is a conversion: a turning about of the mind as from one belief to its opposite, and a turning *ad se ipsum* [to himself]. It is linked to the birth of a sharper self-awareness, and accompanied by apocalyptic feelings. By 'apocalyptic' I mean that there is an inner necessity to cast out nature, to extirpate everything apparently external to salvation, everything that might stand between the naked self and God, whatever risk in this to the self.[40] □

The poet discovers that as the mind grows (or grows up), the transformation from (adolescent) self-consciousness into a richer awareness of self and world involves an acknowledgement of the self's dependence upon relationship, an acknowledgement which, in turn, brings greater (adult) independence. As Hartman notes, it is significant that this realization *does* come as a 'turn', insofar as it has much in common with a religious conversion. Thus, he concludes, in the Alpine episode '[t]he imagination does not find, and strays like Adam, and is then seemingly completed'. And yet, in completion, the prodigal mind

■ still somehow returns to nature. For nature remains in Wordsworth's view the best and gentlest guide in the development surpassing her. It is part of the poet's strength that he faithfully records an experience he did not at the time of writing and still does not control. The greatest [event] of his journey is [...] the spectral figure of Imagination cutting him off, fulfilling Nature's prophecy, and revealing the end of his Negative Way.[41] □

I have devoted a great deal of space to Hartman's work on *The Prelude* because it is his study that opens the gateway to a variety of theoretical readings of the poem over the following decades. This does not necessarily mean that it met with widespread agreement. Indeed, as we shall see in the next chapter, many deconstructionist critics would delight in dismantling Hartman's notion of Wordsworth's phenomenological worldview (as would, ultimately, Hartman himself). For many, the picture of a stable but reflexive consciousness whose own coming-into-being is teleologically determined by a pathway of negative dialectic proved to be as unconvincing an account of what was really going on in Wordsworth's poetry as the existential and broadly idealist thinking upon which this picture was based. These disagreements notwithstanding, many subsequent theoretical approaches to *The Prelude* are indebted to Hartman's 1964 study, if for no other reason than that *Wordsworth's Poetry* is the first to consider seriously that the imaginative activity on display in the poem might be the result of more than what was (supposedly) going on 'in the poet's head' – indeed, that its finer passages might best be understood in terms of a power that both transcended and determined the merely psychological. For Hartman (in 1964, at least) this power was the power of negativity: later, other commentators would come up with different, more radical names for it. Before turning to these, we must consider another critic from this period whose voice is every bit as influential as Hartman's.

In his groundbreaking work in poetic psychology, *The Anxiety of Influence* (1973), Harold Bloom used Freud's account of the Oedipal complex to explain the Romantic poets' ambivalent relationship towards their poetic precursors: the striving for voice and originality, he maintained, is a form of psychic aggression through which great writers such as Wordsworth assert their own visionary independence. While undoubtedly his most influential work, *The Anxiety of Influence* has little to say directly about *The Prelude*. However, in his 1971 collection of essays, *The Ringers in the Tower: Studies in the Romantic Tradition*, Bloom applied his own distinctive take on the relationship between Freudian and Romantic ideas of consciousness to the poetry of Wordsworth, and to *The Prelude* in particular. In an essay titled 'The Internalization of the Quest Romance', he argues that Freud's interpretations of the psyche are a twentieth-century analogue of the 'quest' narratives of romantic literature. By transforming the traditional religious quest narratives of *romance* into explorations of consciousness, Bloom maintains, *Romantic* writers charted the mind's simultaneous attraction and resistance to enchantment in the same way that Freud would a century later. Bloom links Wordsworth with the Romantic poet, painter and graphic artist, William Blake (1757–1827) as precursors of Freud: 'what Blake and Wordsworth do for their readers, or can do', he asserts, 'is closely related to what Freud does or can do for his, which is to provide both a map of the mind and a profound faith that the map can be put to a saving use'.[42]

Freud, Bloom notes, 'thought that even romance, with its element of play, probably commenced in some actual experience whose "strong impression on the writer had stirred up a memory of an earlier experience, generally belonging to childhood, which then arouses a wish that finds a fulfilment in the work in question [...]"'.[43] This pattern of wish-fulfilment is crucial, Bloom finds, in understanding the psychological dynamics of visionary literature. In particular, he is interested in how it might shed light on the revival of the romance genre in eighteenth and nineteenth-century literature. For Bloom, the 'immortal longings of the child, rather variously interpreted by Freud, Blake, and Wordsworth, [...] do seem to be at the sources of the mid-eighteenth-century revival of a romance consciousness, out of which

nineteenth–century Romanticism largely came'.[44] The Romantic res-
urrection of the quest romance, however, is more than just a revival:

■ it is an internalization of romance, particularly of the quest variety, an
internalization made for more than therapeutic purposes, because made in
the name of a humanizing hope that approaches apocalyptic intensity. The
poet takes the patterns of quest-romance and transposes them into his
own imaginative life, so that the entire rhythm of the quest is heard again in
the movement of the poet himself from poem to poem.[45] □

Where traditional quest narratives seek spiritual illumination through
outward action, the Romantic search is directed inwards, towards an
unmediated vision of the mind itself, and thus towards an unmediated vision of the mind *searching* for itself. This attempt of the mind to
stand on its own head, as it were, produces a 'doubling' or alienation
that divides the self 'into passive and active components', a separation
that is evident in Blake's figures of Urthona and Los, or *The Prelude*'s
dim sense of '[t]wo consciousnesses' (1805, II, 32).[46] Given Hartman's
and Abrams' work on the dynamics of consciousness in Wordsworth's
poetry, Bloom's use of the term 'apocalyptic' to describe the unmediated vision desired by the divided ego is suggestive, and far from coin-
cidental. Indeed, *The Ringers in the Tower* is dedicated to Hartman – a
colleague of Bloom's at Yale University – and it is not difficult to find
the latter's influence in 'The Internalization of Quest Romance'. Bloom,
however, resourcefully adapts Hartman's notion of the Wordsworthian
dialectic of consciousness, giving it a Freudian slant. For Bloom, the
dialectic described by Hartman within Wordsworth's mind is not so
much phenomenological as psychopathological, driven by a fundamental instability within the ego itself:

■ In Freud, part of the ego's own self-love is projected onto an outward
object, but part always remain in the ego, and even the projected portion
can find its way back again. [...] [A]ll romance is really a form of what he calls
'Family-romance'; one could as justly say, in his terms, that all romance is
necessarily a mode of ego-romance. [...] All romance, literary and human,
is founded upon enchantment; Freud and the Romantics differ principally
in their judgement as to what it is in us that resists enchantment, and what
the value of that resistance is. For Freud, it is the reality-principle, working
through the great disenchanter, reason, the scientific attitude, and without it
no civilized values are possible. For the Romantics, this is again a dialectical
matter, as two principles intertwine in the resistance to enchantment, one
'organic', an anxiety-principle masquerading as a reality-principle and identical to the ego's self-love that never ventures out to others, and the other
'creative', which resists enchantment in the name of a higher mode than the
sympathetic imagination.[47] □

It is for this reason that the visionary wish–fulfilment of the Romantic quest narrative 'is never the poem itself but the poem beyond that is made possible by the apocalypse of imagination'.[48] It is towards such a 'poem' that *The Prelude* gestures in its celebration of the growing power of the poet's 'supernatural' imagination. Like Hartman, however, Bloom believes that Wordsworth's enduring attachment to nature means that his embracement of the purely apocalyptic imagination is always qualified. Thus, Book XII of *The Prelude*, while ostensibly a paean to imagination, never attains the level of visionary freedom that one finds in Blake's verse:

■ In his crisis, Wordsworth learns the supernatural and superhuman strength of his own imagination, and is able to begin a passage to the mature phase of his quest. But his anxiety for continuity is too strong for him, and he yields to its dark enchantment. The Imagination phase of his quest does not witness the surrender of his Selfhood and the subsequent inauguration of a new dialectic of love, purged of the natural heart, as it is in Blake. Yet he wins a provisional triumph over himself, in Book XII of *The Prelude* [...]. And the final version of *The Prelude* is not of a redeemed nature, but of a liberated creativity transforming its creation into the beloved:

Prophets of Nature, we to them will speak
A lasting inspiration, sanctified
By reason, blest by faith: what we have loved
Others will love, and we will teach them how;
Instruct them how the mind of man becomes
A thousand times more beautiful than the earth
On which he dwells, above this frame of things...[49] □

The seminal studies of Bloom and Hartman define the high–water mark of a certain tradition of *Prelude* criticism, one which, for all its sophistication, continued to trade in the kind of ideas with which Wordsworth himself would have been comfortable: 'consciousness', 'imagination', 'genius', and so on. By the early 1970s, however, criticism was assuming a more suspicious attitude. For some commentators, Abrams, Hartman, Bloom, and others were too ready to adopt of the Romantic–metaphysical nomenclature of 'consciousness' and 'genius', and not ready enough to question the fundamental assumptions (often relating to language, gender, and subjectivity) upon which these terms rested. For others, the application of critical concepts and methodologies derived from twentieth–century phenomenology and history of ideas to writing of the early nineteenth century betrayed an inadequate grasp of both the historical specificity of *The Prelude* and its involvement with the material, social, political, and economic forces of its era. In the following two chapters, I will treat each of these critical tendencies in turn.

CHAPTER FOUR

Writing the Self: Deconstruction, Feminism, and Psychoanalysis

Hartman's *Wordsworth's Poetry 1787–1814* marks a watershed in *Prelude* criticism and commentary. After Hartman, it became increasingly difficult to take Wordsworth's assertions of the unity of the creative consciousness (and its universal validity) at face value, as what once appeared as the confident, visionary poetic acts of the creative imagination now emerged as fraught compromises between an aggressive but homesick intellect and the authenticating but potentially suffocating presence of nature. Where Hartman treated this instability from the viewpoint of the phenomenology of experience, however, many subsequent critics and theorists would interrogate the very concepts of 'consciousness', 'experience', and 'dialectic' at the heart of his approach. In particular, from around the late 1960s, the intersection of three critical orientations helped to shape an axis of interpretation (or, in many cases, *anti*-interpretation) that presented a powerful critique of the notion of subjectivity around which Wordsworth's poem was constructed. Accordingly, this chapter concentrates on the influence of deconstructive, feminist, and psychoanalytic approaches to *The Prelude* in this period. What distinguishes these movements from those that preceded them is not just their commitment to read 'against the grain' of Wordsworth's epic of consciousness, but also a shared attitude of suspicion towards 'subject–centred' writing (that is, writing that took the 'self' as its foundation) in general.

THE RHETORIC OF *THE PRELUDE*

Of these new varieties of critical analysis, the methods and techniques of deconstruction are perhaps the most far-reaching in their ramifications, as well as the most challenging to the 'Romantic ideology' that Wordsworth's poetry is seen to promote. Indeed, some argue that, with its complex compositional and editorial history, *The Prelude* is particularly available to deconstructive analysis. In his 1993 Introduction to the

Open University *Theory and Practice* volume on *The Prelude*, for example (in a section titled 'Does *The Prelude* Exist?'), Nigel Wood (born 1953) meditates on the implications of the myriad variants of the poem – and the lack of an 'authoritative' version – for attempts to unpack its meaning. Crucially, he asks the question: which (or whose) *Prelude* are we reading? In addition to the different manuscripts of the poem available, he notes, the extensive list of its editors further complicates the problem of how it should be interpreted: indeed, 'the roll-call of contributors to the "meaning" derived from *The Prelude* should include Helen Darbishire, Ernest de Selincourt, M.H. Abrams, Jonathan Wordsworth, Stephen Gill, Stephen Parrish, W.J.B. Owen and Mark L. Reed'.[1]

The textual instability of the poem, however, is not merely due to its complex origins. Drawing on the French theorist Roland Barthes (1915–80), Wood argues that the plurality of *Prelude* texts merely indicates that the poem exhibits to an unusually high degree the *textual* indeterminacy that problematizes *all* so-called 'works' of literature:

> ■ If the printed words on the page are the product of necessary editorial intervention as well as the spread of the identifiable 'Wordsworth's' who penned the manuscripts, then we might feel ourselves free to draw a basic distinction, following Roland Barthes's influential wording, between two forms of critical discourse: that interested in *The Prelude*'s existence as a 'work', an object of consumption, knowledge, library classification and integrity, and its existence as a 'text', something *experienced only in an activity of production*' and thus a 'methodological field' that is plural and which is produced in the process of reading [...]. □

Once a literary 'work' such as *The Prelude* is viewed as a 'methodological field' produced by the process of reading, the figure of the author recedes, indeed, vanishes:

> ■ [W]e are consequently left with the conclusion that, ultimately, we are reading ourselves, noting merely the modes of how we 'displace' anxieties on to the text or, in, negotiating with the words we read (however disparate their provenance), how we transfer our own desires on to them.[2] □

Some followers of Barthes went further, arguing that the notion of 'language' was as much of an illusion as that of the 'author'. If a text is in reality an effect produced by material *inscription*, or writing, rather than the ideal, illusory 'presence' of *language*, then this 'meaning' can never amount to more than the indeterminate figure of reading itself. This in turn produces the cornerstone of deconstruction: the only thing supporting our supposedly determinate interpretation of language is the figure of reading produced by the indeterminate materiality of writing.

The writer who is most closely associated with applying this idea to Romantic poetry is Paul de Man. In his searching and often difficult essays, de Man challenges readers to study the relationship between the self and textuality in Wordsworth. De Man rejects the Romantic belief that notions of 'truth' and 'self' are ideal categories that lie 'beneath' the text as the grounds of its meaning. Language, for de Man, does not 'refer' to the world: it *figures* a world: as a result, the only thing that writing refers to, ultimately, is writing itself. Consequently, de Man reads 'against the grain' of Wordsworth's poetry by showing how its *rhetoric* – its figures and metaphors, whether overt or concealed – finally reveal their own role in constituting the very relationships between the 'subjective' consciousness (mind) and the 'objective' world (nature) that they are supposed merely to represent.

Much of de Man's most important work on Wordsworth is contained in his seminal collection *The Rhetoric of Romanticism* (1984), in particular the essays 'Wordsworth and Hölderlin'; 'Autobiography as De-Facement'; 'Wordsworth and the Victorians', and 'Symbolic Landscape in Wordsworth and Yeats'. In 'Autobiography as De-Facement', he argues that the 'specular' nature of autobiography is not the result of the conscious choice of the author, but the product of the inescapably metaphorical structure of language. Like language, which always hovers indeterminately between figuratively *creating* an object and *referring to* an object, autobiography is forever caught in 'a revolving door' between fiction and fact, so that 'the distinction between fiction and autobiography is not an either/or polarity but [...] is undecidable'.[3] This oscillation, he reiterates, stems from language rather than the intention of the writer:

■ Autobiography, then, is not a genre or a mode, but a figure of reading or of understanding that occurs, to some degree, in all texts. The autobiographical moment happens as an alignment between two subjects involved in the process of reading in which they determine each other by mutual reflexive substitution. The structure implies differentiation as well as similarity [...]. This specular structure is interiorized in a text [...]. □

It follows from this, paradoxically, that just as all texts are autobiographical, 'by the same token, none of them is or can be'.[4] Indeed, the image of the revolving door 'aptly connotes the turning motion of tropes and confirms that the specular moment is [...] the manifestation, on the level of the referent, of a linguistic structure. The specular moment that is part of all understanding reveals the tropological structure that underlies all cognitions, including knowledge of self'.[5] What *The Prelude*'s autobiography ultimately confirms, then, is 'the impossibility of closure and of totalization (that is the impossibility of coming into being) of all textual systems made up of tropological substitutions'.[6]

De Man's approach differs markedly from that of Hartman (his colleague at Yale), who had argued in *Wordsworth's Poetry* and elsewhere that the coming-into-being of self in *The Prelude* was fundamentally a problem of consciousness and experience. For de Man, the situation is quite different: the anxieties of Wordsworth's autobiographical poem, he claims, are rooted in the fact that a complete 'unity' of self can never be achieved, given that the 'self' itself is constituted by a textual system 'made up of tropological substitutions'. Indeed, de Man remains dubious, to say the least, about any attempt to find a 'philosophy' of imagination in Wordsworth's poetry. Thus, in his essay 'Wordsworth and the Victorians', he casts a sceptical eye over a history of attempts, initiated by the Victorians, to cast Wordsworth in the role of 'philosopher-poet'. Like Leavis, de Man traces the cause of these (ill-fated) critical enterprises to the texture of Wordsworth's language, which eschews formal argument and yet seems pregnant with philosophical significance. 'It is', de Man observes, 'as if his language came from a region in which the most carefully drawn distinctions between analytic rigor and poetic persuasion are no longer preserved, at no small risk to either'.[7] Attempts by Stephen and Arnold to cast Wordsworth respectively as a 'moral' philosopher and a poet misled by philosophy are 'defensive' strategies that miss the point: ' "Philosophy" is supposed to shelter us from something to which Wordsworth's poetry, unlike any other romantic poetry, gives access, although it remains unnamed and undefined.'[8] This 'something', de Man avers, is the uneasy realization that human awareness – even the most fundamental self-consciousness – depends upon the temporality and contingency of *rhetoric*. There can be no recuperation of 'unity' from such contingency, which is why de Man remains unconvinced by Hartman's displacement of the 'philosopher-poet' model of Stephen into the realm of phenomenology, a 'move to which Wordsworth's texts respond with almost suspicious docility', whereby '[t]he threat from which we were to be sheltered and consoled is now identified as a condition of consciousness'.[9] Against this, De Man insists that what *The Prelude* reveals is that there can in the end be no aesthetic recovery of meaning, since the *aporia* (De Man's term for an irresolvable paradox) of self-knowledge is finally a 'conflict that can no longer be reduced to existential or psychological causes'.[10]

Accordingly, when de Man turns to examine *The Prelude* (as he frequently does in these essays), he is interested less in the mind's struggle to articulate its relationship with nature than those moments in the text when the very grounds beneath the mind threaten to disappear altogether. In his essay 'Time and History in Wordsworth', for example, he focuses on the use the poet makes of the word 'hangs', claiming that it frequently denotes

■ a sudden feeling of dizziness, a falling or a threat of falling, a *vertige* of which there are many examples in Wordsworth. The nest robbing scene from Book I of *The Prelude* comes to mind, where the experience is a literal movement of absolute dizziness which disjoins the familiar perspective of the spatial relationship between heaven and earth, in which the heavens are seen as a safe dome that confirms at all times the earth's and our own centrality, the steadfastness of our orientation towards the center which makes us creates *of* earth. But here, suddenly, the sky no longer relates to the earth.

Oh! at that time,
While on the perilous ridge I *hung* alone,
With what strange utterance did the loud dry wind
Blow through my ears! the sky *seem'd not a sky*
Of earth, and with what motion moved the clouds! □

(1805 *Prelude*, I, 335–339; p. 291)[11]

This feeling of precariousness, de Man suggests, is linked to the mind's unsteady sense of itself as an entity that is figured *spatially* as a 'centre', at least of its own phenomenal world. The possibility of this world being upturned, however, reveals how this spatial self 'hangs' upon complex metaphors of *time*. Such temporality proves essential to the poet's understanding, and yet also threatens it, insofar as it connotes impermanence, contingency, and ultimately, death. As a result, Wordsworth's poetic self in *The Prelude* suffers from a bad case of vertigo: it is always in the paradoxical but inescapable predicament of falling back into temporality, even as it struggles to conceal from itself its dependence upon time. Thus, while Hartman had argued that Wordsworth's 'vision' is enabled by an unsustainable blindness to nature, for de Man, whatever insight there is in *The Prelude* is negative, in the sense that it depends upon an awareness that the very power that sustains imagination is finally at odds with it, since 'time itself', he argues, 'lies beyond language and beyond the reach of imagination':

■ The power that maintains the imagination, which Hartman calls nature returning after it has been nearly annihilated by apocalyptic insight, is time. The key to an understanding of Wordsworth lies in the relationship between imagination and time, not in the relationship between imagination and nature.[12] □

De Man was not the only critic who sought to revise Hartman's theory of the *Prelude*'s 'dialectic' by stressing the importance the uneasy relationship between language and consciousness in the poem. The fundamental claim of Frances Ferguson's 1977 book, *Wordsworth: Language as Counter-Spirit* is that 'Wordsworth thought seriously and coherently about language in both his prose and his poetry'.[13] Ferguson challenges M.H. Abrams' view that Wordsworth's theories of language were based upon an ideal of *organic* form. This theory – advanced by Coleridge – proposes that language is plant-like, and thus that the *form* a poem assumes is determined by its *content* (its origin or 'seed'). For Coleridge, a poem should aspire to the status of a plant, revealing its meaning through its linguistic form in the same way that a flower reveals its essence through the shape into which it grows. The problem with applying this model to Wordsworth's poetry, Ferguson claims, is that it doesn't fit. Rather than the figure of the plant, Wordsworth's writing on language is dominated by the metaphor of 'the epitaph and its inorganic counterpart, the tombstone'.[14] This has two consequences: the first is that Wordsworth's poems typically display a heightened awareness of themselves as *linguistic* creations, taking

■ their metaphors literally only for a time, invariably turning on them with an awareness that their correspondences are things that they have made [rather than things that have emerged from an essential idea]. I describe this turning as *reading* because I know of no better way to convey the sudden detachment which takes place when the correspondences come to seem constructs which can be reread and conned like texts.[15] □

Wordsworth's epitaphic model of language, in other words, is dominated by an image not of growth, but of *reading*. This brings us to the second consequence of Wordsworth's metaphor: the materiality and impermanence of the tombstone epitaph, Ferguson claims, 'suggest that neither human incarnation nor linguistic incarnation is a fixed form which can be arrived at and sustained. The life of language in poetry, like the life of the individual, is radically implicated with death [...].' Consequently, language for Wordsworth can never be (as Coleridge believed it was) 'a salvation to the perplexities of individual consciousness'.[16] Any attempt to trace a 'dialectic' between consciousness and world in Wordsworth's poetry must take account of the poet's own deep realization that the 'counter-spirit' of mind is not life-giving nature, but death-dealing language.

Turning to *The Prelude*, Ferguson immediately focuses on one passage that comes early in Book I:

■ Sometimes it suits me better to invent
A tale from my own heart, more near akin
To my own passions and habitual thoughts;

Some variegated story, in the main
Lofty, but the unsubstantial structure melts
Before the very sun that brightens it,
Mist into air dissolving! □

[I, 221–227][17]

Ferguson is struck by the way in which this passage discloses
Wordsworth's awareness of 'the inadequacy of one's accounts of himself on the basis of memory', and how this inadequacy 'keeps disclosing
the otherness of one's own mind as a force which is divine in its power
and persistence. Precisely the individual's inability to construct himself [...] becomes testimony to the thoughts and language of others as
an Ur-principle [original principle] for the individual.'[18] Rather than
signalling a metaphysical dialectic between consciousness and nature,
it betrays the dependence of consciousness upon language and the contingencies of interpersonal communication. This 'dialectic' (if it can be
described as such) offers no promise of truth or meaning. This is how
Ferguson glosses the lines quoted above:

■ The sun which has been gradually projected from within becomes a
counteragent, an intransigent other which dissolves structure into mist into
air. Thus curious drifting of the sun itself becomes emblematic of an analo-
gous movement which Wordsworth discerns in language – its tendency
to convert itself into a counter-spirit which seems always to threaten the
possibility of the poet's changing his internal story into an external story.
The internality, which is possessing his own past, continually implies an
externality, which is being possessed by a 'mistaken' or 'inadequate' version of that past.
    This dialectic persists throughout *The Prelude*, repeatedly blurring the
boundaries between Nature and (human) nature, so that the boundaries
between externality and internality correspondingly blur.[19] □

Another good example of the materiality of language intruding on
the ideal interchange between mind and world, Ferguson finds, is the
'Blind Beggar' episode in Book VII. This recounts the poet's encounter in London with a man who 'Stood, propped against a wall, upon
his chest / Wearing a written paper to explain / His story, whence he
came, and who he was'. In this image the poet experiences an epiphanic
'spot of time', discovering an emblem or 'type' of all we can know

■ Both of ourselves and of the universe;
And on the shape of that unmoving man,
His steadfast face and sightless eyes, I gazed,
As if admonished from another world. □

[VII, 646–649][20]

For Ferguson, however, this passage is not really about the strengthening of the poet's 'inner' vision and consciousness through the contemplation of an 'external' object. It contains a far more troubling implication for the poet, namely, that what he takes to be his *own*, 'subjective' world is, like that of the blind man, already inscribed or 'written down' for him: it is, in other words, always determined by language. The 'otherness' that the poet detects here, then, recalls the otherness of language encountered in Book I:

■ The imagination of the beggar's internal existence develops into a recognition of the dependency of all internal being. For the label is 'an apt type' of the limits of human knowledge of the self and of the universe precisely because it is an external form pleading for meaning from the reader [...]. For Wordsworth here in the middle of his own 'story', *The Prelude*, the label and the beggar constitute a return to that early indecision in Book I. The tale from his own heart, the account of his 'own passions and habitual thoughts', cannot be written, the description of the beggar would imply. For even the passions which are apparently the most internal of human faculties came to seem dependent, both in their origins and in the external, 'final' form of writing. Just as the passions are derived from others for both the poet and the beggar, so also are the external products of their internal existences – their stories – dependent upon their readers for meaningfulness. The self cannot know itself, because it is ineluctably not really a self but rather a composite of selves intertwined through a chain of the affections and continually reaching out in an appeal to additional selves.[21] □

The troubling conundrum posed by the Blind Beggar passage, then, can be framed in the following question: if one can only know (indeed, *be*) oneself through the intervention of the material and social 'other' of language, how is it possible for *The Prelude* to be an 'authentic' and 'sincere' expression of self? Indeed, as Ferguson concludes, Wordsworth's quest for personal meaning ultimately raises questions about the foundations of meaning itself:

■ The very belief that words mean anything – and have a shared meaning – represents a tacit acknowledgment that the only world and self which we can know is a residue of an unfathomably extensive chain of affections which have led us all to imagine the possibility of meaning in the face of all evidence to the contrary.[22] □

Deconstruction had a significant impact upon Wordsworth criticism during the 1980s, opening up to critics the possibility of dealing with the hidden conceptual tensions and contradictions in the poet's work, rather than with its declared themes. For some critics, however, the implications of a deconstructive approach to Romantic poetry were more far-reaching than de Man allowed. The paradoxes of thought and language that beset *The Prelude* are described by de Man in epistemological terms: they are problems of insight and the (im)possibility of knowledge. Yet it could be argued that this approach as complicit with the foundationalist 'logocentrism' of the western philosophical tradition that de Man ostensibly attacks, insofar as it perpetuates the idea that the most fundamental issue at stake is *knowledge*. In contrast, Mary Jacobus's book *Romanticism, Writing and Sexual Difference: Essays on* The Prelude (1989), takes a different tack, using deconstructive techniques to show how (among other things) an unresolved logic of gender affects *The Prelude*.

Jacobus's approach is epitomized in her essay on the textual and editorial history of the 'Vaudracour and Julia' section of the poem, originally the closing 380 lines of Book IX. This episode tells the tragic tale of a forbidden love between the noble Vaudracour and the plebian Julia. The relationship produces a child, after which Julia retreats into a convent, and Vaudracour to a lodge, 'Deep in a forest' (IX, 900), only for the child to die soon afterwards. Vaudracour thereafter withdraws from all human contact, and 'in those solitary shades / His days he wasted, an imbecile mind' (IX, 935). Commentators have long noted the connections between the story of Vaudracour's enforced separation from Julia and Wordsworth's own abandonment of Annette Vallon and his daughter, Caroline, when the outbreak of war between Britain and France in 1793 forced him to return to England. Jacobus's interest is 'not so much [in] the begetting of Caroline as the beginnings of *The Prelude*'.[23] While revising the 1805 text, Wordsworth decided to excise the story, repackaging it as a separate poem, which was published in 1820. For Jacobus, this decision reflects anxieties relating to questions of genre *and* gender in *The Prelude*.

The origins of this anxiety, she claims, lie in the dubious legitimacy of the new literary form of autobiography. Like Vaudracour, Wordsworth's autobiography defies the patriarchal laws of classification: in Vaudracour's case, these restrictions relate to children produced through marriages across class boundaries; in Wordsworth's, to literary works produced by 'marriages' across genre boundaries. As a result, '[a]t once an endless beginning and always an afterword to the life it narrates, Wordsworth's autobiography seems not to have a proper place after all. It belongs nowhere and has no fixed character [...]'.[24] From this perspective, *Vaudracour and Julia* appears as the illegitimate child of a proscribed mixture of 'high' and 'low' genres, an offspring which Wordsworth must abandon in order to recover his own status within the patriarchal poetic order:

■ The Vaudracour and Julia episode can be seen [...] as the point from which *The Prelude* departs as well as a redundancy; as an opening as well as a cut. A history of error and transgression, the episode is also symptomatic of the errancy of Wordsworth's abandonment of historical and philosophical epic for that mixed and transgressive genre, autobiography.[25] □

Jacobus is influenced by de Man's theory that all writing is, in a sense, autobiographical, insofar as it depends upon the 'mutual reflexive substitution' of reference and figuration: thus, even as language renders meaning possible by positing the figure of a face (as referent), it simultaneously renders it impossible by *defacing* that meaning through the contingent (figurative) play of its signification. Meaning, in other words, is always fatally compromised by its reliance upon its own nemesis: contingency. Jacobus extends de Man's arguments by applying them to the rhetoric that underlies the 'laws' of gender and genre, both of which seek to conceal the dependence of their 'logic' upon contingent figure and metaphor. She finds in Wordsworth a strategy of containment whereby a potentially disruptive 'minor' term (woman, romance) is subordinated to a normative 'major' term (man, history). In the 'romantic' interlude of Vaudracour and Julia, *The Prelude* invokes the otherness of a feminine genre in order to constitute itself as a masculine autobiography. In this way, the 'story of Vaudracour and Julia is also a means of constituting Wordsworth himself as an autobiographical subject, and, specifically, a masculine one'. However, once this identity is established, the dialectic of masculine/feminine can be repressed in the service of a homogenously 'male' discourse:

■ Hence gender (sexual difference) establishes identity by means of a difference that is finally excised. What we end up with is not difference [...] but the same: man, or man-to-man. Like the Vaudracour and Julia episode, and like the feminised genre of romance, woman becomes redundant. Her role is to mediate between men, as the role of romance is to mediate between history and the historian's tale or page.[26] □

A 'bastard' genre, Wordsworth's autobiography attempts to legitimize itself by insisting on its status as the product of an entirely natural act of reflection and expression. However, Jacobus argues that by appealing to *nature* for its legitimacy in this way, *The Prelude*, like Vaudracour, ultimately submits to patriarchal authority:

■ In the last resort, nature proves to be merely the common-law wife of a Wordsworth who subsequently married within the family [...]. If *The Prelude* as autobiography is Romanticism's rebellion against the law of genre, it is a rebellion which ultimately turns back to the order of the past in the interests of a readable text. Engendered by the illicit mixing of aristocratic and middle-class genres [...] *The Prelude* simultaneously defies the Law of the Father and preserves it. □

But this taming of autobiography by the rule of genre in *The Prelude* does not mean that the 'Law of the Father', finally triumphs. Quite the reverse, if we recall de Man's point that autobiography is not a genre as such but the specular form of all writing, in which there is always lodged an ineliminable, indeterminate, and 'feminine' otherness:

■ [T]he Vaudracour and Julia episode reminds us that there is no history without error; that genre is always impure, always 'mothered' as well as fathered, and that 'lodged within the heart of the law itself, [is] a law of impurity or a principle of contamination'.[27] □

THE USES OF GENDER

Jacobus was one of a number of critics who, in the 1980s and 1990s, used theoretically sophisticated techniques to examine configurations of power and gender (sometimes hidden, sometimes overt) in *The Prelude*. Not all of these critics took their lead from the strategies of deconstruction. In 1986, Marlon Ross (born 1956) published an article in the journal *English Literary History* entitled 'Naturalizing Gender: Woman's Place in Wordsworth's Ideological Landscape'. Ross's essay sets out from the assumption that 'the Romantic poet often attempts to dissolve and distort the concrete socio-historical relations (to distance and disorient us from them) that actually constitute his experience'.[28] One of these 'socio-historical relations crucial to Wordsworth's ideological ground, a relation that Wordsworth himself continually attempts to transcend, to dissolve and distort, to mask and forget' is 'the relation between Wordsworth's conceptualization of the development of human identity and the culturally established view of women's role in civilization'. In short, Ross avers, 'the poet exploits the socio-historical experience of women's subordinate position, transforming that culturally fabricated status (a socio-historical fact) into a natural and essential place (a transcendent idea)'. In fact, Wordsworth

■ subtly and quietly reasserts and solidifies the priorities of male needs and desires. The male's need for self-identity is repeatedly reenacted in the poems, and the female always serves that need as the object of his desire; ironically, though she is always unattainable, she is always obtained (meaning held totally) in that she is objectified – hence contained – by the contours of male desire.[29] □

There are a number of points worth noting about these remarks. The first is the way in which they up-end the traditional terms of the debate surrounding Wordsworth's 'philosophy'. Rather than treating this philosophy as the key to the mysteries of Wordsworth's poetry and the source of *The Prelude*'s wisdom, Ross and commentators of a similar persuasion now view it with (political, hermeneutic, sexual) suspicion. In many cases indeed, the problem such critics identify is not with the particular character of Wordsworth's philosophy, but with *philosophy per se*, which is seen as at best complicit with, and at worst constitutive of strategies that further the interests of a specific class of people – generally identified as male, bourgeois, and white. Accordingly, Ross refuses to read Wordsworth's poetry on its own terms. Doing so, he claims, would be to fall into a trap that even 'Wordsworth's best readers (Bateson, Ferry, Hartman, Bloom, to name a few)' have failed to avoid: that of unconsciously inheriting Wordsworth's 'ideological estate', the gender-loaded discourse of his metaphysics. In their turn, by reading Wordsworth metaphysically rather that socio-historically, such critics have 'passed the inheritance on', perpetuating a male legacy that is ultimately complicit in ensuring that 'the female becomes a subspecies of male humanity'.[30]

Ross's article does not examine *The Prelude* directly, but its opening statement serves well as an introduction to the concerns and issues feminist scholarship has brought to the poem. These might be summarized under two headings: (1) The growing imagination of the poet is configured in *The Prelude* as male and autonomous. However, it can be seen that this identity is only able to define itself by reference to a *female* principle or figure, which the poem then conceals or represses. Thus, the so-called 'philosophical' problem of 'otherness' in *The Prelude* is fundamentally a problem of *gender*; (2) More specifically, the story of the growth of the poet's mind is Oedipal in character: that is to say, the process of self-definition traced by the poem echoes the narratives of Freud and Jacques Lacan regarding how the ego of the male child comes to assert itself once it has been wrenched by the father from the protective and immediate presence of the mother. According to Lacan, one of the most important features of the Oedipal complex is the acquisition of language. The poem's concern with, and use of language, then, is also fundamentally a problem of gender.

Both these issues are tackled by Margaret Homans (born 1952) in her 1986 study, *Bearing the Word: Language and Female Experience in Nineteenth-Century Woman's Writing*. Homans approaches the question of gender in Wordsworth's writing by treating it as a problem shared by both William *and* Dorothy. She notes that the relationship between women and language has always been problematic in western culture, due to what she calls the symbolic 'dependence of androcentric culture on the mother's absence'.[31] As far back as the mythology of ancient Greek culture, she notes, 'the death or absence of the mother sorrowfully but fortunately makes possible the construction of language and of culture'.[32] More recently, Lacan gave this mythology a psycholin-guistic twist, describing the acquisition of language by the male child in Oedipal terms. Thus, the son is torn from his blissful, inarticulate union with his mother by the intrusive presence of the father. The son's reward for this is entry into the symbolic order, the world of reference and denotation: in short, the world of language. The *cost* of this passage, however, is alienation from the female, which now becomes merely that which is denoted or signified: woman, quite literally, is objectified.

Unsurprisingly, the repercussions of this mythology affect men and women differently. For men, the quest for meaning becomes bound up with a quest for reunion with the mother. Intervening in the 'poten-tially incestuous dyad of mother and child', the father is symbolized by the phallus, which itself becomes the symbol of symbolization itself, the mark of the *difference* (between male and female) that makes lan-guage possible.[33] Seeking to recover an original (maternal, incestuous) relationship of non-difference rendered impossible by the very nature of language, male language is driven by a desire for an unattainable object: effectively, 'a system for generating substitutes for the forbid-den mother'.[34] This predicament was felt especially keenly by William, whose mother died when he was only eight years old. In Homans' view, this trauma intensified for the young boy the primal association of 'learning representational language [...] with a loss that is equivalent to his mother's death. This loss feels like the mother's death, and it is, paradoxically, both caused by and the cause of the acquisition of repre-sentational language.'[35]

For women, however, the problem is quite different. They are faced with a stark choice: either they fight to gain entry into the male sym-bolic order of language – demanding the right to 'bear the word' as well as the child – or they remain with the mother, which is to say, undifferentiated and mute. In Lacanian terms (which Homans adopts, though she sees Lacan's theories as perpetuating an 'androcentric' dis-course), the dilemma confronting Dorothy is whether to strive to gain access to a paternal and inaccessible 'figurative' language, or to resign herself to the 'literal' language of the maternal. This is a double bind. On one level, according to the 'Lacanian myth', 'language and gender are connected in such a way as to privilege implicitly the masculine and the figurative'[36]; at the same time, the 'positioning of the literal poses special problems for women readers and writers because literal language, together with nature and matter to which it is epistemolog-ically linked, is traditionally classed as feminine, and the feminine is, from the point of view of a predominantly androcentric culture, always elsewhere' – in other words, undifferentiated.[37]

Taking this Western mythology of language as a 'quest romance, based on the boy's postoedipal renunciation of the mother and his quest for substitute objects of desire', and applying it to *The Prelude*, Homans finds that it tells us much about the underlying logic of the poem:

■ As a structure of difference and absence, language is modelled on sexual difference, the boy's difference from and renunciation of his mother. The referent of language is always absent; indeed, the word necessitates the absence of the object. That this is the governing myth of language for Wordsworth is nowhere more clear than in his central account of the acquisition of language in book 2 of *The Prelude* [...]. In this passage, the 'infant Babe' is 'blest' because he 'Drinks in the feelings of his Mother's eye!' (2.237). What the baby 'drinks' is his mother's love of nature. Because her 'Presence' 'irradiates' nature, and because he loves everything connected to her, the baby's love for his mother grants him 'The gravitation and the filial bond / Of nature that connect him with the world' (2.243–44). Empowered by the feelings he drinks in from his mother, the infant 'Doth like an agent of the one great Mind / Create, creator and receiver both' (2.257–58), but his creation is without language: 'by intercourse of touch / I held mute dialogues with my Mother's heart' (2.267–68) [...].

But the entry into the symbolic order causes a 'trouble':

> I was left alone
> Seeking the visible world, nor knowing why.
> The props of my affections were removed,
> And yet the building stood, as if sustained
> By its own spirit!

As we have seen, Wordsworth here equates the acquisition of representational language with a loss that feels like his mother's death, most likely the growing boy's oedipal renunciation of his most intimate bond with her.[38] □

'Ironically', Homans continues, having been separated from the mother, 'the child discovers that he can overcome this crisis with the aid of what has precipitated the crisis: language and personal autonomy'. The result of this (as was seen earlier), is that Wordsworth the adult poet is faced with a paradox, in that the very means of his overcoming his crisis (using language, writing poetry) perpetuates it. As Homans puts it, Wordsworth 'fears that language depends upon and therefore necessitates death, the death of the referential object that is always also the death of his mother, and his project is to forestall the determinate meaning of words so that the object need not die'.[39]

This line of argument enables Homans to offer an entirely new slant on the same quality of vagueness in the language of *The Prelude* that F.R. Leavis noted decades earlier. The famous opacity (and the power) of much of the language of *The Prelude*, she maintains, is the product of an indeterminacy rooted in the psychopathology of William's childhood. Thus, the attainment of imaginative power or 'vision' so painstakingly charted in *The Prelude* is actually the adult poet's attempt to reconnect with the pre-linguistic bliss of early infancy, an endeavour that can only be carried out through 'a language that does not signify but defers signification'.[40] As an example of this strategy of deferral, Homans cites the following passage from Book II of *The Prelude*:

> ■ the soul,
> Remembering how she felt, but what she felt
> Remembering not, retains an obscure sense
> Of possible sublimity, whereto
> With growing faculties she doth aspire,
> With faculties still growing, feeling still
> That whatsoever point they gain, they yet
> Have something to pursue. □

> (II, 315–322)

Homans notes Thomas Weiskel's observation in his book *The Egotistical Sublime* that this kind of language in *The Prelude* aspires to be 'as nonreferential as possible', and finds in Wordsworth's choice of oblique words and phrases like 'obscure sense', 'possible sublimity', 'whatsoever', and 'something' an indication of how 'the language of the sublime defers indeterminate signification indefinitely'. She goes further than Weiskel, however, by maintaining that the poem's 'visionary power, and the forestalling of signification it depends upon, is connected to the ambiguous presence and absence of the mother'.[41]

   Published seven years after Homans's study, Gayatri Chakravorty Spivak's influential 1993 essay 'Sex and History in *The Prelude* (1805)' also takes up the theme of how the figure of the 'feminine' is invoked by the poem only to be cancelled – or, at least, subordinated to a masculine principle. In her long and searching essay, Spivak claims that Wordsworth coped with the disappointment of the French Revolution by 'transforming it into an iconic text that he could write and read', and by convincing himself that 'poetry was a better cure for the oppression of mankind than political economy or revolution'. Of primary interest here, however, is her argument regarding the Oedipal imagination at work in *The Prelude*, to the effect that in this autobiographical poem 'Wordsworth not only needed to exorcise his illegitimate paternity but also to re-establish himself sexually in order to declare his imagination restored'.[42]

   Like Homans, Spivak finds the tools and concepts of psychoanalysis useful for examining the text from a feminist perspective, but remains wary of the gender assumptions of Freud and his disciples. However, where Homans deploys (albeit with reservations) the categories of

Lacanian psycholinguistics, Spivak, like Mary Jacobus, interweaves deconstructive and feminist approaches in her reading of Wordsworth's poem. In particular, she is influenced by the notion of the 'trace', as propounded by Jacques Derrida (1930–2004). Spivak explains this concept in the following way: 'Every origin that we seem to locate refers us back to something anterior and contains the possibility of something posterior. There is, in other words, a trace of something else in seemingly self-contained origins.' This 'trace', although it signals an original meaning, cannot guarantee the presence of meaning; instead, all it provides is an endless deferral of meaning. The trace then, 'since it breaks up every first cause or origin, cannot be a transcendental principle. It would thus be difficult to distinguish clearly between the trace as a principle and cases of the trace, such as writing or a stream.' The problem with thinking about the trace, as Derrida and Spivak recognize, is that one cannot think in the complete *absence* of meaning, of origins. Thus, one cannot attend to the trace fully: something has to be 'taken for granted': 'Since the trace cannot be fully attended to, one possible alternative is to pay attention to the texts of history and politics as the trace-structuring of positions [...].'[43]

This brings us back to Spivak's core argument regarding the 'gender' of the imagination in *The Prelude*. By paying 'attention to the texts of history and politics as the trace-structuring of positions', she finds that in Books IX to XIII 'one may find textual signs of a rejection of paternity, of a reinstatement of the subject as son (rather than father) within Oedipal law, and then, through the imagination, a claim to androgyny'. In other words, a 'deconstruction' of the poem reveals the ways in which 'Wordsworth projects the possibility of being son *and* lover, father *and* mother of poems, male *and* female at once'.[44]

Spivak's analysis is complex, and dominated by the highly technical vocabulary of post-structuralism. She adopts some of Freud's ideas, particularly the notion of the Oedipal complex, but has no truck with psychoanalysis as a general method, considering it to be 'part of the ideology of male universalism'.[45] Instead, she examines this 'trace-structuring of positions' in the poem as a product of repressions and consequent displacements and transferences of meanings. For example, one of the 'textual signs of a rejection of paternity' that she locates is the figure of Vaudracour. Vaudracour, Spivak argues, emerges as an unacceptable *alter ego* for the poet, one which is later 'sublated' or carried over into the figure of Coleridge – who in turn ultimately becomes a guarantor of Wordsworth's 'glimpses of a future world superior to the revolutionary alternative'.[46] More important, however, are the 'traces' she claims to find of *The Prelude*'s hankering for a pre–Oedipal condition where the contradictions and conflicts between the self and world are annulled. The poem registers an awareness that this removal of

contradictions cannot be achieved simply on the command of an isolated ego. Thus, the mediation of a *female* figure is required. At this
point, Spivak claims, Dorothy's role in the poem becomes pivotal, for
it is she who ultimately links the poet to the idea of a feminine centre
of self and thereby 'provides a passage into the rememoration of these
Oedipal events, and finally into the accession to androgyny':

■ Unlike the male mediators who punish, or demonstrate and justify the
law – the teacher, the murderer, the father, Coleridge – Dorothy Wordsworth
restores her brother's imagination as a living agent. And, indeed, William,
interlarding his compliments with the patronage typical of his time, and perhaps of ours, does call her 'wholly free' (XI. 203). It is curious, then, that the
predication of *her* relationship with Nature, strongly reminiscent of 'Tintern
Abbey', [1798] should be entirely in the conditional:

> Her the birds
> And every flower she met with, could they but
> Have known her, would have lov'd. Methought such charm
> Of sweetness did her presence breathe around
> That all the trees, and the silent hills
> And every thing she look'd on, should have had
> An intimation how she bore herself
> Towards them and to all creatures.
>
> (XI. 214–221)

The only indicative description in this passage is introduced by a controlling
'methought'.
  Although Wordsworth's delight in his sister makes him more like God
than like her – 'God delights / In such a being' (XI. 221–2) – she provides a
possibility of transference for him. The next verse paragraph begins – 'Even
like this Maid' (XI. 224) [...]. Dorothy as sister is arranged as a figure that
would allow the poet the possibility of a replaying of the Oedipal scene, the
scene of sonship after the rejection of premature fatherhood. [...] William is
invoking the pre-Oedipal stage when girl and boy are alike [...].[47] □

Like Jacobus, Spivak interprets Wordsworth's interest in nature symp-
tomatologically. The agency of nature is vital to Wordsworth, she
suggests, in that it counters the rigid differences of human *culture* by
representing an anterior state of indeterminacy. In this way, the figure
of nature facilitates the poem's pre-Oedipal blurring of gender boundaries. Still more important to Wordsworth, however, is the assistance of
Dorothy, who, having served as the rhetorical means whereby the poet
can access an androgynous ideal, is confirmed in her position of subordination to the male poet. Finally, then, one can trace in *The Prelude* the
'itinerary of Wordsworth's securing of the Imagination':

■ Suppression of Julia, unemphatic retention of Vaudracour as sustained and negative condition of possibility of disavowal, his sublation into

Coleridge, rememorating through the mediation of the figure of Dorothy his own Oedipal accession to the Law, Imagination as the androgyny of Nature and Man – Woman shut out. I cannot but see in it the sexual-political programme of the Great Tradition.[48] □

For Spivak, the purported 'growth of the poet's mind' in *The Prelude* is in reality a coded fantasy of psychic regression. Rather than synthesize divergent energies, the poem articulates a repressed desire to escape sexual difference, an androgyny uneasily embodied in the figure of Imagination. Moreover, like Jacobus and Homans, Spivak maintains that, for Wordsworth, woman's role in this process – what she terms the underlying 'sexual-political programme of the Great Tradition' – is first to facilitate it, and then be 'shut out'.

Surveying the work of commentators such as Jacobus, Ross, Homans, and Spivak reveals the extent to which modern feminist theory and criticism is able to adapt and incorporate a wide variety of theoretical approaches, including historicism, psychoanalysis, and deconstruction. As a result, perhaps more than any critical trend I have discussed so far, feminist commentary on *The Prelude* resists easy definition and summary. Nonetheless, the two key features I have identified as characteristic of feminist readings of *The Prelude* – namely, close consideration of the way in which the poem appropriates and excludes the figure or 'voice' of the female, together with an interest in the Oedipal dynamics of Wordsworth's consciousness – also play important roles in Anne Mellor's study, *Romanticism and Gender*.

Published the same year as Spivak's essay, Mellor's book does not confine its attention to *The Prelude* – or even Wordsworth, for that matter – but seeks to give an overview of issues relating to the relation of romanticism and gender. In an important chapter, however, Mellor turns her attention to Wordsworth's longest poem. She initially registers how the crises of consciousness described in *The Prelude* lead to a loss that is always somehow, miraculously, recuperated. 'Wordsworth's falls', she notes, 'couched in tropes borrowed from Milton's *Paradise Lost*, are represented as potentially fortunate', leading to 'an ever subtler understanding and more profound conviction of his poetic vocation'.[49] Following Hartman, Mellor infers that this is because Wordsworth's poetic self is constructed upon a 'genetic, teleological model', progressing through childish unself-consciousness, through adolescent self-consciousness, into the fully grown Imagination of adulthood.

Here, however, Hartman's account of the dialectic of consciousness is inflected with an awareness of gender: this putatively higher self or consciousness, Mellor maintains, is 'a specifically *masculine* self'.[50] Like Spivak, she draws the reader's attention to 'the Oedipal pattern of exclusively masculine childhood development and regression that is embedded in *The Prelude*'. The sense of loss that follows the passing of childhood 'produces in Wordsworth a never-satisfiable desire for reunion with that originating mother'. This in turn results in the 'construction of an autonomous poetic self that can stand alone'. Thus, we have what Keats called the 'egotistical sublime' in Wordsworth, whereby the 'self or subjectivity must transcend the body and become pure mind, become a consciousness that exists only in language'.[51] There is a price for this transcendence, however, one which the logic of the poem, by insisting upon the pre-eminence of the male intellect, demands from all that is 'other', including the very figure of the female – the maternal principle, nature, Dorothy – upon which it covertly depends:

■ Precarious indeed is this unique, unitary, transcendental subjectivity, for Wordsworth's sublime self-assurance is rendered possible, as many critics have observed, only by the arduous repression of the Other in all its forms: of the mother, of Dorothy, of other people, of history, of nature, of 'unknown modes of being', of that very gap or 'vacancy' which divides his present from his past identity. To sustain such a divine intellect, unspeaking female earth must be first silenced, then spiritually raped [...], colonized, and finally completely possessed. By the end of *The Prelude*, female Nature is not only a thousand times less beautiful than the mind of man but has even lost her gendered Otherness.[52] □

In his endeavour to evolve an essentially masculine imagination and identity in *The Prelude*, then, Wordsworth is fighting a losing battle. There is, in the end, no escaping the Oedipal character of his struggle: every attempt to assert the male character of his transcendent poetic subjectivity merely betrays, through its very assertiveness, its longing for an original maternal presence. Consequently, the more Wordsworth strives to gender his imagination as male, the more it appears to be constructed around the figure of the female:

■ Wordsworth recognizes that his hold on male supremacy is as insecure as his hold on his autonomous self. At the very end of his poem dedicated to a revelation of the male poet's possession of a godlike imagination 'in all the might of its endowments' (VI, 528), Wordsworth acknowledges that this very imagination, 'the main essential power' which throughout *The Prelude* he has tracked 'up her way sublime' (XIII, 290), is resistantly female. Wordsworth thus reveals the stubborn Otherness of all that he has labored so long and hard to absorb into his own identity: the originary power of the female, of the mother, of Nature.[53] □

THE STORY OF THE PSYCHE

One of the things that has already emerged from our survey of *Prelude* criticism is the prevalence and longevity of psychoanalytic methods of reading the poem. We have seen how early versions of these strategies were pioneered by critics such as Read and Bateson, and how they later influenced commentators like Bloom. Reading the work of Homans, Jacobus, and Spivak, however, one becomes aware of the considerable diversity within this strain of critical approach: thus, the methodological gulf that separates Read and Bloom is in turn rivalled by that which divides Bloom and Jacobus. And yet, aside from their varying degrees of indebtedness to Freud, these writers do indeed have something in common, namely, a tendency to keep the great psychoanalyst at arm's length. Thus, while many of the approaches discussed above import the techniques of psycho-analysis, these remain ancillary or even subordinate to other theoretical paradigms and agendas. Some critics, however, wholeheartedly embraced Freudian procedures in their analysis of *The Prelude*, and it is to these, more full-blooded psychoanalytic approaches that I now turn.

In his Introduction to the *Theory in Practice* collection of essays on *The Prelude*, Nigel Wood muses on the reasons why Wordsworth's poem has proved to be so amenable to psychoanalytic interpretation:

■ Psychoanalytic criticism [...] regards the poetic text as composed of negotiations between the unconscious and the repressive forces of the drive to represent and so control it. For Freud this tension exists to a greater or lesser extent in every narrative, or, in terms more familiar to his own work, 'case history'. The identification between a patient's account of anxiety and a piece of writing is a common one and lends itself to adaptation by any commentator on *The Prelude*. While the poet seems to give a faithful or sincere account of his formative years, the distinction between truth and falsehood in these matters is a fruitless one if we are to understand how he, in 1798, 1805 or 1950, is 'making sense' of his past and so of his present, that is, the adult he has become.[54] □

The textual instability of Wordsworth's verse autobiography, Wood observes, makes it ripe for psychoanalytic investigation. In particular, commentators who bring a Freudian eye to the poem see in the poet's endeavour to 'make sense' of his own history an (increasingly desperate) attempt to keep at bay the threat of his own mortality by making something coherent out of the scattered fragments of the past: '*The Prelude* represents, therefore, a proposition about the past that emerges from this anxiety to construct it *in the present*'. Wood continues:

■ 'Anxiety' is an apt word for this reordering, as it involves a working through of the displaced fears and repressed desires, a full coming to terms (in a

quite literal sense) with these shadows of authority or Otherness that cannot be faced directly, either because they only now exist in a language that
is metaphorical (and so require extensive interpretation) or because they
need to be reassembled out of their chronological order in order that they
can emerge for the conscious mind. This listening to the new grammar or
language of the unconscious is what Wordsworth often associates with the
'sense of God' – either as an external power or one that is apprehended
internally. After climbing Snowdon, Wordsworth reports how the original
experience was transformed by his 'meditation' on the 'lonely mountain'
(1805, XIII: 66–7), where there formed

> The perfect image of a mighty mind,
> Of one that feeds upon infinity,
> That is exalted by an under-presence,
> The sense of God, or whatsoe'er is dim
> Or vast in its own being – above all,
> One function of such mind had Nature there
> Exhibited by putting forth, and that
> With circumstance most awful and sublime... □
>
> (1805, XIII: 69–76)[55]

On this account, the moments of 'insight' that *The Prelude* commem-
orates are not the privileged occasions of awareness synthesized and
memorialized by a commanding consciousness. Rather, they represent
displaced eruptions of the unconscious, transferred in their significance into a 'sense of God', the sublime, or 'spots of time'. In all such
instances

> ■ the fear of the uncharted disturbs Wordsworth and forces its concep-
> tualization as another of his 'spots of time' that will actually supply spir-
> itual health. Often, using Freudian terminology, there is an Oedipal fear
> of the Father, where the uninterrupted enjoyment of mother nature [...]
> with its promise of full identification and loss of individuation, is rudely
> dislocated.[56] □

A good example of the 'Oedipal fear' driving the poem is the 'Stolen
Boat' episode of Book I. Here, the 'troubled pleasure' (I, 389) of the
boy's journey across the lake – leaving, as he dips his oars, 'Small circles
glittering idly in the moon' (I, 392) – represents the 'uninterrupted
enjoyment of mother nature'. This is rudely cut short by the intervention of the patriarch, violently and phallically symbolized by the 'huge
cliff' (I, 409) that seems to rise up and pursue the boy across the water.
    Nonetheless, Wood claims, no matter how persuasive such inter-
pretations may appear at first, there remains a danger lurking within
psychoanalytical readings, namely, that they are often apt to approach

a literary text as little more than an exotic 'case study' for diagnosis. Moreover, in so doing, they buy into rigid and 'essentialist' notions of gender and subjectivity that have been subjected to fierce attacks since Freud's day. It is for this very reason that critics like Jacobus and Spivak are wary of relying solely upon psychoanalytic models in their own readings of *The Prelude*:

■ In addressing form and its metaphorical freedoms psychoanalytic readings 'enter the frame' and educe a new 'unintended' order to construct the particular language of the unconscious. The temptation emerges, however, to rest content with this, to render the work as part of some complicated effusion of personality.[57] □

Wood writes in the early 1990s, when literary criticism in general was still reeling from the effects of two decades of the 'theory wars'. Psychoanalytic criticism, however, had a much older pedigree, and as we have seen in Read and Bateson, Wordsworth's longest poem was a favoured target. Thus, when Richard Oronato came to write a systematic psychoanalytic study of *The Prelude* in 1971, he did so without any of the misgivings registered later by Wood, Jacobus, or Spivak. Steeped in the technicalities and subtleties of Freud's work, Oronato's study offers itself partly as a corrective to 'the kind of intuitive psychologizing that offers no real account of itself but is implicit in many literary studies'.[58] In doing so, he attempts to take seriously Wordsworth's own conviction (as expressed in the poem 'My heart leaps up') that 'The Child is Father of the Man' (7), suggesting that, instead of seeing the young Wordsworth through the eyes of the older poet, 'we should be reading *The Prelude* differently, allowing [...] more attention to the child'.[59]

Like Homans, Onorato identifies the keystone in Wordsworth's unsteady psychological architecture as the moment of separation from the mother. It is this psychic 'trauma' that structures the adult Wordsworth's consciousness and echoes through his concepts of imagination and nature:

■ The relationships to be observed in Wordsworth's poetry between Imagination and Revelation [...] are present in this difficult sense of the self's beginnings in relation to what is real:

> his mind,
> Even as an agent of the one great mind,
> Creates, creator and receiver both,
> Working but in alliance with the works
> Which it beholds

(II, 271–275)

This is a characterization of the earliest sense of the poet's mind, which 'half-creates' what it perceives. The relationship of self and soul, then, is to be understood in the traumatic disruption of this ideal state of being. Imagination and Revelation, as Wordsworth characterizes them, are experienced as attempts of the pre-conscious mind to reunite the self and soul by giving to consciousness a knowledge of the traumatic disruption of one's being.

It is only one step further in psychological thinking to say that a severely traumatic disruption of this relationship may be only a special case of the general human case [...]. When Wordsworth says

> Such verily, is the first
> Poetic spirit of our human life;
> By uniform controul of after years
> In most abated or suppress'd, in some,
> Through every change of growth or of decay,
> Pre-eminent till death.

(II, 275–280)

he has rightly observed that most people seem to lose, in the exigencies of growth, not only the powers initially fostered in that ideal relationship, but even the capacity to realize or be concerned about their loss. The Poet as a special case, in Wordsworth's account of himself, acquires early in life an elaborately 'privileged' relationship with fostering Nature and a permanent concern with the ideal of growth. In our account of Wordsworth he is seen as fixated to a trauma, obsessed by a vital relationship with Nature which has come to stand unconsciously for the lost mother.[60] □

Put simply, Oronato reads *The Prelude* as an attempt at self-analysis. Because Wordsworth does not understand as Freud does the cunning of the unconscious, however, his quest for self-understanding is doomed to failure. The 'obstinate questioning' of the 'Intimations' Ode thus becomes another name for *The Prelude*'s peculiar form of repetition compulsion, whereby the poet repeatedly misrecognizes the symptoms of his psychopathology:

■ But if we say that his poetic obsession failed to reveal its meaning to him and that his unconscious intention to reveal the truth to himself was never successfully expressed, we are nevertheless saying that a stronger and opposite unconscious intention succeeded instead. The negative aspect of the repetition compulsion had effectively resisted and denied the trauma; it had rationalized the traces of repressed matters that had remained in memory, revealing them only in disguised form. Wordsworth was depressed by the result, but the depression did not last.[61] □

The depression 'did not last' because having failed to come to terms with his psychic trauma through memory and consciousness, the older

Wordsworth eventually turned back to the bland pieties of Victorian Christianity, much to the detriment, Oronato claims, of his later verse. Here, the obstinate questioning and self-analysis of *The Prelude* that made Wordsworth's obsession 'poetic' – and thus more than merely neurotic – subsides in the face of an imposed normative order:

■ The abnormality of a poetic obsession is [...] to be contrasted with the abnormal individual states of neurosis and psychosis which produce fantasy but not art. The aging Wordsworth, cultivating a Christian selflessness and impersonality, effected normality through resignation, with great difficulty, and wrote bad poetry.[62] □

Oronato's study of *The Prelude* systematically psychoanalyses the poem from as broad a perspective as possible. In comparison, David Ellis's 1985 monograph *Wordsworth, Freud and the Spots of Time* is less doctrinaire in its methods and (at first sight, at least), more limited in its choice of subject. Thus, while he he agrees with Oronato that 'although Wordsworth has the diversity of all great writers, his main strength is "psychological"', Ellis carefully positions his own reading of the poem 'very broadly in the tradition of Read and Bateson'.[63] Like these writers, whose methods Oronato dismissed as 'intuitive psychologizing that offers no real account of itself', Ellis consciously adopts an unsystematic approach to *The Prelude*, eschewing the temptation to reduce it to the dramas of the Freudian unconscious. Similarly, his principal concern is

■ not with *The Prelude* as a whole, but its so-called 'spots of time' and the extent to which they can be understood or 'read'. For it is on these episodes where Wordsworth's self-understanding appears stretched to its limits [...] that the claims he implicitly made for himself have to rest.[64] □

For Ellis, any attempt at a complete and comprehensive psychoanalysis of *The Prelude* risks uncritically aping that poem's doomed struggle to make comprehensible a life in which the only certainty is death. 'Like any autobiography', he maintains, '[Wordsworth's] poem represents an effort to make sense of a life: to deduce order and meaning from the discontinuities of experience. In doing so, he necessarily builds up an explanatory framework within which certain terms ("power" is an obvious example) become vital.'[65] Ellis's wariness of what might be called 'global' explanations means that his analysis of the 'spots of time' resists the temptation to push his own 'explanatory framework' too far. All theories and interpretations are mortal, so it is no coincidence, he claims, that the 'spots of time', *The Prelude*'s most commemorated moments of insight, are 'evidently concerned with death'.[66] He cites as one example of this the episode of the 'Drowned Man':

■ The succeeding day –
Those unclaimed garments telling a plain tale –
Went there a company, and in their boat
Sounded with grappling-irons and long poles:
At length, the dead man, 'mid that beauteous scene
Of trees and hills and water, bolt upright
Rose with his ghastly face, a spectre shape –
Of terror even. And yet no vulgar fear,
Young as I was, a child not nine years old,
Possessed me, for my inner eye had seen
Such sights before among the shining streams
Of fairyland, the forests of romance –
Thence came a spirit hallowing what I saw
With decoration and ideal grace,
A dignity, a smoothness, like the words
Of Grecian art and purest poesy. □

[1805, V, 466–481]

This passage appears in Book V of the 1805 text. In the Two-Part *Prelude*, however, it is the curtain-raiser to Wordsworth's reflections on 'spots of time', a passage which, in turn, was later moved to Book XI:

■ There are in our existence spots of time
Which with distinct preeminence retain
A fructifying virtue, whence, depressed
By trivial occupations and the round
Of ordinary intercourse, our minds –
Especially the imaginative power –
Are nourished and invisibly repaired;
Such moments chiefly seem to have their date
In our first childhood. □

[1799, I, 288–296]

Ellis argues that, taken together, these passages should be read as the poet's coded meditation on his own mortality: thus, 'the record of the murderer's execution suggests to Wordsworth the imminent possibility of his own destruction. The death which provides its subject-matter is Wordsworth's own.' In seeking to protect himself from this intolerable knowledge, however, Wordsworth in *The Prelude* utilizes the very psychic strategies that Freud has since identified as part of the defensive armoury of consciousness. Ellis notes Freud's observation that 'a mode of thought which is normally associated with very young children and

which allows them to believe themselves immortal, can coexist or alter-
nate with later understandings'. It is just such a 'mode of thought' that
Ellis detects in the 'inner eye' of Wordsworth's younger self, bestowing
'a spirit hallowing what I saw / With decoration and ideal grace'. Once
recalled, this mode enables the adult Wordsworth to transfer or (more
accurately) *translate* a meditation on death into 'the words / Of Grecian
art and purest poesy' – specifically, the 'poesy' of *The Prelude*. In his
commentary on the Drowned Man, then, Wordsworth illustrates 'how
it could be that a death whose immediate effect he admits was terrifying became no longer a threat'.[67]

From this, Ellis educes that the most important function of imagination in the poem is to act as a charm against the constant threat of
annihilation. Non-existence, he argues, is clearly the real subject of *The
Prelude*'s 'spots of time':

■ This is because, on several occasions [...] he presents what it is conveni-
ent here to call imagination as the one power in the mind which is death-
defying. The effect of these is to suggest that, if Wordsworth did have one
overriding, specific motive for insisting that [...] he had exerted power rather
than been the victim of it, it was likely to have been his feeling that 'imaginative power' was an antidote to the threat of extinction [...].[68] □

None of this means that Ellis does not value or even admire Wordsworth's
heroic effort to contain the threat of death in *The Prelude*. The fact that
the poet ultimately fails to deal with the problems of mortality is not
in itself as interesting as *how* he fails: 'The interest lies in how deeply
he ponders them, not in his solutions [...].'[69] Indeed, in this respect
Ellis finally finds much to applaud in Wordsworth's endeavours. As he
concludes: '*The Prelude* would not be so absorbing if he had found the
task easy.'[70]

Ellis's sympathy and admiration notwithstanding, the rise of deconstructive, feminist, and psychoanalytical methods during the 1970s and
1980s convinced many commentators on Romantic period literature
that the language and the categories of *The Prelude* could no longer be
treated on their own terms. Instead, Wordsworth's poem was increasingly read 'against the grain'. In other words, rather than trying to
understand what Wordsworth was trying to 'express' or 'communicate'
in *The Prelude*, critics increasingly read the poem with an eye to what
the poem *betrayed* about its deepest anxieties, regarding the definition of
masculinity, the (in)stability of the self, and the (im)possibility of meaning. Charting the strategies – the evasions and displacements – whereby
Wordsworth attempted to cope with these problems soon brought criticism into direct conflict with the core notion which (it was argued)
underpinned the anxious logic of *The Prelude*: the Romantic concept of

ideal subjectivity as a unified field of consciousness. However, while the three critical currents discussed in this chapter posed powerful challenges to Romantic idealism, arguably none of these was as enduring or as influential as that mounted by another strain of *Prelude* criticism that emerged during the 1980s. It is to this strain that we must turn now.

CHAPTER FIVE

Spots of Time: The New Historicism

Notwithstanding the latest developments in *Prelude* commentary discussed in the following, final chapter of this volume, critical debate over the poem continues to be influenced (positively or negatively) by the methods and agendas of the New Historicism. Originally a reaction within Renaissance studies against the textual formalism of both the New Criticism and the 'Yale School' of deconstruction, New Historicism emerged in North America in the early 1980s, and soon formed a British offshoot (sometimes termed 'Cultural Materialism') with its own distinct characteristics. It had its roots in the theory of the fluid interrelationship between representations and 'regimes' of truth and power advanced by the French thinker Michel Foucault (1926–84); the account by the American anthropologist Clifford Geertz (1906–2006) of the indispensability of 'thick' evaluative descriptions in interpretation, and the concept of 'metahistory' as the ineliminably rhetorical narrative of history, as propounded by the American historiographer Hayden White (born 1928). Accordingly, New Historicists such as Stephen Greenblatt developed a form of literary criticism that (1) emphasized the involvement of literary texts in the (material, capitalistic) economies of their period; (2) eschewed the standpoint of critical objectivity, and (3) refused to distinguish between 'literary' and non-literary texts. This historical method swiftly found its way into – and was in turn transformed by – Romantic studies. The extent and influence of the various strands of New Historicism that propagated themselves throughout the 1980s and 1990s is too wide to catalogue here. Instead, I will concentrate on those works that were to have lasting impact upon the critical reception of *The Prelude*. First, however, a little more needs to be said on the emergence of a peculiarly 'Romantic' historical method.

In some respects, the differences between the Renaissance and Romantic breeds of New Historicism mirrored the different cultural topographies of their respective historical periods. Thus, where Renaissance scholars were generally more concerned with how power is configured and circulated through representations in Elizabethan and Jacobean court and culture, Romanticists tended to patrol the agonistic relationship between two distinctive phenomena that grew out of the cultural discourse of late eighteenth-century and early nineteenth-century Western Europe: the discipline of history and the new idealism of the 'aesthetic'. I use the adjective 'agonistic' here to describe the peculiar relationship of attraction and repulsion between these discursive vectors: seen from one perspective, they appear mutually dependent; seen another way, however, they contest each other. In the Romantic period, the site of this struggle is the arena of the 'imagination'.

As many critics have noted, it is no coincidence that the very culture that elevates the significance of *art* to an unprecedented pitch of pre-eminence is also deeply embroiled in an attempt to understand the role of *history* in shaping human life. Since for many writers of this period (not just Wordsworth) imagination was the distinguishing, if not the defining characteristic of humanity, it became tremendously important to determine whether this faculty was purely ideal and 'aesthetic', transcending the materiality of history and politics, or whether it was in some way the product or outgrowth of these domains. At stake in this equation is the epistemological and political status of literary representation. Considered as the creation of the author's imagination (and no poem wears its status as the creation of the imagination more openly than *The Prelude*), what kind of relation could it be said to have to both the time in which it was produced, and the time(s) it depicts? Does a poem such as *The Prelude* rise above its own era (by virtue of its ineffable aesthetic properties, perhaps, or through its power as the sincere expression of private consciousness)? Is history, indeed, just an aspect of consciousness, 'the growth of the poet's mind'? Or is the journey into creative consciousness a flight from history, an attempt to escape material reality?

If these were obstinate questions for Wordsworth, they are no less the bugbears of Wordsworth's modern readers. Indeed, it has not gone unnoticed that the tensions within the Romantic concept of imagination has had far-reaching and determining effects upon criticism and scholarship today. The uneasy relationship between the 'aesthetic' and the 'historical' echoes through the modern, *critical* imagination. One consequence of this is that, depending on which side of the 'aesthetic/historic' debate they incline towards, commentators tend to separate (speaking very roughly) into two camps. First, there is the long tradition of critics (many of whom we have examined above) who were, for the most part, happy to treat the poem formally. New Critics, deconstructionists, and out-and-out formalists saw (and some continue to see) literary works as operating primarily on an aesthetic, textual, or rhetorical level. Most of these commentators regard the historical or political as at best marginal to the meaning (or 'abyss' of meaning) in the work. Even scholars with an interest in Wordsworth's biography (difficult to avoid in a poem such as *The Prelude*) pursued their researches in a way that foregrounded 'personal' history at the expense of cultural or political events.

Next, then, comes the class of critics who emphasize the 'historical' vector in literature. Again, drawing very crudely, we might further divide this camp into two species: 'old' and 'new' historicists. Nigel Wood's distinction between these two sects is useful here:

> ■ The 'old' historicism can be defined in several ways, but, in outline, it involves certain working principles: a belief that the investigator can be empirically neutral if she/he is scrupulous about source materials by quoting contemporary or primary authorities for historiographical conclusions. This presupposes the removal of the self from one's investigations so that the evidence may have a chance of 'speaking for itself', and ensures the even-handedness of one's approach, yet it is also regarded as a historian's duty to trace a coherent account (with agents and reagents) of what happened, to instil causes and effects that supply a global explanation of why and how. Overall, historicism deals in structure and direction. What New Historicists point out is that this is narration and that History is inextricably bound up with textual effects: it is *written*.[1] □

Another way of thinking about the difference between the 'old' and 'new' historicisms is in terms of a disagreement about 'context'. Traditionally, literary historians attempted to interpret texts by placing them in their historical (biographical, philosophical, political) context. What many New Historicists reject, however, is the notion of *con*-text as a kind of background or frame that is external to the text itself. They argue that dropping the dichotomy between the literary and the non-literary means that no clear dividing line can be drawn between text and context: instead, they maintain, *discourse* permeates everything. Texts are historical and history is textual. This interweaving of text and context means that commentators have no stable grounds upon which to conduct an 'objective' framing of the text they are interpreting. As the products of language and history no less than Wordsworth, modern critics must relate their own historical situatedness to that of the poem. Thus, as Wood observes, '[w]hether we choose to interrogate the structures of feeling from the (constructed) past or our own neck of the academic woods, there is this radical edge to the historical account: that history is traced by us in the forms by which we find it intelligible [...]'.[2]

We should, however, proceed with caution. As Wood warns us, there is always the 'danger of herding all those writers together who have tried to return to history with the insights gleaned from deconstructive, feminist or psychoanalytic studies'.[3] We have already studied some of these writers in Chapter 4. In the rest of this chapter, I focus on three different kinds of 'New' Historicist commentary on *The Prelude*. In the first section, I examine a number of commentators whose work on the poem in the 1980s signalled a renewed interest in the question of its historical context, whether this was handled (as in the case of Roger Sales) from a Marxist perspective, or (as in the case of Nick Roe) with a view to offering a more nuanced account of Wordsworth's own political philosophy. In the second section, I turn to studies by the critics Jerome McGann, Marjorie Levinson, James Chandler, and David Simpson, all of which, to a greater or lesser degree, treat the problem of history in *The Prelude* as a problem of 'displacement', arguing that the poem is governed by the 'Romantic ideology' in its evasion of historical, social, and political realities. Finally, I discuss attempts by two critics – Alan Liu and Clifford Siskin – to read the poem in the light, not of 'history', but of 'historicity' – that is, with an eye to the historical contingencies of the present, as well as those of the past.

THE SOCIAL CONTEXT

First published in 1981, Marilyn Butler's *Romantics, Rebels and Reactionaries* is one of the founding texts (if not the founding text) of the 'return to history' in Romantic studies. The scope of Butler's ambitious book takes in the politics of Romantic literature as a whole, but she has significant things to say about Wordsworth – and *The Prelude* in particular – that changed the ways in which the poem would be read in the coming decades. At first sight, Butler's general appraisal of the poem's politics might seem familiar: *The Prelude*, she claims, manifests the increasingly conservative mindset of the poet in a country that was quickly jettisoning the revolutionary ideals of the eighteenth century. What is fundamentally new in Butler's approach, however, is the level of socio-historical detail that she amasses to support this interpretation. Most notably, she reads *The Prelude* in the context of the 'counter-revolution' that occurred in the Britain in the late 1790s, during which period popular political opinion swung away from qualified support for the French Revolution to outright opposition. *The Prelude* is itself a product of this counter-revolution: as a result, Wordsworth's poem treads a tightrope between the secular revolutionary ideals of his youth and the new atmosphere of assertive conservatism that stressed 'the emotional appeal of traditional religion'. The commencement of the poem, then, marks a pivotal point in Wordsworth's career: the beginning of a gradual but inexorable turn towards conservatism.

■ Wordsworth from 1797–8 ceases to see others as social phenomena; they are objects for contemplation, images of apparent alienation which the

poet's imagination translates into private emblems of his troubled commu-
nion with nature. In Books x to xɪɪɪ of *The Prelude*, the great poem he began
now and published in 1850, Wordsworth himself analysed the all-important
transition from external to internal goals, which to him seemed to follow
disillusionment with the Revolution, but to us looks equally like a response
to the deep new current of conservatism in English thinking. Looking back
with an increasingly orthodox religious perspective, he felt that there had
been a period in which his eye, dwelling on external things, had meant
too much. Gradually his vision internalized itself: he perceived that significance lay not in the simple object in the world of Nature, but in the power
of his imagination to work upon the impression he retained, fully to appropriate to his own thought these 'spots of time'. Thus a pagan, external this-
worldliness is transformed into a habit of mind compatible with acceptance
of religious truth.[4] □

For Butler then, the 'all-important transition from external to internal
goals' is signalled by the poet's abandonment of the 'pagan, external this-
worldliness' of the *Lyrical Ballads* in favour of the Protestant introspec-
tion of 'Tintern Abbey' and *The Prelude*. Here, we see another theme
that will become central to New Historicist readings of *The Prelude*:
the idea that the displacement of empirical, 'external', historical reality into the domain of the 'internal' psyche is typical of the politically
reactionary strategy of the ideology of Romanticism. I will return to
this argument in the following section, 'Ideology and Displacement'.
Not all of the 'political' readings of *The Prelude* that rode the wave of
New Historicism adopt such a suspicious outlook. Howard Erskine-
Hill's 1996 monograph, *Poetry of Opposition and Revolution: Dryden to
Wordsworth*, for example, concentrates on the political significance
of the poem's inception by examining the Two-Part *Prelude* of 1799.
Beginning at the beginning, Erskine-Hill notes that the poem opens
with a curiously opaque rhetorical question, 'the antecedent of which
is never formally identified'.[5] In the lines with which the original version of the poem commences, 'Was it for this / That one, the fairest of all rivers loved / To blend her murmurs with my nurse's song'
(I, 1–3), a clear referent for the term 'this' remains lacking, leaving
the reader unclear about the precise nature of the poet's predicament.
Commentators have generally interpreted these lines as an expression
of disappointment and self-doubt in the face of an unfulfilled poetic
vocation. But Erskine-Hill claims that it is also possible to read the
lines as a complaint about the outcome of the French Revolution, and
that 'the 1799 *Prelude* (whether Wordsworth originally envisaged its
subsequent extension or not) had as its goal the consolation available for
those who have undergone political disappointment, and the reorientation of faith in − something radical perhaps for the times − Human
Nature'.[6] Seen this way, the recollections of early childhood experiences

(the emergence of a 'Human Nature') in the Two-Part *Prelude* take on an embryonic political significance:

■ The early episodes of the 1799 *Prelude* are indeed not political (nor apolitical), but prepolitical. They are physical experiences, sporting activities, but with spiritual and moral awareness growing out of sensation and energy. Yet they also have political implications. They concern the primal awareness of the untaught human being ('the naked savage'), the earliest predatory impulses, conscious guilt, enterprise, and rebuff, free enjoyment both social and solitary. They contain the germs of political ideas capable of being experienced later in practice, in specific historical situations, later still of being meditated upon and generalized.[7] □

Another facet of this nascently political current in the Two-Part Prelude is exemplified by the card-playing episode in Book I. Wordsworth, Erskine-Hill claims, was fully aware from his reading of the anti-Jacobinical philosopher and politician Edmund Burke (1729–97) that the game of cards had a strong political resonance at that time:

■ The metaphor of politics as a game of cards remained fully current: as Burke had put it in his *Letters on a Regicide Peace* (1795): 'What signifies the cutting and shuffling of cards, while the Pack still remains the same?' This is another social episode, and another sport, this time an outdoor social one:

I would record with no reluctant voice
Our home amusements by the warm peat fire
At evening ...
We schemed and puzzled, head opposed to head,

                     sate in close array,
And to the combat – lu or whist – led on
A thick-ribbed army, not as in the world
Discarded and ungratefully thrown by
Even for the very service they had wrought,
But husbanded through many a long campaign.

                                        (I, 206–19)

Consistently with the view that *The Prelude* of 1799 is a poem seeking the fount of political engagement in early experience, the card-game embeds in childhood recollection a series of images for high affairs of state.[8] □

When the occasion demanded it, Wordsworth, it seems, was not averse to deploying the dependable weapons of an earlier era: irony and allegory. The hierarchy of kings, queens, and 'common' numbers (and the ability of all to be shuffled or trumped in unlikely combinations) was in itself a potent political metaphor. A few lines later, however, this playful allegory becomes more urgent and contemporary:

■ Oh, with what echoes on the board they fell –
Ironic diamonds, hearts of sable hue,
Queens gleaming through their splendour's last decay,
Knaves wrapt in one assimilating gloom,
And kings indignant at the shame incurred
By royal visages. □

[I, 220–225]

The reference at line 222 to 'Queens gleaming through their splendour's last decay', Erskine-Hill suggests, is a clear allusion to a well-known section in Burke's *Reflections on the Revolution in France*, in which he mourns the fate of Queen Marie Antoinette:

■ Burke lamented the situation of the Queen, 'once glittering like the morning star, full of life, and splendour, and joy', now with 'disasters fallen upon her'. Wordsworth [...] gives the humble card-game of the lakeland children a pastoral role in prefiguring the downfall of regal splendour. The poet, one might suggest, had seen and felt the 'assimilating gloom' of Robespierre's ascendency, and witnessed the reaction among the other crowned heads at the imprisonment and execution of Louis XVI. Quietly and with some humour, without revolutionary zeal, the card-game marks the two-part *Prelude*'s awareness of itself as the poem of a revolutionary era.[9] □

Erskine-Hill maintains (pace Butler) that, rather than diverting his poetic gaze away from revolutionary events, Wordsworth in 1799 was engaging with them directly. He did so, moreover, in a form of language that would have been understood by his contemporaries.

Erskine-Hill is one of a number of historicist critics who remain broadly sympathetic (or at least, not hostile) to the broad aims of Wordsworth's poetic endeavour. Another is Nicholas Roe, whose 1992 essay, 'Revising the Revolution: History and Imagination in *The Prelude*, 1799, 1805, 1850', charts the shifting politics of the poem through its various incarnations as the poet revised it over the course of his life. Roe begins by revisiting the verdicts of some of the first formal reviews of *The Prelude*. Among these, he is particularly struck by the claim of the historian and essayist Babington Thomas Macaulay (1800–59), who, upon the publication of the poem in 1850, declared it to be 'to the last degree Jacobinical'. The reason why this opinion is surprising, Roe notes, is that the 1850 *Prelude* is commonly considered to be a politically diluted version of the more 'revolutionary' 1805 poem. Nonetheless, Roe insists, Macaulay got it right: the 1850 *Prelude*, like its predecessor, is a politically radical poem. Modern commentary has lost sight of this radicalism because 'the critical debate about the 1799, 1805, and 1850 versions of *The Prelude* has been polarized in a manner that has obscured the continuity of the revolution in Wordsworth's imagination over more than half a century'.[10]

In defending this thesis, Roe focuses on the ways in which Wordsworth registers his encounters with the poor, the dispossessed, and the socially marginalized. He is especially interested in the 'view / Of a blind beggar' that Wordsworth recounts in Book VII of the 1805 Prelude, and how this meeting is revised in later versions of the poem. This is how the episode appears in 1805:

> ■ 'twas my chance
> Abruptly to be smitten with the view
> Of a blind beggar □

> (*1805* VII, 610–12)

By 1850, Wordsworth describes the incident differently:

> ■ lost
> Amid the moving pageant, I was smitten
> Abruptly, with the view (a sight not rare)
> Of a blind Beggar ... □

> (*1850* VII, 636–9)

This alteration appears minor, but for Roe it is highly significant:

> ■ I shall use Wordsworth's revisions [...] to show how the quotidian strange-
> ness of the beggar relates to the poet's earlier democratic aspirations as
> an English Jacobin in the 1790s. My larger purpose will be to suggest that
> spots of time in *The Prelude* disclose a *continuousness* in Wordsworth's
> vision that substantiates Macaulay's criticism of his 'Jacobinical' imagin-
> ation in 1850.[11] □

What Roe finds striking about the 1850 Blind Beggar passage is the added observation that to see a beggar on the streets of London at that time was 'a sight not rare'. By adding this deceptively parenthetical remark, Wordsworth reminds us of 'a world in which beggars are to be found at every street corner'. Taken in isolation, such a comment is not surprising. As Roe notes, '[i]n protest poems and pamphlets the beggar was a stock figure of human misery, the cause of political complaint'. Through the mediation of Wordsworth's 'imaginative idiom of the spots of time', however, this radical figure of suffering is transformed, initiating 'an inward process of psychic revolution and self-reproach' – a claim Roe supports by documenting the poet's frequent use of terms like 'admonished' and 'reproached'. The upshot of this rhetoric, Roe concludes, is the forging of a link 'between revolutionary impotence and Wordsworth's later imagination of suffering in his poetry'.[12] This brings him to the fulcrum of his argument:

■ These monitory encounters might appropriately be described as an introspective Jacobinism. [...] In each of these poems the poet's self-involvement is the condition for a sudden, intense revelation of ordinary existence. That instant of awakening marks the interpenetration of history and imagination, and the resurgence of visionary 'progress' that had been deadlocked in the public, political world. Manifest social 'injustice' (formerly the concern of protest literature) has been assimilated as an obscure sense of personal blame, and Wordsworth's former commitment to political enlightenment has been similarly involved as the personal revolutions of 'admonishment', 'reproach', and spiritual insight. Such moments constitute 'the growth of the poet's mind' [...].[13] □

Roe concludes his essay with a close analysis of the revisions that Wordsworth made to passages describing his return from France in December 1792. Comparing the 1805 and 1850 manuscripts, he finds that only in the latter do we find an attempt to blend 'two sorts of radicalism': 'One is "the allegiance to which men are born" (*1850* VII, 530), which derived from Burke. The other is the radical equality of mankind, which was the basis of Paine's [Thomas Paine (1737–1809), radical writer and politician] political theory and an essential principle of Wordsworth's spots of time as representative of human experience.' By combining these perspectives, Roe argues, Wordsworth's 'introspective Jacobinism' attempts to come to terms with the revolutionary debate in light of 'his own experience of revolutionary optimism and defeat'. The tendency of many modern commentators to concentrate their critical attention on the 1799, 1805, or 1850 versions of the poem on the basis of perceived political allegiances means that they neglect this development. By doing so, they overlook the crucial fact that these manuscripts are merely snapshots of a *process* of work that continued throughout most of Wordsworth's adult life. Thus, '[t]o champion one or other version of *The Prelude* on the basis of politics, religion, or style is to lose sight of *The Prelude* in progress. It constitutes a narrowing of critical perspective, perhaps a scholarly dead-end'.[14]

While Roe and Erskine-Hill use historical material to defend Wordsworth's reputation as a political thinker, Roger Sales's objective in his 1983 survey of Romantic period literature, *English Literature in History 1780–1830: Pastoral and Politics* is not to praise the poet, but to bury him. Sales's interrogation of *The Prelude* in 'William Wordsworth and the Real Estate' follows in the tradition of Marxist critics such as Raymond Williams (1921–88) and E.P. Thompson (1924–93). He is, indeed, even less inclined than these critics to pull his punches, complaining that 'Wordsworth toadied the counter-revolutionary line with the worst of them towards the end of his career'. Worried that the neglect of cultural props and buttresses and a lack of 'moral cement' was causing social edifices to crumble, Wordsworth's 'breathtakingly unoriginal solution was to try to persuade everybody to support their local landed aristocrat'. Here, Sales alludes to Wordsworth's support of the Lowthers in the 1818 election, a family who five years earlier had used their considerable influence to secure Wordsworth an administrative appointment as distributor of stamps for Westmorland.[15] Earlier, Lord Lowther had helped Wordsworth to buy a freehold in Westmorland: 'No wonder', Sales observes wryly, 'he was strangely prejudiced in favour of the landed aristocracy. They helped William to pay the bills with a handful of silver.'[16]

As John Williams observes, such uncompromising language 'unambiguously reminds us that Marxism fundamentally threatens much that is normally taken for granted in other traditional critical approaches'. Sales's book, he notes, was 'given a rough ride by most reviewers' when it was first published. Nor is this surprising, since

■ his approach uncompromisingly insists on the primacy of economics and class when it comes to the analysis of literature, and the assessment of literary figures [...]. His attack on Wordsworth's personal integrity is in fact a way of challenging a whole set of value-judgements underpinning capitalist society and its cultural superstructure.[17] □

As a consequence, what appears to be an *ad hominem* assault on Wordsworth is part and parcel of Sales's rejection of the very aesthetic values that the poet represents, values Sales sees as an expression of the poet's conservatism. For Sales, treating *The Prelude* primarily as the poetic expression of a private consciousness is to concede to such conservatism the terms in which the debate will be conducted before it has even begun. By pursuing instead a social and economic approach, he insists, we can see how politically regressive the poem really is. Sales is particularly suspicious, for example, of Wordsworth's celebration of rural values and vaunting of the intimacy and familiarity of the 'small, face-to-face community' against the impersonality and alienation of urban life. This pastoralism, he believes, is merely the vessel of an inherently conservative outlook that seeks to maintain traditional social inequalities by monitoring individual identity: in Wordsworth's rural utopia, every face is *known*, and *knows* its place. This regime is unsettled, however, by the fluid anonymity of modern urban life, as described in Book VII of *The Prelude*:

■ Wordsworth is lost in the streets of London town because the good old days when everybody knew each other and their place appear to have gone altogether.

> How often, in the overflowing streets,
> Have I gone forwards with the crowd, and said
> Unto myself, 'The face of every one
> That passes by me is a mystery!'
> Thus have I looked, nor ceased to look, oppressed
> By thoughts of what and whither, when and how,
> Until the shapes before my eyes became
> A second-sight procession, such as glides
> Over still mountains, or appears in dreams;
> And all the ballast of familiar life,
> The present, and the past; hope, fear; all stays,
> All laws of acting, thinking, speaking man
> Went from me, neither knowing me, nor known.

(VII. 594–606)

The city is 'dissolute' because it dissolves personal identity. Wordsworth is swept into the ebbing and flowing tide of street life against his will. He is carried along by the crowd and feels as if he is drowning. His identity and will are being submerged. He is being literally reduced to a part of the mainstream. This passage is often interpreted as a great poet's affirmation of individual, nay human, values, which is both of its time and for all time. Wordsworth is all for reason when he stands there feeling 'oppressed' in those city streets. Such interpretations accept Wordsworthian propaganda as the whole truth. They firmly believe, for instance, that familiarity does not breed contempt. They do not question assumptions that villages and policemen are good things. Like the village bobby, Wordsworth only feels at home when he knows all the faces on his patch or manor. He can then successfully interrogate them with 'thoughts of what and whither, when and how' as they pass by. This rescues him from drowning, but it means that most other people are swamped by a parochial paternalism.[18] □

By contrast, when Wordsworth retreats 'to the safe, secure and predictable community of the Lake District',[19] described at the beginning of Book VIII, he is able to view the economic processes of a country fair with a benignant eye. Fairs such as these were major trading hubs in the rural economy, and thus 'also places where the "little Family of Men" bought and sold each other', a fact that Sales claims is barely registered by the poet. Wordsworth 'was obviously feeling far too fragile after being oppressed up in London to want to deal with economic oppression'. Perhaps, he muses (with somewhat heavy-handed irony), 'the mountain mists actually obscured all but the quaint and folksie from neighbour Wordsworth's eye'.[20]

IDEOLOGY AND DISPLACEMENT

Sales's final remark demonstrates how, for him, Wordsworth's political rhetoric is best described in terms of obscurement and evasion. What *The Prelude* obscures, he argues, is social reality and thus the possibility of progressive change. Other critics, while broadly sympathetic to Sales's approach, detect different, and often more complex strategies at work in Wordsworth's poetry. Jerome McGann sets the terms of this debate in his landmark work *The Romantic Ideology* (1983). McGann does not discuss *The Prelude* at length in this book, but his highly influential chapter 'Wordsworth and the Ideology of Romantic Poems' urges the critic 'to expand the concept of the poem-as-text to the poem as a more broadly based cultural product: in short, to the poem as poetical work'.[21] With Romantic poems, this means attending closely to the means by which they endeavour 'to occlude and disguise their own involvement in a certain nexus of historical relations'. To detect such an 'act of evasion', the critic 'must make a determined effort to elucidate the subject matter of such poems *historically*'.[22]

In Wordsworth, this evasiveness appears as a form of 'displacement'[23] whereby the concrete particulars of social and historical reality are transferred into the purely mental theatre of the poet's consciousness. Here the difference between a New Historicist such as McGann and a Marxist like Sales is evident: both take material history as the foundation of their method, but while Sales interprets and evaluates *The Prelude* positively, that is, as direct expression of Wordsworth's (misbegotten) views on contemporary socio-economic reality in Britain, McGann reads the poem as the *negative* embodiment of history. Displaced into the aesthetic, history makes itself felt in the *absences* of Wordsworth's poetry. McGann is not interested in scoring points here: that Wordsworth's is a 'false consciousness', he maintains, does not detract from the 'greatness' of his poetry.[24] The *poetry* speaks to us with a historical voice, not a personal one: 'If Wordsworth's poetry elides history, we observe in this "escapist" or "reactionary" move its own self-revelation.'[25] Indeed, what makes a poem like *The Prelude* 'beautiful' is the very struggle between the material and transcendental realms that shape it. Nonetheless, one can only arrive at this realization by reading *against* Wordsworth, rather than with him. Only then can one see that Wordsworth's cultivation of an internal space as a refuge for an unbearable external reality 'is a very emblem of the tragedy of his epoch, for in that conceptualization Wordsworth imprisoned his true voice of feeling within the bastille of his consciousness'.[26]

The work of McGann and Butler encouraged many to make fundamental reassessments of the politics of *The Prelude*. One of the more common stories told about Wordsworth is that, as he grew older and more conservative, his early enthusiasm for the work of the philosopher Jean-Jacques Rousseau (1712–78) was gradually eclipsed by an increasing admiration for the great critic of the French Revolution, Edmund Burke. In his 1984 book *Wordsworth's Second Nature*, James Chandler endeavours to overturn this conventional wisdom by contending that, far from being a late convert to conservatism, Wordsworth was a disciple of Burke from the start. In this respect, Chandler stands directly opposite Roe in the debate over Wordsworth's politics. While Chandler and Roe both refute the 'conversion' narrative (maintaining that the poet's political views remained more or less consistent throughout his life) they disagree about the nature of the views to which he remained committed. For Roe, Wordsworth remained true to his radical, Jacobin instincts; for Chandler, Wordsworth's poetry 'is from its very inception impelled by powerfully conservative motives'. Thus, in chapter 3 of *Wordsworth's Second Nature*, Chandler argues 'that *The Prelude*, the magnum opus of the great decade and Wordsworth's fullest attempt to deal with the French Revolution, is written from an ideological perspective that is thoroughly Burkean'[27]:

■ Burke's writings on the Revolution offer a scheme that explains the course not only of Wordsworth's decline in The Prelude but also of his crisis and recovery. France is the land of abstract speculation. Young Wordsworth is introduced to such speculation early, but his moral sentiments, formed on the strength of ancient, homebred, English experience, preserved him from moral harm through even repeated exposure to danger.[28] □

Among the evidence that Chandler produces to support his case is the influence upon Wordsworth's thought of the key Burkean concepts of 'prejudice' and 'second nature'. These related notions formed the basis of an index for reasonable human behaviour and value that Burke developed to counter the abstract rationalism of the French revolutionaries. Burke argued that sometimes it is more reasonable to trust to prejudice rather than throw one's lot in entirely with pure abstract reason – that there is a latent wisdom in feelings and intuitions built up by generations of accumulated but unsystematized experience. Consequently, Burke maintains that the British are right (unlike the French) to cling to their 'just' prejudices, even as the so-called age of 'Enlightenment' is calling for all preconceptions to be swept away. In the same way, the idea of what is 'natural' for Burke is determined by culture, custom, and habit, as much as by the qualities associated with our original, innocent, and primitive condition. Contrary to Rousseau, then, Burke argues that human nature 'includes both our (naked, shivering) "nature" and our "second nature" '.[29]

Burke's definitions are carefully hedged and not always clear. As Chandler argues, however, this imprecision is itself an important component of his argument:

■ Burke does not spell out the difference between nature and second nature for the same reason he does not spell out the difference between prejudice and just prejudice. In each case he would debilitate the power of the pure, simple noun and thereby undercut the rhetorical force of his argument.[30] □

'Second nature' and 'just prejudice', then, are not concepts defined by coherent, logical conditions. Instead, they are rhetorical terms whose validity rests upon the very affections Burke is defending as the essence of the British constitutional settlement since the 'Glorious Revolution' of 1688. Opposing French logic with British 'feeling', Burke's arguments deliberately appeal to the 'heart' rather than the 'head'. As Chandler puts it, 'second nature is for Burke not so much an identifiable fact in the world as a way of thinking that conveniently collapses certain troublesome oppositions'.[31]

How do these ideas influence *The Prelude*? Chandler notes the 'long tradition in Wordsworth criticism that would have us believe that Wordsworth's natural feelings are, like Rousseau's, moments when he divests himself of all habits, prejudices, and customs'.[32] He pays particularly close attention to those passages in *The Prelude* that have been seized upon by M.H. Abrams and others as 'condemnations of habit and custom' – and thus, by extension, of Burke's theories:

■ One of those which Abrams has in mind is no doubt Wordsworth's introductory comment for the 'spots of time' section in the latter part of book 9. This is where Wordsworth explains more fully what he means by the assertion that 'Nature's self' revived the feelings of his earlier life. Referring one last time to his practice of bringing all his passions and beliefs before the seat of judgement, Wordsworth recounts:

> I shook the habit off
> Entirely and for ever, and again
> In Nature's presence stood, as I stand now,
> A sensitive and a *creative* soul.[33] □

[11, 253–256]

On the face of it, this passage appears unmistakeably anti-Burkean in its celebration of the poet's ability to shake off the 'second nature' of acquired human custom and habit, in order to stand once again 'in Nature's presence'. However, Chandler notes, all is not as it seems:

■ Before we rush to claim these lines as corroboration for the notion that Wordsworth simply needed to free his natural, native feelings from the tyranny of custom and habit, we should look to the similar passage that brackets the 'spots of time' section on the other side: 'Behold me then / Once more in Nature's presence, thus restored, / Or otherwise, and strengthened once again / ... To habits of devoutest sympathy' (392–96). Being in Nature's presence does not mean being in an original, naked, or habitless condition, or even in an approximation of such a condition. It means being in the condition of one's authentic habits and of their attend-ant feelings. And this is not a Rousseauist state of nature but a Burkean state of second nature.[34] □

Chandler's claim that the ideology of *The Prelude* is essentially Burkean-conservative tallies with the substance of McGann's argu-ments in *The Romantic Ideology* and elsewhere. In more obvious har-mony with the *methods* of McGann's book, however, is David Simpson's 1987 *Wordsworth's Historical Imagination: The Poetry of Displacement*. In this book, Simpson argues that, regardless of his intentions, Wordsworth's imagination is ineluctably historical. In other words, his 'exposition of the nature and exercise of the most essential faculty in human nature makes constant reference to limiting or enabling conditions of time and place'.[35] As Simpson frames it, imagination in Wordsworth is historical in three ways: first, it is 'significantly both formed and maintained by empirical circumstances, human and geographical'; second, poems such as *The Prelude* 'address themselves to fairly precise events and circum-stances: the French Revolution, the condition of England, the plight of the poor, and so forth'; third, there is a history 'evident in the details of his writing':

■ This writing, at least in the early Wordsworth, transcribes a subject in conflict, a subject defined by a condition of acute alienation, both vocational and social. It is a writing that continually falls short of what it aspires to be, but reveals in that falling short its greatest intelligence and its most coherent messages.[36] □

This is the 'self-revelation' of Romantic poetry to which McGann refers in *The Romantic Ideology*: Wordsworth's imagination reveals itself to be historical in its very flight *from* history. In order to describe the strategy whereby this revelation is effected, Simpson (like McGann, adopting a Freudian category) argues that 'it must be traced in the forms of its displacement, as much in its radical incoherence as in its life within the tidy language of propositional argument'.[37] Wordsworth's language, then, does not reveal its historical status straightforwardly: instead, it betrays it through the slippages of thought and contradictions that are produced by the 'conflict' and 'alienation' within *The Prelude*'s construction of subjectivity. Thus, while 'the topic of *The Prelude* announces itself as singular and individual', the self in this poem 'is always conceived of as a social or intersubjective entity'.[38]

Take, for example, the recollections of Cambridge in Books III–VI:

■ Cambridge introduced him to an alienated world of superficial pastimes and unsubstantial social distinctions, all the 'surfaces of artificial life' (3: 590) that the surplus economy could support. Participating in his own undoing, his life became 'rotted as by a charm' (3: 339), and his subsequent return to the rural environment was appropriately compromised. Thus, he experienced an 'inner falling off' (4: 270), a cultural schizophrenia resulting from the baffled attempt to assimilate two different worlds with different and antithetical values, habits and pleasures:

> Strange rendezvous my mind was at that time,
> A party-coloured shew of grave and gay,
> Solid and light, short-sighted and profound,
> Of inconsiderable habits and sedate,
> Consorting in one mansion unreproved. □

(4, 346–50)[39]

For Simpson, the 'strange rendezvous' described by Wordsworth reflects his anxious sense of the fundamental incompatibility of two forms of social existence in Britain around the beginning of the nineteenth century: rural/feudal and urban/industrial. In *The Prelude*, however, this socio-economic conflict is *displaced* into a mental struggle between two states of consciousness: the solitary and the social. The problem with this rhetorical feint, however, is that it merely transfers the contradiction from a material reality to an ideal one. Inevitably, the two forms of subjectivity with which Wordsworth grapples prove as impossible to reconcile as the social phenomena they displace:

■ There is much in *The Prelude* that argues against the possibility of closing the gap between the solitary and the social forms of restitution that Wordsworth investigates. To do so would clearly alleviate the more anxious symptoms of the poet's displacement. It would create an audience, a public validation of the author's labours; and it would afford Wordsworth a reciprocally reconstituted self.[40] □

In response to this dilemma, Simpson argues, there are 'two prospective forms of renewed consensus that *The Prelude* explores as alternatives to the incumbent culture of alienation'. The first of these 'is the philosophical idealism that was for the poet associated with the early days of the French Revolution; the second, brought in as a second line of defence, is dependent upon the owner–occupier society of rural Westmorland and Cumberland'. Like Sales, Simpson finds the pastoral utopia unconvincing, a 'confused and ambivalent' response to social change: thus, he observes, '[i]t is involved with nature, but it is nature alone that finally emerges as the poet's best hope'. Thus, though the first form of consensus gives way to the other, 'neither achieves conviction, either historically or rhetorically'.[41] This impossibility of 'closing the gap between the solitary and the social forms of restitution' ultimately means that the 'reciprocally reconstituted self' so earnestly prospected by *The Prelude* remains, as Simpson concludes, 'richly inscribed with the symptoms of his own displacement'.[42]

Terms such as 'inscribed', 'symptoms', 'displacement' feature prominently as part of what Marjorie Levinson calls the 'heterodox' approach of the New Historicism. In the Introduction to her 1986 book *Wordsworth's Great Period Poems*, she claims that what distinguishes New Historicist readings of Romantic literature from their precursors is that 'they position themselves as demystifications of Romanticist readings as well as of Romantic poems'. Levinson sees the resurgence of historical methods in the 1980s as reaping the most valuable insights (and jettisoning the illusions) of both deconstruction and the more traditional historicism of previous generations of scholars and critics. Thus, while historicists of the new school 'use history, or sociopolitical reconstruction, to resist the old control of Yale [deconstruction]', they also 'repudiate the empiricist, positivist concept of historical fact, in that they focus textual antinomy and erasure rather than manifest theme and achieved form'.[43] This means, among other things, that New Historicists like Levinson insist that an adequate criticism must account for the historical situatedness of both the poem *and* the critic. Levinson agrees with de Man that there is no neutral standpoint from which to interpret Wordsworth, but insists that this is because every 'standpoint' is determined historically as well as textually. Consequently, New Historicism attempts in its procedures to avoid repeating the Romantic trick of transcending – by objectivizing or idealizing – its encounter with the text. The result is a historical method that seeks to incorporate a reflexive knowledge of its own relativity:

■ It is a self-consciously belated criticism that sees in its necessary ignorance – its expulsion from the heaven of Romantic sympathy – a critical advantage: the capacity to know the work as neither it, nor its original readers, nor its author could know it. It is a criticism that uses the devices of deconstruction to materialize a greatly idealized corpus; or, to locate the body in Wordsworth's poetry.[44] □

For Levinson, the need to locate the 'body' in Wordsworth's poetry was initiated by her 'persistent feeling that Wordsworth's most general-ized representations owed their pronounced ideality to some disturbing particular and the need to efface or elide it'.[45] Wordsworth's representa-tions efface uncomfortable material (social, political) realities, she finds, by replacing 'the picture of the place with "the picture of the mind", such as might be at any time and in any place'.[46] Faced with unpalatable facts, Wordsworth's poetry seeks a 'boon' that he can offer to his reader: 'the displacement of ideological contradiction to a context where resolution could be imagined and implemented with some success'.[47] Like McGann and Simpson (but unlike Sales), Levinson's project is not to denigrate Wordsworth's writing, but to allow it to speak to the reader with all the power of its historical and ideological contradictions. 'Far from seek-ing to depreciate Wordsworth's transcendence or to trivialize profoundly moving works', she maintains, 'I hoped to renew our sense of their power by exposing the conditions of their success: that recalcitrant facticity with which they had to contend, explicitly and unconsciously'.[48]

The drama of *The Prelude*, then, lies not in that poem's expressions, but in its 'displacements', the 'symptoms' of the antinomies that it 'inscribes'. While none of the four essays in *Wordsworth's Great Period Poems* is devoted to *The Prelude*, much of Levinson's analysis is under-taken with one eye on that poem, particularly in the essay 'Chronicles of Heaven: "Peele Castle"'. Here, Levinson explores the way in which both 'Peele Castle' and *The Prelude* reject the unacceptable, 'Napoleonic', face of the poet's earlier revolutionary politics. In doing so, however, they offer an alternative every bit as oppressive and tyrannical: an *ideal* of imaginative power created as the negative image of a threatening *material* reality. In *The Prelude*, she claims, '[t]he mind that keeps its own inviolate retirement [...] does not exclude sinister social fact, but installs it securely *in*, and worst of all, *as*, psyche. The subjectivizing and objectivizing impulses are effectively identical.'[49] One passage that illustrates this paradox, Levinson claims, is the poet's reflection on tyrants in Book X. Here, the poet's meditations on political tyranny swiftly segue into lamentations for

■ the 'oppression' of his 'passion' for Nature ([...] Nature was for Wordsworth the Enlightenment *idea* of Nature as presiding genius, or gen-eral, of the Revolution) as compared to the less egotistical sublime of social love. The passage continues, offering additional, more topical instances of oppressive passion: 'I felt a kind of sympathy with power – / Motions raised up within me, nevertheless, / Which had relationship to the highest things. / Wild blasts of music thus did find their way / Into the midst of ter-rible events, / So that worst tempests might be listened to' (*Prelude*, 1805, Bk. 10, 416–21).

Or saw, like other men, with bodily eyes,
Before them, in some desolated place,
The wrath consummate and the threat fulfilled;
So with devout humility be it said,
So, did a portion of that spirit fall
On my uplifted from the vantage-ground
Of pity and sorrow to a state of being
That through the time's exceeding fierceness saw
Glimpses of retribution, terrible,
And in the order of sublime behests,

But, even if that were not, amid the awe
Of unintelligible chastisement,
Not only acquiescences of faith
Survived, but daring sympathies with power,
Motions not treacherous or profane, else why
Within the folds of no ungentle breast
Their dread vibration to this hour prolonged?

(*Prelude*, Bk. 10, 444–60)

One cannot help noticing the chiasma formed by the two systems: a crossing of the poetry axis (psyche, subjectivity) upon the political axis (Nature, History, the object world). By 'crossing', I mean a back and forth reciprocally imbricated or paired figuration.[50] □

Like Hartman, Levinson observes that the dialectic of self and nature in *The Prelude* betrays Wordsworth's anxieties regarding the power of Imagination, the 'chiasma' or 'paired figuration' referring to the way in which the language of subjectivity always crosses into the discourse of the objective world, only for the objective world to cross back into consciousness. Levinson, however, offers a different take on the consciousness/nature dialectic (whereby, according to Hartman, Mind in *The Prelude* is able to draw ever nearer, without ever reaching, a terrifying apocalypse of Imagination). She claims that in Wordsworth's poetry, 'autonomous Imagination is demonically doubled in the figure of Napoleon'.[51] Despite Wordsworth's attempt to narrate the growth of the poet's mind in terms of a hypostasized reciprocity between self and nature, *The Prelude* reveals that its fundamental anxiety is *political*, not epistemological. By attempting to abstract mind from material history, the poem ultimately effects 'a deconstruction of the very mechanisms of the poet's mundo. Wordsworth's fear of Imagination – Reason in its most exalted mood – signifies a fear of the History in and as Imagination.'[52]

In the end, then, the sense of crisis that pervades *The Prelude* is that of a subjectivity that has severed its links with society, from history, and made itself the captive of its own ideality. The poet's life-raft, launched

to escape the shipwreck of history, soon becomes his prison, a comprehensively interiorized subjectivity cut adrift from material, social reality. Wordsworth's 'crisis', Levinson maintains, is really 'the crisis of the
autonomous ego alone in the universe of conceptual objects, with nothing to reflect itself upon and therefore nothing – literally, no-thing – to
reflect'.[53] And yet, she adds – echoing McGann and Simpson – the
poem's very negation of history is what gives it its powerful *historical*
voice. In the end, the beauty of *The Prelude* stems from the fact that
the poem itself possesses a historical knowledge (in negative form) that
Wordsworth does not. As she puts it, 'for Wordsworth to have grasped
this meaning would have meant giving up that special blindness which
produces his great poetry: that hypostasis of a Mind of Man and [...]
Nature'.[54]

THE SENSE OF HISTORY

More than McGann and Simpson, Levinson's work openly embraces
the influence of deconstruction as well as historical materialism. At
the heart of her analysis, nonetheless, remains the idea that Romantic
poetry (the *Prelude* especially) is the *displacement* of history. By diag-
nosing the symptoms of displacement, the modern commentator gains
access to the historical knowledge to which Wordsworth's 'ideology'
blinded him. Other New Historicist critics, however, have been less
sure that 'displacement' best describes *The Prelude*'s relationship with
history. Correspondingly, they are more sceptical about the notion
that the critic accesses a form of knowledge by historicizing the poem.
Heavily influenced by the philosopher Michel Foucault, such commentators make the relativity of their own critical and historical perspectives a central concern in their criticism. As a consequence, they are
interested less in the 'displacing' activities of Wordsworth's poetry, and
more in that poetry's engagement with problems of language history,
and contingency that recur in all writing. In this section, I examine
two examples of such criticism: Clifford Siskin's 1993 essay, 'Working
The Prelude: Foucault and the New History', and Alan Liu's monumental work *Wordsworth: The Sense of History* (1988).

　　Siskin's essay was written for Wood's *Theory in Practice* collection of
essays on *The Prelude*, and, as the latter notes in his editorial preface,
it draws a number of lessons from Foucault's work. The first of these
regards the *historicity* of criticism itself. According to Foucault, Wood
claims, '[u]nless we own up the problem of the relativity of frames of
reference, our criticism will be in bad faith: it will always derive its
authority from premises that pose as universals yet are always historically *situated*'.[55] This relativity of historical discourse means that there

is no neutral perspective from which the historian or literary critic can dispassionately and objectively 'observe' his or her subject. The second of Foucault's notions that Siskin incorporates stems from the first, and regards the nature of the author. For Foucault, the 'author' is not a subject, an autonomous individual defined by the possession of a single consciousness, but is constituted *in and by* historical discourse. Consequently, the 'heading "Wordsworth"', does not refer to some unitary item': for Foucault and Siskin, the author is not a subject (or a subjectivity), but a *function* of discourse. Discourse shapes the self of the author as narratives of subjectivity twist and turn throughout history, intersecting with other figures and narratives. Thus, a key intersection in the Romantic period occurs between two narratives: that of the authorial self as 'subject' and that of the 'aesthetic'. A truly '*historical* New Historicism,' Siskin agues, should be aware of these discursive intersections, and of its own situation within them:

■ Attending historically and theoretically to these changing combinations must, I would argue, be a central task of a *historical* New Historicism, one which is most simply defined as occupying the current intersection of literary history and literary theory. Aware of itself as a kind of writing, a particular combination of features, that criticism would engage such signs as the dissolution of boundaries and the construction of a subject as local manifestations of an informing concern with boundary-making, classification, grouping as a process rather than a category – the problem, that is, of genre.[56] □

One tendency of the theory that Siskin practises is for it to reject the very distinction in literary criticism between 'theory' and 'practice'. Concomitant with this is a repudiation of the tendency of academics and critics to divide judgements into the 'personal' and the 'professional'. Accordingly, Siskin's discussion of *The Prelude* seeks not only to make its point 'in the *very act of making it*', but to do so in a way that does not take the 'professional' voice of the critic for granted:

■ I will assert the ongoing power of Wordsworth's *Prelude* – the way it continues to configure our professional and personal behaviours – by engaging in two quintessentially Wordsworthian habits: using my own personal experience as evidence; and framing that experience within a tale that contrasts the present with the past.[57] □

Siskin believes that the critic must constantly problematize the objectivity of his or her own critical stance by placing it in the full glare of its historical situatedness. Only in this way can we, first, appreciate the extent to which our own literary–critical endeavours are determined by the very poem we are interpreting, and, second, encounter the incommensurable difference or otherness of the discourse within which Wordsworth worked, and which in turn worked upon him. Failure to do this means that when we come to interpret the evolution of *The Prelude*, we unselfconsciously repeat the discourse of Wordsworth's own time. By treating *The Prelude* in psychological or philosophical terms, we end up parroting Wordsworth instead of criticizing him:

> ■ Traditional literary histories have explained the Wordsworthian changes the way Wordsworth taught us to understand them: we have psychologized them. [...] These histories become 'gratulant' Preludes, echoing the very past they are supposed to analyse.[58] □

Siskin proposes to break this habit 'by locating all assumptions within a *political* space by articulating how, since the eighteenth century, acts of knowledge production are exercises of power' in a 'political economy of knowledge'.[59] Siskin is particularly concerned with *The Prelude* 'as a text prescribing particular kinds of work – the division of labour that authorizes modern professionalism'.[60] As we have seen, at the centre of this question is the dimension of historical discourse referred to by Foucault as the 'author function', and the way in which the emergence in the eighteenth century of 'certain narratives linking aesthetic depth and individual development' ultimately produce the function of 'that most familiar form of the subject – the Creative Author'.[61] This function does not work in isolation. A second crucial concept for Siskin is Foucault's notion of 'discipline'. As Siskin points out, this concept has two interrelated meanings: 'discipline as a field of study connects to knowledge, while discipline as regimentation invokes power'.[62] For Siskin and Foucault, these two senses, pertaining to knowledge and power respectively, cannot be prised apart. With the addition of a third category, '*commentary*' – namely, the consolidation of a discourse by a *reader*'s repetition – the triad of 'knowledge' is complete. It is this triad that determines both how *The Prelude* inscribes its knowledge, and how modern readers understand the poem.

Like most New Historicists, Siskin is at pains to point out that his objective in using Foucauldian categories to deconstruct the 'discipline' of knowledge in Wordsworth is not to make some value judgement about *The Prelude*, but to relativize the context of the poem's ideology and of his own critical analysis:

> ■ For Foucault all three – Author, Commentary, Discipline – are 'principle[s] of limitation' that constrain discourse, and thus configure regimes of truth, even as they further its proliferation [...]. The point in using them to organize my practice upon *The Prelude* is *not*, I must emphasize, to condemn the

text as bad, aesthetically or politically, compared to some unconstrained alternative or some 'real' truth, but to identify what configurations of power it may have helped to produce and may be continuing to naturalize.[63] □

The chief 'configuration of power' that Siskin finds in the poem is the domain of literature as a discipline. *The Prelude*, he argues, is a founding document in the professionalization of literature that began in the late eighteenth century. As an extended autobiographical reflection on Wordsworth's discovery of – and growth into – his vocation as a poet, the poem is 'quite simply, the most extraordinary résumé in English literary history [...]. Its primary function then, was to present an individual's training and qualifications for performing his life's work [...].'[64] Wordsworth rejected the neoclassical notion that the function of poetry was to delight and teach by presenting the reader with morally instructive narratives in the pleasing shape of verse. *The Prelude* is not, in this sense, a 'didactic' poem. Instead, it offers a celebration of imaginative activity as the consummation of human intellectual development. In so doing, the poem reconfigures the relationship between literature, knowledge, and power: 'Literature's job as a discipline was to produce the right kind of understanding. It helped, that is, to construct and naturalize new relationships between knowledge and power [...].'[65] The result is a new concept of 'professionalism', which Siskin finds in an early passage from the 1850 *Prelude*:

■ [I]n the passage

> It was a splendid evening, and my soul
> Once more made trial of her strength, nor lacked
> Æolian visitations; but the harp
> Was soon defrauded, and the banded host
> Of harmony dispersed in straggling sounds,
> And lastly utter silence! 'Be it so;
> Why think of any thing but present good?'
> So, like a home-bound labourer I pursued
> My way beneath the mellowing sun...

(1850, I, 94–102)

I read a prescription for the two most important characteristics of the professional ideal. First, it presents professional work as desirable work – an edenic georgic [a form of poetry written for the purpose of instruction, often on rural and agricultural subjects]. Since the pastoral is not offered as a separate source of happiness, the georgic activity with which it is intertwined is taken to be a means to that end. Second, the mixture naturalizes what many sociologists consider to be the distinguishing characteristic of modern professionalism: the claim to autonomy. When the domain of work is assumed to be a personal Eden, the professional assumes ethical sway over his or her own actions: the Wordsworthian phrase 'Be it so' signals the self-authorizing power of professionalism [...].[66] □

Siskin's final claim is, then, that *The Prelude*'s realignment of para-digms ultimately helped to establish the very academic discipline of English Literature from which so many critics of the poem (himself included) now view the poem. In this sense, Wordsworth was tremen-dously successful in his declared aim of *creating* the tastes and the audi-ences by which his poetry would be judged. It is this very audience from which (by foregrounding the poem's role in the creation of his own disciplinary perspective and thereby relativizing his own insights) Siskin's analysis seeks to escape.

A similar determination to break away from 'Romanticist' interpret-ations of *The Prelude* by attending closely to the historical reflexivity in all literary criticism is evident in the work of Alan Liu's comprehensive study, *Wordsworth: The Sense of History* (1989). Like Levinson (whose term 'deconstructive materialism' he borrows to describe his own work), Liu ambitiously attempts to bring two powerful intellectual tra-ditions to bear on his reading of Wordsworth.[67] The first of these is essentially Marxist: it insists that material history (i.e., what happens in society rather than what goes on in people's heads) determines reality, and thus the meaning of literary works. The second has its roots in the linguistic theories of Ferdinand de Saussure. This tradition (a branch of which we examined in the work of de Man) maintains that all know-ledge is mediated by language, but that language is radically indeter-minate. Aware of the lessons of both traditions, Liu is wary even of certain tendencies in New Historicism. Indeed, he argues that at worst, new Historicism has been every bit as abstract and 'formalist' in its approach to historic texts as the New Critical methods that dominated literary criticism for much of the mid–twentieth century:

■ Where the New Criticism propagated the forms of ambiguity, paradox, irony, texture, unity, and imagery, the New Historicism, in rough parallel, studies subversion, transgression, oppositionality, textuality, power, and ideology. Though conceived as situated *in* past literatures and cultures, these critical forms – none of which 'live / Like living men' – function as semi-technical abstractions cutting the modern interpreter off from the less clearly or differently shaped forms of experience in the past.[68] □

Liu is deeply suspicious of such 'abstractions'. By marrying histori-cism and deconstruction, he offers instead 'a historical epistemology grounded on what may be called denied positivism'.[69] According to this theory, literary texts are determined by contexts, not *positively* (through the direct influence of an event, a text, or writer), but *negatively*, through what he calls the 'absent cause' of history. Like theorists such as Frederic Jameson (born 1934) and Louis Althusser (1918–90), Liu sees history as a peculiar phenomenon, which, while it determines reality, cannot be experienced immediately or through 'ordinary means of verification such as sight or touch'. History is not 'present' to us, but determines our being through its *absence*. As Liu puts it: 'History is the absence that is the very possibility of the "here and now." ' [70] He unpacks this idea further:

■ [I]t is not the case that contexts cue texts in the way that a stick imparts spin and direction to the billiard ball. Rather, contexts are themselves constituted as masses of difference – as collisions or discontinuities with other contexts or with aspects of themselves. And it is this dynamic mass of marked breaks and shaped absences that determine the text by spelling out in advance the shaped *absence* of context – negative yet determinate – that is the defamiliarized text.[71] □

The key idea behind Liu's epistemology of 'denied positivism', then, is that historical context is not a *thing*, but a determining absence. For Liu, 'the context of "real" history is unknowable. It becomes knowable only insofar as it is acted upon by the collective process of arbitrary structuration – or arbitration, as we might call it – by which cultures interpret reality'.[72] By treating history as the absent cause that determines how arbitrary structures of language and discourse ultimately come to be determined as truth and ordered knowledge, we can, Liu claims, settle on 'a negative, but nevertheless determinate, explanation of how we know the relation between text and context'.[73]

This 'denied positivism' throws up some challenging thoughts about *The Prelude*'s relationship with history, some of which, at first sight, appear paradoxical. One of the more striking of these is the idea that texts *realize* history in the very act of *denying* historical reality. Since history is an absent cause – in its negativity, 'the very category if denial' – Wordsworth's poetry cannot *help* but deny history. And yet, it also follows from this that by denying history, Wordsworth's poetry 'is ipso facto a realization of history'. By pursuing this paradox, Liu's analysis endeavours to highlight the fact 'first, that Wordsworth's largest, most sustained theme is the realization of history; and, second, that his largest theme is the denial of history'.[74]

At the core of Wordsworth's strategy of 'denial' is the concept of nature. Liu makes his own position on this idea plain from the start, baldly asserting that '[t]here is no nature'. Indeed, to 'believe that nature "is" in the way a tree "is" is to abstract the notion of essence while concealing the abstraction'.[75] In Wordsworth, however, abstract nature becomes a kind of epistemological red herring whereby the poet endeavours to erase his own (and by extension, his reader's) sense of *history*. As Liu puts it, nature is 'an imaginary antagonist against which the self battles in feint, in a ploy to divert attention from the real battle to be joined between *history* and self'.[76] More specifically, it becomes

> ■ the name under which we use the nonhuman to validate the human, to interpose a mediation able to make humanity more easy with itself. To invoke *The Prelude*:
>
> > Ye Brooks
> > Muttering along the stones, a busy noise
> > By day, a quiet one in silent night,
> > And you, ye Groves, whose ministry it is
> > To interpose the covert of your shades,
> > Even as a sleep, betwixt the heart of man
> > And the uneasy world, 'twixt man himself,
> > Not seldom, and his own unquiet heart,
> > Oh! that I had a music and a voice,
> > Harmonious as your own, that I might tell
> > What ye have done for me. □
>
> > > > > > > > (II, 12–22)[77]

By choosing as his main theme the relationship between imagination and nature (what 'Brooks' and 'Groves' have 'done' for the poet), Wordsworth evades a more troubling inquiry into how *history* determines the relationship 'betwixt the heart of man / And the uneasy world'.

   Nowhere is this denial of history more pronounced, Liu argues, than in Books IX and X (the 'Revolutionary' books) of *The Prelude*. Here, Liu is especially interested in the way in which, taken together with the final three books on Imagination, these books convert 'history into myth' by telling 'a story of deluge followed by lyric peace'.[78] The memories of France that fill these books, in other words, are given a particular narrative shape by Wordsworth, whereby initial recollections of the turbulent 'deluge' of the French Revolution are swiftly contained by a 'bewildering succession of story forms – most importantly, romance, drama, and epic', before Wordsworth reasserts the power of retrospective meditation and 'a peculiar grace of lyric at last subsumes their enactive agony'.[79] This crucial shift of narrative genre, he claims, arrives early in Book X. Having recounted in Book IX the catalogue of betrayal, apostasy, and war that characterized the later stages of the French Revolution, Book X proceeds 'to envision a new shape of history about to begin'.[80] In this way, according to the logic of the poem, 'the false passage of history acts as a prelude to the new':

> ■ Wordsworth launches a 'separate chronicle' (X, 471), a fresh kind of history. The deluge-sea recedes, and he shows us his younger self walking

home over Leven Sands estuary beneath a prospect of Miltonic splendour: 'creatures of one ethereal substance, met / In Consistory, like a diadem / Or crown or burning Seraphs' (10, 480–2). But the prospect of Miltonic glory is not the core of the experience. Prospect originates in a retrospective moment that makes 'fancy more alive' (X, 488): the poet's morning visit to Carmel Priory and the grave of his Hawkshead teacher, William Taylor. At the center of this retrospection is his reading of a certain kind of history on Taylor's tombstone:

> A plain Stone, inscribed
> With name, date, office, pointed out the spot,
> To which a slip of verses was subjoin'd,
> (By his desire as afterwards I learn'd)
> A fragment from the Elegy of Gray.
> A week, or little less, before his death
> He had said to me, 'my head will soon lie low;'
> And when I saw the turf that cover'd him,
> After the lapse of full eight years, those words,
> With sound of voice, and countenance of the Man,
> Came back upon me; so that some few tears
> Fell from me in my own despite.

> (X, 495–506)

This is epitaphic, or self-epitaphic, history. The passage, we notice, begins by alluding to a pastoral elegy sealing off, rather than releasing, the history of the dead.[81] □

In order to register the thrust of Liu's argument, we need to be clear about the full significance of the notion of 'self-epitaphic history'. Wordsworth was fascinated by the art of epitaphs, and among his few formal prose compositions are the three *Essays on Epitaphs* (1810), in which he explores the relationship between poetic language and death, and between memory and memorialization. Liu's interest in the genre stems from the political significance of elegy within the broader framework of *The Prelude*. The moment Wordsworth sets out his 'separate chronicle' in Book X is the moment he ceases to describe himself as a participant in historical events and begins to refashion himself as a detached observer. Focusing on the 'Elegy of Gray' inscribed on Taylor's gravestone allows the poetry of *The Prelude* itself to slip from the more 'enactive' modes of romance, drama, and epic (through which genres it has hitherto recounted much of the poet's experiences of the Revolution) into the retrospective contemplation of elegy. This, Liu observes, immediately has the effect of 'memorialising' the past: that is to say, sealing it off by making a monument (a gravestone) in which the self can be interred in the form of elegiac memory. For Liu, *The Prelude* is this monument, and the consciousness that is engraved upon it is 'self-epitaphic'. Wordsworth thus writes about his 'self' as if it were dead, as if it existed *outside* history:

■ Thrice-compounded as if in some magic spell, self-epitaphic consciousness at last wholly seals off the enactive quality of narrative history, causing a shift of perspective by which the self, caught up in the deluge of contemporary events, suddenly elegizes itself in past tense. [...] Epitaphic history creates such a sense of elegiac finish, that is, that even the present becomes *as* if past.[82] □

As so often, however, Wordsworth's 'finishing' of the past, his efface-ment of political history, is itself a deeply political gesture. For as the subsequent passages in Book X reveal, the poet uses the contempla-tive, tranquilizing mode of elegy as a foundation upon which he can base his authoritative vision of the future. Thus, it is Wordsworth's very denial of history (his making a monument out of it) that enables his prophetic voice. Liu argues that this generic change in gear is typ-ical of Wordsworth's poetry generally. Indeed, '[m]odulating in this fashion from pastoral elegy to prophetic hymn, Wordsworth's epitaph contains in seed the whole span of his characteristic lyricism'.[83] In *The Prelude*'s Revolutionary books, the poet's subtle modulation of verse from history to drama, and from drama to lyric, enables what Liu calls the transformation of 'history into myth'. History now speaks only through the poet and the mediating forms of self and nature:

■ The function of Wordsworth's lyric return of the dead is to allow the voice of past history to utter again only in the service of leading us to a purer, eter-nal history ruled by a transcendent authority. In actual epitaphs, of course, the realm of eternity is heaven and its authority God. But in Wordsworth's epitaph for Revolutionary history, there is a new heaven and God: nature and self.[84] □

From the perspective of New Historicism, then, Wordsworth's ele-vation of 'nature and self' in *The Prelude* sheds new light on the 'dia-lectic of consciousness' first described by Geoffrey Hartman. For Liu, Levinson, McGann, and other historicists, this 'dialectic' is not really a dialectic at all, but more of a smokescreen. Hartman had suggested that the *via naturaliter negativa* was the poet's way of describing the growth of a consciousness that avoided the Scylla of suffocating self-consciousness and the Charybdis of imaginative 'apocalypse', or unmediated intuition of absolute reality. For Liu and like-minded critics, however, the dance between mind and nature in *The Prelude* amounts to a highly evasive strategy for nullifying the political and *material* reality of history. The poem's visionary moments are characterized not by dialectic, but by 'displacement' and 'denial'. Consequently, as Liu sums up, 'denial is the threshold of Wordsworth's most truly shocking act of Imagination: the sense of history. The true apocalypse will come when history crosses the zone of nature to occupy the self directly, when the sense of history and imagination thus became one, and nature, the mediating figure, is no more.'[85]

Liu's verdict encapsulates the position taken by late twentieth-century historicism on the significance of *The Prelude*. Crossing the threshold of the twenty-first century, however, Wordsworth criticism takes some new and distinctly unhistorical turns. In the next chapter, I examine these developments and review the condition of contemporary *Prelude* commentary.

CHAPTER SIX

The Prelude and the Present

As Wordsworth himself discovered while writing *The Prelude*, the closer historical events press on the writer, the more difficult it becomes to represent them with a sense of coherence and direction. And so, as we turn to survey the most recent and 'present' *Prelude* criticism, detecting 'developments' and 'new directions' inevitably involves more than a modest amount of guesswork and a certain amount of divination. At the close of the first decade of the twenty-first century, it is probably fair to say that no new theory or methodology has emerged to dominate Romantic literary criticism in the manner that New Criticism did in the 1950s and 1960s, or the way that New Historicism managed to do in the 1980s and early 1990s. It may be, indeed, that the age of major critical orthodoxies, those master narratives of literary studies, is itself at an end. That said, it is possible to descry certain movements in the types of debate being conducted about the poem over the past decade or so, and the purpose of this chapter is to introduce students of *The Prelude* to the most significant and interesting of these.

The single biggest factor behind the changing debate in recent years has been a distinct ebbing in the tidal surge of historicism. As this has drawn back, many readers have been left to reorientate themselves around a transformed critical landscape, and to pick over concepts, like 'ideology' and 'displacement', which have washed up on the shore. Associated with historicism's recession is the emergence of new – in some instances, resurrected – critical vocabularies, which in turn have created a fresh set of methodological assumptions and sites of interest in recent readings of *The Prelude*. Below, I provide an overview of some of these developments. In the first two sections, I outline how *Prelude* criticism and commentary has been influenced by two innovations in literary theory: first, a revival of interest in form and the aesthetic, and second, the rise of ecocriticism. In the third and final section of this chapter, I examine in turn two of the most prominent thematic concerns taken up recently by critics: the poem's treatment of 'vagrancy' and the social predicament of the homeless, and its relation to contemporary discourses of geography and geology.

FORM AND THE AESTHETIC

The mid-1990s witnessed the emergence of a number of studies that sought in various ways to roll back the wave of political and historicist criticism that had enveloped *The Prelude* in the 1980s. Many of these works tried to develop a new conception of how the 'aesthetic' and the political / historical are related. One way in which this was attempted was by revisiting the question of *form*. Since the demise of New Criticism under the onslaught of deconstruction and New Historicism in the 1970s and 1980s, 'formalism' had become something of a byword for a discredited critical method: one which, by treating any poem as aesthetically autonomous, failed to appreciate how aesthetic form is involved in, and produced by, social and discursive forces. In 1997 however, Stanford University Press published two books that were to prove influential in redrawing the boundaries between form, history, and politics in Wordsworth studies: Susan Wolfson's *Formal Charges: The Shaping of Poetry in British Romanticism*, and Thomas Pfau's *Wordsworth's Profession: Form, Class, and the Logic of Early Romantic Cultural Production*.

The central claim of Wolfson's book is that 'Romanticism addressed, debated, tested, and contested' the question of 'what is at stake in poetic formings of language'.[1] New Historicist accounts of the so-called Romantic ideology purport to critique the formalism that they see as complicit with certain class interests: 'what is missing from the story thus told', Wolfson counters, 'is any sense of how Romantic formalism itself is involved in this kind of critical project'.[2] Following the Russian critic and theorist Mikhail Bakhtin (1895–1975), New Historicism typically maintains that a poet does not *select* linguistic forms, merely the evaluations posited in them. This originally insightful idea, Wolfson complains, has hardened into a dogma. One result of this is that historicist commentators have become blind to the agency of form in their own critical constructions. Agreeing with Alan Liu that New Historicism is itself a (repressed) kind of formalism, Wolfson notes that '[c]ultural formalism has replaced aesthetic formalism in these reports as the universal, always subsuming all other formalisms to itself'.[3] However, where Liu's response to this predicament is to urge historicism to put its house in order by rooting out the final vestiges of formalism, Wolfson concludes that New Historicism is a busted flush. Any critical method that attempts to dispel or explain away the agency of form in literary works, she claims, blinds itself to 'the dialectical interaction of aesthetic imagination and social information'.[4]

Consequently, Wolfson contends that any study of the relation between ideology and poetic form needs to be attuned to 'the capacity of poetry to strengthen critical understanding by engaging attention with its constructedness, making a reading of its forms fundamental to any reception of or quarrel with its power'.[5] Accordingly, *Formal Charges* advocates a 'cogent historicist criticism' capable of registering how Romantic forms 'reflect on rather than conceal their constructed-ness'.[6] By rejecting the historicist view of the 'Romantic Ideology' as the displacement or denial of history, she maintains, we can see that Romantic poems 'are more various than monolithic, and their poetic practices are alert to form as construction'.[7] Indeed, far from being complicit in a history-denying 'ideology', Romanticism's 'involvement with poetic form [...] participates in central discussions of its historical moment', especially in

■ the articulation of form, not merely as a product of social evaluations, but as a social evaluation itself, one of the texts in which culture is written. My deepest claim is that language shaped by poetic form is not simply conscriptable as information for other frameworks of analysis; the forms themselves demand a specific kind of critical attention.[8] □

The Romantic concern with the autonomy of poetic form is not, then, an attempt to escape the domain of material culture, but the expression of a desire to explore how such cultural knowledge is in*formed*. Indeed, Wolfson argues, Romanticism's self-conscious engagement with form as the mediator of representation is so deep-rooted that it appears even in one of its most 'antiformalist' poems: *The Prelude*. According to Wolfson, *The Prelude* is antiformalist in two ways: first, as an auto-biography it is shaped by the contingent development of a human life, and thus resists many of the conventional literary structures associated with other genres. Second, no 'definitive' form of the poem exists: Wordsworth left behind a number of different versions of the poem, among which two, three, or even four (depending upon which critic one agrees with) are contenders to be considered as best representing Wordsworth's poetic vision. This raises an immediate problem for the formalist critic of the poem who endeavours to determine '[w]hat kind of form [...] its plural texts, none published in Wordsworth's lifetime, define'.[9] The reader of *The Prelude* must remain alert to the effects of revision:

■ And with [...] revision comes a host of related alterations: tinkerings with syntax and punctuation, recastings of metaphor and invocation, expan-sions or elisions of narrative detail, as well as important rearrangements of the preliminary context. The effort to secure 'perfect form' is never secure from the pressure of 'second thoughts'. [...] Writing as an autobiographer, Wordsworth summons this memory into textual recollection with a power-ful sense of import; but writing in poetic form acquires its own subversive agency, bearing information that eludes rhetorical mastery and thwarts exact imaginative supervision.[10] □

Significantly, Wolfson argues that these two aspects of formlessness in *The Prelude* are related. This is what makes it such an important poem. Following de Man, she maintains that *all* writing is in a sense autobiographical. The 'life' that shapes the written poem only achieves formal coherence through the act of inscription. For this reason, the process of revision is itself 'not just compositional; it is the very trope of autobiography'.[11] And yet, it is this very vision of the self as paradoxically both *forming* language and *formed by* language that Wolfson finds in *The Prelude*. As she puts it, the poem 'stages the subject in important ways both as constituted and made legible by form'.[12] Consequently, 'to read the network of Wordsworth's texts is to extend his activity as reader in the network of recollection. Formalist criticism, if it is to be relevant, has to enter into this network and follow its temporal process.'[13]

Fundamentally then, Wolfson's claim is that the forming vision of *The Prelude* is of form as *re*-vision. Revision, like autobiography, is a never-ending process, not a product. Accordingly, Wolfson is particularly attentive to the poem's suggestion that the stability of a perfectly formed vision is somehow akin to death:

■ There is another kind of death that is always impending in autobiography: the fact that its text escapes revision only when its writer dies. Wordsworth intuits this end of revision in lines first drafted in 1804, as he was expanding his autobiography. Its textual site has to do with a frustrated imagination in the Alps [...]. Here is the form of this simile in 1805, when Wordsworth moved it to book 8:

As when a traveller hath from open day
With torches pass'd into some Vault of Earth,

* * *

He looks and sees the Cavern spread and grow,
Widening itself on all sides, sees, or thinks
He sees, erelong, the roof above his head,
Which instantly unsettles and recedes
Substance and shadow, light and darkness, all
Commingled, making up a Canopy
Of Shapes and Forms, and Tendencies to Shape,
That shift and vanish, change and interchange
Like Spectres, ferment quiet, and sublime;
Which, after a short space, works less and less
Till every effort, every motion gone,
The scene before him lies in perfect view,
Exposed and lifeless, as a written book.

(1805: 8.711–27 [...])

> Once a specter shape is given a definite form and is turned into a simulac-
> rum of a literary artifact, the life of the subjective eye and I, produced by
> motion and ferment, dies. Long before de Man articulated the negativity
> behind language, Wordsworth staged as much in passages such as this:
> mastery is death.
>   But as the flux of his revisions demonstrates, mastery is also an illusion
> that inevitably dissolves into the ferment against which it asserts itself, and
> revision – that ceaseless play of shifts and vanishing, changes and inter-
> changes – coincides with life, the energy that postpones death and quick-
> ens the mind, and writing, with a hope for limitless adventure.[14] □

What *The Prelude* tells us, according to Wolfson, is that there is no
escaping the agency of form – that is, form as process, as revision, rather
than the 'Exposed and lifeless' closure of the 'perfect view'. From this
perspective, Wordsworth's repeated revisions of *The Prelude* manuscripts testify to a truth inherent in all writing, namely that all autobiographical formations of the self are dominated by the *metaphor* of the self
reading and re-reading itself:

> ■ Wordsworth's revision of forms yields a form of revision in *The Prelude*
> that, in effect, theorizes form *as* revision. If revision sustains the illusion
> of formal stability, it also persists in postponing that achievement as each
> review of the hoped-for 'perfect view' disrupts the possibility of closure.
> Revision is thus an endless opening of poetic form, not simply because any
> vision is open to numerous, potentially infinite interpretations and organiza-
> tions, but because each review discovers within itself new motions and
> forms of reading.[15] □

This insistence on form as process rather than completion is one of
the things that separate the neoformalism of Wolfson from the 'old'
formalism of the New Criticism. Another distinguishing feature is her
continuing commitment to the significance (though not the centrality)
of historical context in shaping the meaning of a poem. By contrast,
earlier formalists such as Wimsatt and Beardsley had questioned the
relevance of such 'external' considerations in interpreting and evalu-
ating poetry. Tellingly, both these identifiably neoformalist perspectives are shared by Thomas Pfau, whose book *Wordsworth's Profession*
appeared the same year as *Formal Charges*. Pfau is all in favour of looking
to history in order 'to understand, not indulge, the motives underlying
and shaping our interpretive practice'. In particular, he is concerned
with 'analyzing how in the late eighteenth and early nineteenth century cultural behavior shifts from a paradigm of leisure and consump-
tion to an increasingly formalized, canonical, and "deep" interpretive
investment in literature and the arts'.[16] However, he rejects as self-
defeating the methods employed by historicists, many of which, as we

saw in the previous chapter, are based on a deep suspicion of the hidden political motives behind Wordsworth's poetry. Instead, Pfau attends to the 'formal-textual presentation' of *The Prelude*, 'its figural and philological movement – as a multilayered process of composition, expansion, and revision'.[17] By avoiding talk of 'its "subtext" or "historicity"', he claims, his analysis 'refrains from imputing conspiratorial or unconscious motives (e.g., a displacement of history or an elision of economic, psychological, or cultural "desire") to Wordsworth's text and thus from burdening it with the incongruous, retroactive wisdom of postmodern theories of the subject'.[18]

Avoiding historicism's flawed but seductive 'retroactive wisdom' for Pfau involves highlighting modern criticism's uneasy awareness of its own debt to *The Prelude*. Like Siskin, he believes that this in turn means understanding how Wordsworth's poetry contributed to the 'professionalisation' of literature in Britain, and thus, ultimately, the emergence of 'literary criticism' as an intellectual discipline. Towards the end of the eighteenth century, Pfau argues, the English middle class found itself in a paradoxical position: caught 'between the consciousness of its political and spiritual disenfranchisement' on one hand, and, on the other, 'the vivid experience of its economic and cultural ascendancy'. Deliberately distancing itself from 'the hedonistic and consumptive materialism' of the aristocracy, the bourgeoisie 'devised new symbolic forms and inward experiences' in order to augment its already growing cultural power. In this way, the modern concept of the *aesthetic* was born.[19]

The aesthetic object was like no other cultural commodity: it was to be, as Pfau puts it, 'interiority as spiritual capital'.[20] This interiority – the expression of the artist-poet's consciousness – was to be experienced by the reader in a unique way, one that signalled that the appreciator possessed 'a superior, because productive, form of subjectivity'.[21] Aesthetic appreciation thus gave rise to a very peculiar product: one that attained its commodity value through its very *denial* of its own status as a commodity. As Pfau argues, for Wordsworth and other Romantics, 'genuine poetry could only be properly appreciated as the supreme anticommodity'.[22] Indeed, the ability to engage with interiority is what, for Wordsworth, distinguished his 'true' readers from mere consumers seeking information or amusement. Training his (largely bourgeois) readers to respond to 'displays of authorial productivity' with 'a corresponding interpretive proficiency', Wordsworth set about creating the taste by which his poetry would be appreciated, and in doing so set the agenda for aesthetics and criticism for the following two centuries.[23]

For Pfau, the way in which this agenda is manifested in *The Prelude* helps to explain the poem's celebrated referential opacity. *The Prelude*,

he claims, follows a strategy whereby it 'legitimates its vocational fic-
tions (i.e., durable poetry, sincere poets, and capable readers) by means
of a language that is deliberately provisional and vague, though never
abstract'. The object of this strategy was to apply 'aesthetic therapy on
a social unconscious beleaguered by profound transformations within
England's political and cultural economy' through the development of
'a model of representation that would imply rather than argue a general consensus among its readers'.[24] Central to such transformations
is the concept of *self-interest*. This idea, theorized by thinkers such as
Burke and Hume, had been 'the only relevant paradigm of agency in
the public discourse on moral and political issues' during the eighteenth century.[25] Following the French Revolution, however, many
intellectuals – Wordsworth included – were urgently searching for a
new model of human action. By writing in the most 'self-interested'
genre of all – autobiography – Wordsworth sought to develop a different conception of self-interest, one which was not justified rationally,
but which attempted to build 'a strictly formal–aesthetic solution' to
the problem.[26] The genius of this solution, according to Pfau, was that
it enabled the poet to escape 'the charge of excessive self-interest by
dramatizing in its rhetorical form how spontaneous recollection inevitably merges with the aesthetic and discursive capital of its demographic
end point: the Nation'.[27] *The Prelude*, in other words, sought to replace
an Enlightenment notion of self-interested reason with a Romantic
idea of self-interested imagination. Such an idea could not, by definition, be logically demonstrated. Hence the opacity and reflexivity of
Wordsworth's poem: far from indulging obscurity for its own sake,
Wordsworth's poetics 'claims an instrumental relation to the philosophical, civic community [...] by positing "style" as the encryption of
an ultimately *social* knowledge'.[28]

For Pfau then, the form of *The Prelude* – including its elusive style,
with its 'customary tone of indirect and understated assertion' – acts
like a dog whistle for a disoriented middle-class readership, alerting
it to the *aesthetic* (rather than rational) basis of its identity and cohe-
sion.[29] In this respect, Pfau, like Chandler, sees the poet as an ally of
Burke:

■ The issue at hand, in other words, involves never really the content of a
given narrative but the reader's fitness for deriving from the text at hand
the expected spiritual gain. Such a gain, it now turns out, requires not a
greater application but, on the contrary, the almost complete suspension
of all analytic narrative:

Oft in those moments such a holy calm
Did overspread my soul that I forgot
The agency of sight, and what I saw

Appeared like something in myself – a dream,
A prospect in my mind.

(P 1799, bk. 2, ll. 397–401)

In collapsing the ideal of a spiritual or poetic authority into holistic affective response to one's historical inheritance, Wordsworth indirectly allies himself with Burke's hostility to explicit and theoretically self-conscious forms of political and cultural argumentation. [...] In so potentiating personal recollection into communal Scripture, Wordsworth substantially expands the poet's spiritual mandate precisely by declaring it permanently beyond the reach of all public and enlightened discourse ('Who knows the individual hour?') [...]. What remains supposedly undemonstrable at the level of public discourse is thus said to become intuitively, indeed empirically apparent as an exemplary psychological equilibrium [...].[30] □

Ultimately then, the significance of *The Prelude* is that it presents for the first time a concerted attempt to define a national identity around a (bourgeois) concept of ineffable consciousness. By privileging the intuitive realm of the aesthetic as the ground of this consciousness, and elevating the poet to the position of its custodian (documenting the growth of his own mind), Wordsworth changes the nature of poetry, effectively *professionalizing* what was once a leisure activity. Since access to this realm is now characterized by difficulty – only the most attentive, reflective, and reflexive readers need apply – Wordsworth's hope is that he has placed it beyond the reach of commodification. As Pfau concludes in the book's final paragraph,

■ [T]he ideological core of the bourgeois middle class, 'feeling', has been transmogrified into the self-interpreting text of private development, a strategy enabling the middle class to experience itself *aesthetically*. In so doing, the Wordsworthian imaginative community eschews theoretical inquiry and its contingent bodies of knowledge in favor of a confessional narrative punctuated by moments of lyric epiphany: in short, a literary reverie allowing its bourgeois readers to dream their post-apocalyptic, elegiac answers to questions that bear no conscious asking.[31] □

In the face of such critiques, historicism gradually changed its terms of reference. While the New Historicism of the 1980s had virtually worn its resistance to theoretical speculation as a badge of honour, during the 1990s historicist critics and commentators working in the field of Romantic literature became increasingly theoretical and reflexive. Indeed, in some writers this tendency is so pronounced that it is debatable whether their work can any longer be characterized as 'historicist' in any meaningful sense. A good example of this trend is Geraldine Friedman's 1996 monograph, *The Insistence of History: Revolution in*

Burke, Wordsworth, Keats, and Baudelaire. Like Marjorie Levinson and Alan Liu, Friedman's book attempts to reconcile the tenets of New Historicism with the methods of deconstruction, thereby responding to 'the oft-issued call that post-structuralism speak to history'.[32] However, unlike Levinson and Liu, Friedman finds that Romantic texts reveal 'a puzzling fact that cannot be comfortably accommodated within historicism: namely, that in the texts under consideration historical occurrence is struck by a strange absence at the moment it is most intensely engaged'.[33] The underlying reason for this 'strange absence', Friedman finds, is that, fundamentally, history just *is* this absence. Here, like Spivak, she adopts Derrida's notion of the 'trace', the endlessly deferred origin of meaning upon which all communication and knowledge depends. Historical occurrence is just such a trace, a referent that is absent from the text but without which the text would have no 'meaning'. Thus, while, as a trace, history does not *exist*, as the condition of possibility for writing, it *insists*:

■ Consequently, revolution cannot be directly written *about*; it must rather be written *around*, but, by the same token, not ignored. In short, if literature is the impossible witness to history, history functions in these works as literature's missed appointment with a traumatic Real; yet the appointment still remains, if only to be missed again and again.[34] □

At this point, Friedman's approach can be seen to have more in common with neoformalists like Wolfson and Pfau than with historicists such as Levinson and Liu. If history is a trace, she infers, then social and political questions are always 'already involved in "formal" patterns of figuration and narrative'. Correspondingly, 'the status of the referent itself becomes complicated because reference is revealed to be inseparable from the aesthetic'.[35] It is this dynamic that Friedman, by teasing out 'through close reading aporias structuring the aesthetics of the work', finds in Wordsworth's poetry.[36] For Friedman, the insistent absence of history is the paradox that undermines the poet's visionary history in *The Prelude* even as it makes it possible. The manner in which this indeterminate logic or 'aporia' arises is itself shaped by the way in which the poem reads the French Revolution and its aftermath as a *text*: more specifically, the manner in which revolutionary history is recovered in *The Prelude* through a 'Christian biblical typology'. This typology imposes a form − a 'coherent narrative' − of the Revolution that envisages 'a shift from the ancien régime's vengeful justice, based on the letter of the law, to a new, merciful dispensation, based on a spirit of love associated with figural interpretation'.[37] Just as the ideals of the Revolution gave way to the reality of the Terror, however, the materiality of the letter returns to haunt *The Prelude*'s idealist utopia.

Viewed this way, *The Prelude* appears to be a doomed attempt at revisionary history. For Friedman, the poem's principal strategy is to contain the arbitrary violence inherent in language and the Revolution by liberating the 'spirit' of both. Wordsworth's metaphysics of consciousness, however, remains hopelessly dependent upon the very *absence* of (ideal) presence that it seeks to conceal. To demonstrate this, in the third chapter of *The Insistence of History*, Friedman examines in detail 'how an explicitly Revolutionary episode from book 10, "Carrousel Square", gets mapped onto a purely personal experience in a later part of *The Prelude*: the first of the episodes designated "spots of time", the Penrith beacon scene'.[38] Originally a purely lyrical passage in the 1799 *Prelude*, 'the "spot" is subsequently pressed into service as the desired resolution of a political and linguistic problematic that "Carrousel Square" poses in the 1805 and 1850 narratives'.[39] This 'problematic' arises from the poet's recollection of passing through Carrousel Square following violent clashes between the Swiss palace guard and Parisian crowds in 1792. The 'empty scene of this violence' offers a direct challenge both to the young Wordsworth's utopian idealism and to the older poet's model, developed through the narrative of *The Prelude*, of a purposeful, constructive dialectic between mind and society. 'In an effort to effect the monumentalizing closure that events in France elude', Friedman claims, 'he defensively restages the enactive conflict of politics as the contemplative activity of interpretation':

■ I crossed – a black and empty area then –
The square of the Carousel, few weeks back
Heaped up with dead and dying, upon these
And other sights looking as doth a man
Upon a volume whose contents he knows
Are memorable but from him locked up,
Being written in a tongue he cannot read,
So that he questions the mute leaves with pain,
And half upbraids their silence.[40] □

(10, 46–54)

Friedman glosses this passage as follows: 'Wordsworth is trying in these lines to imagine the past, which means to read it by the spirit, but since that past appears as an illegible foreign text, he has no possibility of getting at its meaning.'[41] The poet's strategy for coping with this incomprehension, she claims, is to idealize the meaningless materiality of the scene before him into something of significance. One of the ways Wordsworth does this is to transform the absence of a historical referent into the presence of a psychological 'crisis', a crisis that is commemorated and repaired by the 'spots of time' passages. In this way, 'the Terror of history could now be resituated on the level of a subject's cognition and perception', a level more susceptible to poetic comprehension and closure.[42]

However, because this idealization is fundamentally the effect of a rhetorical sleight of hand, traces of the materiality of language and history inevitably resurface to disturb the textual logic that dominates Wordsworth's narrative of his 'recovery' from the political disappointments of the 1790s. Through detailed and subtle rhetorical analysis, Friedman shows how traces of the violent and chaotic Revolution persist in Wordsworth's reworking of the 'Gibbet' spot of time for Book XII of the 1850 *Prelude*. In this way, the meaningless 'letter' of the law that the poet encountered in the 'Carrousel' episode continues to undermine the poem's attempts to liberate a spiritual significance from history. Ultimately, all that *The Prelude* reveals about history is its *insistence* as the material 'trace' or absent referent of writing. This is the true 'Terror' that *The Prelude*'s narrative of the 'Growth of the Poet's Mind' attempts, unsuccessfully, to outmanoeuvre:

■ The trajectory of the referent, in its uncontrolled and violent returns, is the political aspect of the text, the most radical revolution it stages, and its historical dimension. Thus as much as Wordsworth would like to evade history, he finds that history will not evade him, for politics turns out to be the site where the action being read or written inevitably breaks in on the reading or writing subject. Precisely because of the indeterminate relation between text and context, the Revolutionary context can never be escaped.[43] □

Unlike Wolfson, Friedman reads *The Prelude* 'against the grain' of its avowed concerns, combining the ideas of historicism and deconstruction in a way that shows that these methods did not simply disappear in the 1990s. Further evidence of the durability of such approaches can be found in Richard Bourke's *Romantic Discourse and Political Modernity: Wordsworth, the Intellectual and Cultural Critique* (1993). Bourke's work has more in common with a British tradition of cultural materialism (associated with critics like Raymond Williams) than with the largely American phenomenon of New Historicism. Consequently, his work is not content simply to go hunting for symptoms of the displacement or denial of history in Wordsworth's poetry: rather, he is concerned with the broader question of how modernity in general came to associate the concepts of the aesthetic and the political, or, as he puts it in his Preface, with 'the complexities of the entanglement of aesthetics with public morality'.[44] Like Siskin and Pfau, Bourke believes that the answer to this question lies in the relation between Romanticism and the 'professionalisation' of literature, a relationship that Wordsworth, more than most, helped to forge.

Stated briefly, Bourke's argument is that in the wake of the French Revolution, Wordsworth was faced with two equally unacceptable discourses: on the one hand, a discredited radicalism, and on the other, the increasingly influential language of utility associated with the capitalist economy. In response, writers such as Wordsworth attempted to define a new ideal of national consensus and community, one in which the creative writer rather than the philosopher, scientist, or trader enjoyed a privileged voice. Thus, as Wordsworth sat down to write *The Prelude*, '[t]he option presented itself of submitting his project to the judgement of a new and self-regulating discipline – of inaugurating a sympathetic literary profession'.[45] For the first time, 'the literary statement was considered to be the locus of its own legitimacy; its valuation was to have recourse to neither the position of its purported interlocutor nor the configuration of its own status'.[46] For Bourke, however, the tensions inherent in this project doomed it to failure from the start. Politically motivated and yet based on an idea of the priority of the aesthetic over the political, Wordsworth's new discipline of poetry 'never quite manages to free itself from contradiction'.[47] It is these contradictions that Bourke sets out to uncover through his reading of *The Prelude*. 'Ultimately', then,

■ my interest lies in the viability of poetic renovation at that moment when poetry recognises its own ideological status, its irrevocable articulation through a political idiom. The argument that follows might be summarised as an exploration of the poet's inability to prosecute a sustained reconciliation between aesthetic and political value; to conciliate literary recompense with political resolution.[48] □

The political/aesthetic tension at the heart of *The Prelude*, Bourke argues, is rooted in the ambiguous nature of Wordsworth's depiction of the sublime. Usually applied to landscape, the idea of the sublime originally emerged in the eighteenth century as a term for whatever was terrible, overpowering, or fitted to inspire feelings of awe in a beholder. Also implied in the concept was the idea of disorder. As Bourke describes it, 'the object of that [sublime] experience [...] might loosely be designated by the terms convolution and perplexity'. Like Margaret Homans, however, Bourke finds Wordsworth's depiction of the sublime in *The Prelude* to be deeply ambivalent. On one hand, it harnesses the figure of revolutionary power; on the other – at least in Wordsworth's hands – any 'destabilising' potential is annulled by the concord imposed by the poet's mind. In Wordsworth, the disruptive power of the sublime is neutered by the harmony of its antitype, beauty. As such, the sublime 'becomes a mute hypothesis: for it is always on the way to being something else'.[49]

To illustrate this point, Bourke turns to the episode of the Drowned Man in Book V of the 1805 *Prelude*. Having initially introduced the sublime sight of the body emerging from the lake, its 'ghastly face, a spectre shape – / Of terror even', Wordsworth proceeds to neutralize the scene. In so doing, Bourke claims, 'the dead figure is subject to an idealized "hallowing"':

> ■ ... no vulgar fear,
> Young as I was, a child not nine years old,
> Possessed me, for my inner eye had seen
> Such sights before among the shining streams
> Of fairyland, the forests of romance –
> Thence came a spirit hallowing what I saw
> With decoration and ideal grace,
> A dignity, a smoothness, like the words
> Of Grecian art and purest poesy.
>
> [1805, V, 473–481]

Later, in the eleventh book, the extension of 'ideal grace' to terror defines the poetic enterprise itself: the poet would give a 'substance and a life' to feeling, he 'would enshrine the spirit of the past' for 'future restoration'. The past event retains a 'renovating virtue'; its rehabilitation leaves us 'nourished and invisibly repaired'. But the issue remains that of the means of rehabilitation. This rehabilitation requires the preservation of the mind as 'lord and master'. Dignity, smoothness, virtue: these are attained through the exercise of the adolescent mind: it ensures that the image will be restored to health; that feeling will be given the form of detachment, an 'independent life' released from the decay which menaces rural history. The 'inner eye' abstracts, modifies and repairs.[50] □

These tensions within the Wordsworthian sublime (finding an 'ideal grace' in terror) reflect the deeper contradictions within the poet's attempt to synthesize the aesthetic and the political in the form of a self-generating poetic power, what Bourke calls 'autogenesis'. At least, 'this is the hope held out by the promise of community in the 1805 *Prelude*'.[51] As Bourke proceeds to argue, the hope is a forlorn one. In the end, *The Prelude*'s aspiration to provide a foundation for communal values through a new, self-validating 'literary' discipline is brought down by the incongruity of the notion of the 'aesthetic' itself, a paradox which, Bourke claims, continues to haunt the discourse of modernity. Thus, as he concludes: 'The judgement of modernity, coming to rest in the spontaneity of autogenesis, is out of joint.'[52]

GREENING *THE PRELUDE*

The entry of 'ecocriticism' into Wordsworth studies is marked by Jonathan Bate's *Romantic Ecology: Wordsworth and the Environmental Tradition* (Routledge, 1991). Bate rejects the historical–materialist equation of social reality with economic reality. In a counterblast to New Historicist criticism, he complains about the 'constant implication in all this work that Wordsworth *ought* to have written about real economic conditions'.[53] Liu, for example, is far too ready to dismiss the existence of 'Nature' as a fictional category deployed by the poet in his denial of history. '[N]ot even the most ardent advocate of entrepreneurship and the free market' he maintains, 'can privatize the air we breathe [...]. The particles of water which form clouds [...] cannot be possessed or sold.' For Bate, *nature* rather than economic history is the fundamental condition of the poet's existence – something Wordsworth appreciated rather better than his historicist commentators.

This brings us back to the question: 'What, then, are the politics of our relationship to nature?' In answering this, Bate looks not to the economic historian, who deals in facts, but to the poet, who deals in *genres*. 'For a poet, pastoral is the traditional mode in which that relationship is explored. Pastoral has not done well in recent neo–Marxist criticism, but if there is to be an ecological criticism the "language that is ever green" must be reclaimed.' Consequently, Book VIII, the most overtly 'pastoral' of *The Prelude*, becomes crucial to Bate's analysis. This book, cast as revolutionary by critics such as Abrams and counter-revolutionary by New Historicists, is, according to Bate, neither. What Wordsworth does in this 'pivotal' book, he argues, is build 'an account of the pastoral [...] in order to forge a link between the holistic values of his native vales and the "social meliorism" that underlay the French Revolution'.[54]

Bate takes pains to show that Wordsworth's depiction of rural life in Book VIII is in no way idealized. Quite the reverse, in fact. Gone is the detached language of the 'gentleman' observer and the Arcadian typography of eighteenth–century pastoral, to be replaced by a more authentic view of the struggles undergone by the poor in the course of making a living in the country:

■ Despite the absence of alienation and appropriation, Wordsworth's image is not that of a pre-lapsarian Eden. This is a *working* paradise [...]. Wordsworth transposes the pastoral from the fictional Arcadian golden age to the severe life and landscape that he knew:

> the rural ways
> And manners which it was my chance to see
> In childhood were severe and unadorned,

The unluxuriant produce of a life
Intent on little but substantial needs,
Yet beautiful – and beauty that was felt.
But images of danger and distress
And suffering, these took deepest hold of me,
Man suffering among awful powers and forms.

(VIII, 205–13)

The poem itself performs the act Roger Sales demands of literary criticism: it divests pastoral of its silver-tongued language and myths of the golden age. It is the fortitude of the Lakeland shepherd that Wordsworth singles out for praise.[55] □

The reference to Roger Sales reminds us of the latter's swingeing critique of the pastoral politics of Book VIII (see the section on Social Context in Chapter 5). Defending Wordsworth, Bate maintains that such reductively political readings miss the point. To put it simply, the poet is writing a poem, not a documentary:

■ For Wordsworth, to demand 'realism' or 'reportage' from poetry is to misapprehend its function; the purpose of book 8 of *The Prelude* is not so much to show shepherds as they are but rather to bring forward an image of human greatness, to express faith in the perfectibility of mankind once institutions and hierarchies are removed and we are free, enfranchised, and in an unmediated, unalienated relationship with nature.[56] □

What the shepherd comes to represent for Wordsworth is the inextricable involvement of humans with their natural environment. It is this unmediated relationship between people and nature that underlies historical and political reality. Thus, to return to nature, Bate argues,

■ is not to retreat from politics but to take politics into a new domain, the relationship between Love of Nature and Love of Mankind and, conversely, between the Rights of Man and the Rights of Nature. The language of *The Prelude* is fleetingly red but ever green.[57] □

Bate's work is cited by Karl Kroeber as an important influence on his own book, *Ecological Literary Criticism: Romantic Imagining and the Biology of Mind* (1994). In his Introduction, Kroeber presents ecological criticism as a type of criticism which, 'escaping from the esoteric abstractness that afflicts current theorizing about literature, seizes opportunities offered by recent biological research to make humanistic studies more socially responsible'. Kroeber sees green criticism as 'holistic', in that it 'concentrates on linkages between natural and cultural processes' and 'resists current academic overemphasis on the rationalistic at the expense of sensory, emotional, and imaginative aspects of art'.[58] Yet while Bate is generally content quietly to draw a veil over the theoretical approaches to the Romantics that he found unhelpful, Kroeber engages with them more directly and aggressively, accusing earlier 'Cold War critics' in particular of being 'under the spell of antagonistic oppositionalism'.[59] Yale School deconstructionists depicted the Romantics as 'anxiety-ridden prophets of nihilism', while New Historicists condescendingly cast them as 'seekers after an unattainable transcendence'. In fact, Kroeber counters, they were neither, 'but rather forerunners of a new biological, materialistic understanding of humanity's place in the natural cosmos'.[60]

One of the reasons why the more bloodless varieties of modern academic criticism has overlooked this fact, he claims, is that they have found difficult to get to grips with 'the British romantic poets' extraordinary emphasis on *pleasure* as the foundation of poetry, even political verse'. Because they 'made pleasure fundamental to human accomplishments', he argues, the Romantics 'believed that humankind *belonged* in, could and should be at home with, the world of natural processes. This is the foundation of what I shall call their proto-ecological views.'[61] In introducing the term 'proto-ecological', Kroeber means to evoke 'an intellectual position that accepts as entirely real a natural environment existent outside of one's personal psyche', a reality which can, however, only 'be fully appreciated and healthily interacted with only through imaginative acts of mind'.[62] It is this position that he finds fully expressed in the poetry of Wordsworth.

Kroeber argues that Wordsworth's poetry reveals and explores the connections between the ideal processes of consciousness and the material reality of the biological ecosystem in which the poet lives, thinks, and writes. In effect, Wordsworth tells his reader: 'recognize oneself not as an isolated being but as one fully existent only insofar as reciprocally interacting with one's environment'. The cure for alienation and solipsism then, 'is afforded by the pleasure to be found in bestowing my humanness – which means exercising my self-awareness, entering it into the interactivity of an ecosystem's operations – on other elements in my environment'.[63] From this perspective, 'Wordsworth's literary originality consists principally not in his recording of new perceptions into nature but in his representing with acute self-awareness unique qualities of human responses to natural phenomena'. A good illustration of this kind of proto-ecological awareness, Kroeber claims, is the Winander Boy episode from *The Prelude*:

■ These lines from *The Prelude* (but first published separately) change the poet's original representation of the experience as his own to that of another boy. This transposition blocks his readers from escaping into mere vicarious subjectivity. We can identify with 'the boy' only at one remove. By 'withdrawing' himself from what was in fact his own experience Wordsworth encourages his reader to recognize the special 'bias' of the experiencer to be part of the experience reported. This is what makes the unexpected-ness of the major occurrence so persuasive.

> when a lengthened pause
> Of silence came and baffled his best skill,
> Then sometimes, in that silence while he hung
> Listening, a gentle shock of mild surprise
> Has carried far into his heart the voice
> Of mountain torrents; or the visible scene
> Would enter unawares into his mind,
> With all its solemn imagery, its rocks,
> Its woods, and that uncertain heaven, received
> Into the bosom of the steady lake.
>
> [1850, V, 379–388]

The boy's intent purposefulness (to evoke the owls' responses) leaves him vulnerable, as it were, to the unsought entry into him of the 'sounds of mountain torrents' and the imagery of the dusky scene. Because the poem has enabled us to perceive 'objectively' both the experiencer and what he experiences (not just a subjective perspective), it dramatizes powerfully the reciprocality of encounter, showing how a human being may enter into nature and nature may enter into a human being.[64] □

In response to this upsurge in 'Green' writing on Romanticism, the online 'Romantic Circles' *Praxis* Series devoted one of its numbers to the subject of 'Romanticism and Ecology'. In his introduction to the volume, James McKusick argues that revolutionary sentiment among Romantic writers 'was accompanied by a dawning realization of the interconnectedness between human beings and all other living things'.[65] As he explains, for many poets of this period the natural world was a key participant in the struggle for liberty:

■ For the English Romantic poets, nature is more than just a passive beneficiary of human endeavors to bring about social and political trans-formation. The natural world is pervaded by revolutionary energies that contribute to the cause of human liberation. Poised on the brink of revolu-tionary possibility, nature is imbued with an awesome life-giving potential, as well as a terrible power of destruction.[66] □

McKusick detects within the discourse of 'Romantic ecology' an underlying ambivalence between two views of the relationship between humanity and the environment. The first and more gloomy of these finds its clearest expression in the work of the economist and political

theorist Robert Malthus, who wrote pessimistically about the pros-
pects for humanity in the face of – in McKusick's words – 'potentially
limitless demand for scarce resources'.[67] The second tendency is typi-
fied by the utopian social vision offered by the novelist and philosopher
William Godwin. In particular, it was the 'Godwinian aspiration to
create a sustainable society on the basis of an agrarian mode of production in local communities' that influenced the young Wordsworth,
as well as Coleridge, Shelley, and others, and which underwrites
what McKusick identifies as Romanticism's 'environmental ethic',
namely that 'the ideal of community among all living creatures is
essential to our own survival as a species'.[68] For Bate, Kroeber, and
McKusick, then, it is this commitment to the environment that plants
Wordsworth's poetry firmly in material reality, and gives the lie to
the New Historicist's claim that *The Prelude*'s ideology is 'idealist' or
escapist.

VAGRANTS AND BLANKS: SOME RECENT DEBATES

In this closing section, I want to look at two aspects of *The Prelude* that
have attracted an unusual amount of commentary over the past decade
or so. In the following subsections, I examine the growth of critical
interest, first, in *The Prelude*'s depiction of 'vagrants', and, second, in
the ways in which the poem conceptualizes geological and geographical space.

Romantic Vagrancy

Since the mid-1990s, a number of attempts have been made to re-
examine *The Prelude*'s treatment of one of Wordsworth's perennial
subjects: the marginalized sections of society. First to be published was
Gary Harrison's *Wordsworth's Vagrant Muse: Poetry, Poverty and Power*
(1994). Bucking the trend of New Historicism, Harrison endeavours
to show how Wordsworth's poetry constitutes 'a direct engagement
with and intervention into the politics of poverty and reform that
swept the social, political and cultural landscape during the 1790s
in England'. Specifically, Harrison believes, Wordsworth's 'poetry
of encounter with vagrants and solitaries reproduces and empowers
in literary form, elaborates and diffuses in its aesthetic texture, features of a discourse on poverty that shaped the attitudes toward the
poor well into the nineteenth century [...]'.[69] Unlike McGann and
Levinson, who maintain that Wordsworth's work 'rigidly reaffirms
bourgeois attitudes' towards the poor, Harrison argues that the poet's

representation of an 'agrarian idyll [...] shows the radical potential of
those representations to confer a sense of legitimacy and dignity upon
an emergent working class':[70]

■ Instead of meeting rustic paupers as distant aesthetic objects,
Wordsworth's reader encounters the poor as mirrors of his or her own precarious subjectivity and as reminders of the fragility of the reader's own
social status. Wordsworth's poetic spectacle, then, disturbs the compla-
cency of the spectator-reader and places him or her in a position of uncertainty that opens the borders of the aesthetic to the onslaught of the social
and political. If Wordsworth's poetry removes the poor into a marginal
space, it does so in such a way as to invest those marginals with a certain,
if ambiguously realized, power – a power that radicals and reactionaries
alike have claimed as their own.[71] □

   In this way, 'in its double vision of social alienation and natural
harmony, Wordsworth's poetry produces a kind of utopian surplus
that, despite its complicity and origin in middle-class ideology, can be
harnessed by the subordinate classes as a means of self-empowerment
[...]'.[72] There is in Wordsworth's poems a 'dialectic between ideology
and utopia, reaction and revolution'.[73] The poet, in effect, seeks out a
'vagrant muse' 'among marginal or liminal figures', capitalizing on 'the
cultural valuation of poverty as a sign of poetic truth and authenticity'.
Marginality and exile is thus 'a sign of value and affective power for the
poet'.[74]
   Harrison's reading of the treatment of the poor in *The Prelude* is
influenced by Burke's treatment of love in his *Philosophical Enquiry into
the Origin of Our Ideas of the Sublime and the Beautiful* (1758). Burke distinguishes between two forms of power: overwhelming power and power
under domination. While the latter inspires feelings of sublimity, 'non-
threatening forms of power' inspire at best affection and love: they 'may
even cause contempt'. As Burke frames it: a bull is sublime, but an ox
is pitiable. Wordsworth's relationship with the poor is governed by this
ambiguity: are they sublime or merely picturesque? The poet's vacilla-
tion here is important, and differs crucially, Harrison claims, from the
more straightforwardly patronizing treatment of the poor meted out
by another long poem from this period, *The Task* (1785) by William
Cowper (1731–1800). In Cowper's poem, he argues, the poet com-
mands the scene: he is an observer who disempowers the rural labourers he spectates upon by treating them as objects of aesthetic pleasure.
Harrison contrasts this approach to that adopted by Wordsworth in
the scene in Book VIII of *The Prelude*. Here, the poet describes 'his
youthful encounters with shepherds who appeared in the mountain
mists as gigantic forms, as "solitary object[s] and sublime" (8, 407)'.[75]

What this signals is a reversal in the power relationship between viewer and object:

■ In Wordsworth's poem [...] the inversion of the relationship between spectator and spectacle invests the apparently powerless with an alarming power. In the encounter with the giant shepherd figures the boy stands in awe of their spectral sublimity. Unlike Cowper's narrator, the boy cannot contain the shepherd as an object of his cognitive grasp. Escaping the boy's powers of naming, the shepherd appears rather as an object to which the boy submits in a moment of cognitive erasure. The boy can feel, but cannot know the shepherd's power:

> A rambling schoolboy, thus
> Have I beheld him: without knowing why,
> Have felt his presence in his own domain
> As of a lord and master, or a power
> Or genius, under Nature, under God,
> Presiding – and severest solitude
> Seemed more commanding oft when he was there. □

(8, 390–96)[76]

By placing the spectator 'in a realm of uncertainty and doubt, a Burkean state of "obscurity," [...] Wordsworth's encounter, then, involves a kind of ritual of status reversal in which the spectator trades places with the indigent to whose gaze he or she is now subject'.[77]

   If Harrison's book might be seen as broadly sympathetic to the poet's utopian aspirations, the same cannot be said of Celeste Langan's *Romantic Vagrancy: Wordsworth and the Simulation of Freedom* (1995). In her 'Methodological Preamble', Langan clarifies what she means by 'vagrancy' in relation to Wordsworth's writing. Vagrancy is a double-edged concept in Wordsworth, she argues, because it describes not just what he writes about, but *how* he writes: Wordsworth doesn't just write *about* vagrancy; he writes, so to speak, vagrantly. What Langan means by this is that the logic of Wordsworth's arguments in *The Prelude* and elsewhere is always based upon *analogy*. The problems with analogical arguments, however, is that they lack firm foundations: relying solely upon similarities, they easily slip into metaphors and figures of speech. Analogy can quickly lose direction and purpose, thereby, in effect, becoming a 'vagrant' kind of logic. Nonetheless, Langan maintains, '[a]rgument by analogy [...] stands as the logic – and the methodology – of the liberal subject' in general.[78] For this reason, the idea of 'vagrancy' is for Wordsworth a problem of both style *and* substance.

   This logic of analogy confronts the liberal 'subject' of the early nineteenth century with something of a paradox, however: how can a *stable* self be underpinned by such a 'vagrant', contingent discourse?

Underlying this paradox, Langan argues, is the contradiction inherent in the very idea of a 'free subjectivity'; that is, between the ideal of the individual subject as the possessor of an *autonomous* consciousness (embodied in *The Prelude* by the narrative charting the growth of the poet's mind), and the notion of freedom as the embracement of *contingency* (symbolized by walking and travelling). Consequently, liberal freedom easily becomes 'vagrancy – the condition of having nothing to do and nowhere to go'.[79] The vagrant becomes, in romantic poetry, the 'formal imitation of an abstract concept: negative liberty'.[80] The basic assumption behind *The Prelude*, however, is that the poet's mind grows *into* something, that is, that it has *somewhere* 'to go'. By depicting his poetic subjectivity as both autonomous *and* free (vagrant) in *The Prelude*, the poet risks undermining the stability of the 'self' itself.

The consequences of this predicament are twofold. First, vagrancy is idealized: 'The poet and the vagrant together constitute a society based on the twin principles of freedom of speech and freedom of movement', Langan observes. But in this idealization the vagrant is subsumed by the poet, becoming a mere alter ego. Appropriated, 'vagrancy describes not an external object but an internal condition'.[81] Second, through the same process of idealization, the 'metaphysic of liberalism' reduces everyday human activities to abstractions. For Langan, Romantic logic is simultaneously abstracting and analogical. In this way, 'walking and conversation' become, respectively, 'social mobility, freedom of speech'.[82] Romantic 'freedom', then, is not a reality, but a *simulation*.

In using the term 'simulation', Langan draws upon the work of the postmodern commentator Jean Baudrillard (1929–2007). Baudrillard argues that modern consumer society has become so saturated with signs and representations that, in western countries at least, to experience reality *just is* to experience what he terms an endless 'precession' (i.e., a precoding succession) of signs of reality: 'hyperreality'. For Baudrillard, the 'thing itself' has no essence as such, but is merely the effect of repeated simulations of the thing: simulacrae. The same phenomenon of simulation masquerading as objectivity is what Langan claims to find in the Romantic idea of freedom. As she puts it, the 'formalization of freedom – the reduction and abstraction of walking to produce the concept of "freedom" – is a simulation in Baudrillard's sense: "to feign to have what one hasn't" '.[83]

Unable to make its ideals of freedom and subjectivity 'present' to its reader, then, *The Prelude* can only figure them negatively. As a consequence, we get the paradox that in *The Prelude* the least empowered and least purposeful individuals become signifiers for a 'transcendental surplus' of a powerful imagination.[84] Lacking a purpose, an identity, and a destination, Wordsworth's vagrants are inversions of the Enlightenment ideal of the Universal Man. Such figures, simulating freedom, can only

ever be written about in the future perfect tense: '[h]istorical experience registers the identity of the subject freed from determination as
one that "will have been", a registering that requires the rhetorical form
of the negative litany [...]'.[85] In this way, '[b]y figuring the "man" of
whom we read, *The Prelude* only conjures the vagrant'.[86]

   Like Liu, Langan believes that Wordsworth's secret anxiety was not
that the mind should encounter *nature* with apocalyptic immediacy, but
that it should realize itself as *history*. Evading this intuition produces the
referential opacity with which readers of *The Prelude* in particular are
so familiar. Constantly attempting to outmanoeuvre historical reality,
'[r]eference becomes a kind of crossroads, and enables the "shock" of
wrong-turning'.[87] As a result, as Langan puts it, 'because the position
of the speaking subject is perpetually destabilized, the poem offers to
translate or expose such a condition [...] as vagrancy'.[88] In this way, *The
Prelude* is always on the verge of exposing its own deeper ideological
tensions and its own 'vagrant' liberal logic:

   ■ Wordsworth's obsessive representation of the poet as one who talks
   and walks at the same time may be regarded as shorthand for an implicit
   argument that the determinant contingencies of time and place [...] disrupt,
   intersect, and rupture the desire for formal completion and autistic self-
   enclosure that the poem may thematically represent.[89] □

The logic of vagrancy in *The Prelude*, then, ultimately guarantees that the
'Growth of the Poet's Mind' can never formally be completed. Indeed,
in coping with the contingencies of time and place, Wordsworth invents
'an infinitely mobile subject who bears more than a passing resemblance
to the postmodern subject for whom identity is rather a tactic or performance than an investment'.[90]

   If Langan's study focuses on the 'performative' qualities of
Wordsworth's poem, *Romanticism on the Road: The Marginal Gains of
Wordsworth's Homeless* (2000) by Toby Benis (born 1963) aims to offer
'a cultural history of vagrancy in the Georgian period as refracted
through the early poetry of William Wordsworth, whose interest in, or
obsession with, the homeless outdistanced that of any other writer of
his generation'.[91] Traditionally 'a catch-all category for anyone besides
the rich whom inclination, occupation, or the search for employment
kept on the move', the vagrant came under increased scrutiny from
officialdom during the politically nervy 1790s. Vagrancy laws 'aimed to
bring the homeless, lacking a clear station or role, within the realm of
law and under control of the crown'.[92] What is interesting about representations of the homeless during this period, Benis claims, is their
ambiguity, depicting vagrants as both victims and outlaws. In this way,
he argues, the 'unresolved implication of the homeless in conflicting

roles – in short, their social and moral polyvalence – subverts the utility of binary thinking'.[93] It is this 'binary thinking' that Wordsworth's engagement with the homeless also subverts, thereby exposing 'the limitations of political discourse organized around expedient yet inadequate oppositions'.[94]

Wordsworth himself, however, is far from unambiguous on this issue, as the changing outlook of *The Prelude* attests. Thus, the earliest drafts of the Two-Part *Prelude* use imagery of vagrancy (for example, the poaching activities of the young poet) 'to insist on political and moral ambiguity as defining and aesthetically empowering features of a homeless life'.[95] Thus, as Benis later puts it, '[i]n the 1799 *Prelude*, vagrant behaviour's legal polyvalence dramatizes how social norms themselves are often far from monolithic but rather liable to widely differing interpretations by people from various socio-economic strata'.[96] However, when Wordsworth came to write the later books of the 1805 poem, he charted his development less in its 'ambiguous relation to cultural constraints' and more 'within a consistent framework or clearly defined social norms'.[97] As a result, the discourse of vagrancy is 'cleansed of all ambiguous potential', portraying vagrants 'as embodiments of virtue and fellow-feeling'.[98] Nowhere is this shift in attitude signalled more clearly for Benis than in the Blind Beggar episode in Book VII:

■ The treatment of London life and the vagrant narrator who is drawn to it is transformed by the poet's subsequent encounter with a blind beggar standing in a London street. [...] Why does this beggar make a stronger impression than even the discharged soldier or than the other, equally destitute beggars seen in London? The narrator begins by remembering the feeling that made the city unique for him, that in the street 'The face of everyone / That passes by me is a mystery' (VII, 597–8). He has felt this before in lines 171–5 when seeing beggars earlier. What makes this feeling significant later in the book is its location in an unusual context.

> ... all the ballast of familiar life –
> The present, and the past, hope, fear, all stays
> All laws of acting, thinking, speaking man –
> Went from me, neither knowing me, nor known.
> And once, far travelled in such mood, beyond
> The reach of common indicators, lost
> Amid the moving pageant, 'twas my chance
> Abruptly to be smitten with the view
> Of a blind beggar, who, with upright face,
> Stood propped against a wall, upon his chest
> Wearing a written paper, to explain
> The story of the man, and who he was.
> My mind did at this spectacle turn round

As with the might of waters, and it seemed
To me that in this label was a type
Or emblem of the utmost that we know
Both of ourselves and of the universe,
And on the shape of this unmoving man,
His fixed face and sightless eyes, I looked
As if admonished from another world. □

(601–23)

If we are to see the beggar as the poet's alter ego, Benis continues, then
we cannot avoid the conclusion that the latter is equally determined by
social and linguistic conventions:

■ Like the narrator in the early books, the beggar occupies a marginal
position. Though he may have a home, the law would hold him a vagrant
simply for going through the streets to beg [...]. If nothing else, the beggar's
position initially goes hand in hand with *The Prelude*'s implicit hope: the
activities and lifestyle of vagrancy confer a certain freedom from established social strictures and conventions. All this changes when the narrator considers the significance of the sign the beggar wears. [...] This is a
question not only of self-knowledge but of self-definition. The blind beggar
cannot be sure what his sign says, or if it tells the truth about his past. He
has depended on others to write it, and he must rely on others to read it
aloud to him, much as he also relies on them for sustenance. This imperfect system, prone to misunderstandings and inaccuracy, is the only way
he can apprehend his story, through the filter of other people, with their
judgements and prejudices. The vagrant's life is as bounded by social interpretation and convention as language itself, including the language of the
label that defines him for the world.[99] □

Like Frances Ferguson, Benis argues that the Blind Beggar episode
demonstrates Wordsworth's sudden realization that his own poetic
wanderings are always already 'socialised': the significance of *The
Prelude* is beyond the poet's control in the same way that the inscription
on the sign is not determined by the blind beggar. Thus, the motto
that subtitles the subsequent book – 'Love of Nature Leading to Love
of Mankind' – indicates the poet's increasing concern with integrat-
ing the potentially radical, 'vagrant' consciousness or imagination into
a social mainstream. It is this preoccupation that separates the visions
of the 1799 and 1805 versions of the poem. The Blind Beggar episode
introduces into *The Prelude* a 'new tone, dependent upon a conventional
moral vocabulary hostile to ambiguity',[100] whereby '[t]he homeless are
now seen as unfortunate but good people unfairly labeled as degener-
ates'.[101] By recovering the figure of the homeless wayfarer from the
margins of society, the poet metaphorically returns his own mind to its

family home: 'Mankind'. Thus, 'the conclusion of *The Prelude* is careful to emphasize that the imaginative faculty, along with the vagrancy
with which it has been so long identified, now partakes of the values
and limitations of the society within which it operates'.[102]

Geology and Geography

A recurring theme in *Prelude* criticism and commentary over the past decade has been the way in which spatial metaphors affect the poem's rhetoric
of 'borders' and 'boundaries'. This in turn has encouraged some readers
to engage – as Amanda Gilroy puts it in *Romantic Geographies: Discourses of
Travel 1775–1844* (2000) – 'in materialist terms with the desire to extend
the boundaries of Romanticism, signalled by the recent critical flavour
extended to terms like boundary, margin, position, site, place, space'.[103]
John Wyatt (born 1931), for example, in his *Wordsworth and the Geologists*
(1995), suggests that Wordsworth's interest in contemporary geological
theory led him to conceive of eternal time in spatial terms:

■ In a passage in book vi of *The Prelude*, which has attracted critical attention in respect of Wordsworth's understanding of contemporary geological
theory, there is a richly romantic sequence of the opposition of permanence
and destruction, rather more important an issue than the meagre evidence
it gives of specific knowledge of mineralogy:

>   The immeasurable height
> Of woods decaying, never to be decayed,
> The stationary blasts of waterfalls,
> And everywhere along the hollow rent
> Winds thwarting winds, bewildered and forlorn,
> The torrents shooting from the clear blue sky,
> The rocks that muttered close upon our ears –
> Black drizzling crags that spake by the wayside
>   ...
> Were all like workings of one mind, the features
> Of the same face, blossoms upon one tree,
> Characters of the great apocalypse,
> The types and symbols of eternity,
> Of first, and last, and midst, and without end. □
>   [1805, VI, 556–563, 568–572]

In these lines Wyatt hears 'echoes of a geological theory which is cyc-
lical and renewing':

■ *The Prelude*, a document of a relationship between the developing inner
life of a man and the 'active universe' of the earth's various forms, presents

here a world in torment, expressing itself in human terms. The ever-changing, but persisting universe is thwarted, bewildered, forlorn. The very rocks 'mutter' and speak. What they pronounce is about first and last and 'midst' but also about the never ending.[104] □

A more extensive examination of Wordsworthian spatiality, however, is provided by Michael Wiley, in *Romantic Geography: Wordsworth and Anglo-European Spaces* (1998). For Wiley, Wordsworth is first and foremost a *utopian* writer. This does not mean, however, that he sees the writer as a hopeless dreamer. Rather, Wordsworth's talent as a poet was the ability to imagine alternative spatial realities. Following theorists of space such as Henri Lefebvre (1901–91), Wiley argues that representations of space 'are constituted socially, politically and [...] imaginatively', and that they can in turn 'affect how, where and why people relate to the land and each other'. Wiley is particularly interested in how imaginative configurations of space 'can affect reality by demonstrating "real possibilities" for alternative modes of social and political life'. Unlike New Historicists then, Wiley does not see Wordsworth's utopianism as merely precipitating a withdrawal into idealism: 'while Wordsworth clearly became disillusioned with the course of the Revolution', he argues, 'by turning to nature, solitude and the imagination he did not forsake his early Revolutionary hopes, but attempted to develop new strategies to realize them'.[105] Key to such strategies was the imaginative reordering of space:

■ Nature, solitude and the imagination, I argue, are material concerns for Wordsworth, grounded in the land he lived and walked upon, inseparable from physical, social and political place. In this sense they are geographical concerns, and Wordsworth himself is a geographical poet. When he describes nature or enters into the realm of the imagination, he still situates himself in relation to named physical geographical sites. When he describes solitude, he locates his solitude geographically and explains his spatial relation to others from whom he is separated. Wordsworth maps out a complex geography, which is recognizably related to the actual world even when transforming it.[106] □

Specifically, 'much of Wordsworth's work reveals the spatial boundaries of the ideological and "imaginary order" instituted within the British landscape and imagines an alternative to it'.[107] One way in which such alternatives are imagined is through the creation of what Wiley terms 'imaginative blank spaces', through which the poet 'can reveal and critique the limitations of the world that we already inhabit. He explores the possibility of making such critiques, for example, when he discusses blank spaces in his own and others' experiences of this world – often in passages that have been seen as some of his most idealizing and world-denying.'[108]

One of the most notable instances of 'Wordsworthian blanking' occurs in the Crossing of the Alps episode in Book VI of *The Prelude*. Like Wolfson, Wiley is particularly drawn to the 'cave simile' passage, originally included in this sequence, but by 1805 transplanted into Book VIII. Wiley – again, like Wolfson – focuses on the description of the traveller's disordered perceptions upon entering the cave, 'until all settles and the place "lies in perfect view, / *Exposed and lifeless, as a written book*" [my emphasis] (see the 1805 *Prelude*, 8. 711.27). Predictably, Wordsworth associates this lifeless book [...] with a "blank sense of greatness passed away" (8. 744).'[109] Wiley continues:

■ Just as the traveler configures the living scene into a lifeless book by focusing his eyes, he *re*configures the lifeless book into a utopian living geography by *re*focusing his eyes with the evident expectation that an alternative configuration is potential (that there is a blank where there might be 'greatness'). If the traveler 'look[s] again' at the cave, he will see on its uneven surface a new

> type
> Or picture of the world; forests and lakes,
> Ships, rivers, towers, the Warrior clad in Mail,
> The prancing Steed, the Pilgrim with his Staff,
> The mitred Bishop and the thronèd King –
> A Spectacle to which there is no end.
>
> (8. 736–41)

In the 1804 manuscript draft of this passage (MS X), the scene appears explicitly as a mapped or re-mapped one: here Wordsworth imagines 'Ships trees whole territories visible in maps.'[110] □

For Wiley, these passages reveal the way in which the rhetoric of blank spaces in *The Prelude* becomes the basis for imagining real social and political change. 'Wordsworthian blanks' form the interface between actual and imagined spaces, or, as Wiley puts it, '[t]he world of sense experience [...] engages with the reimagined world through the blank space which separates them.' Moreover, Wiley argues, since '[t]hese two worlds must be understood *relationally*', it is unfair to accuse the poet of having abandoned the 'real', empirical world, 'even though his geography may seem to suggest that the unrealized world fully replaces the real one'. He concludes:

■ Wordsworthian blanks, then, are informed by images of the earth as contemporaries inscribed and understood it. Wordsworth configures these blanks in critical relation to the familiar world, establishing spaces in which he can describe alternatives to it. This is the general dynamic of Wordsworth's utopianism.[111] □

As mentioned above, Wiley reads Wordsworthian geography in *The Prelude* through the prism of Lefebvre's theories of space. Other methods, however, have been pursued. In his 2000 essay 'Wordsworth's Grand Tour', Keith Hanley approaches the topic by way of Lacanian psychoanalysis. The key moment in all of Wordsworth's poetry, Hanley claims, is the point where consciousness leaves the maternal, 'Imaginary' realm, and enters the paternal, 'Symbolic' realm of language.[112] This transition is repeatedly figured as a journey of 'self-fulfilment', but what Hanley finds remarkable about Wordsworth is the extent to which the writer attempts to conceal the sacrifice made in this move. According to Lacan, the emergence of the infant mind into linguistic reality is characterized by the trauma of an encounter with the threatening otherness of the father-figure. Once the phallic intervention of the father has introduced 'the original self-division of symbolic castration', there is no way back to the Imaginary sense of oneness with the mother. Wordsworth, however, takes pains to avoid any suggestion of conflict between the maternal–imaginative and paternal–symbolic.

This phenomenon gives rise to the two principal planks of Hanley's argument. First, he claims that Wordsworth's poetry resists the reality-principle upon which the Symbolic Order of the father insists. By denying the 'primary rupture' between imagination and language, Wordsworth's verse preserves a 'rudimentary formation of the Imaginary which took the form of a lasting preoccupation with the experience of derealisation'. Second, unwilling to leave the maternal presence, the 'journeys' described in Wordsworth's poetry are always destined to return to an Imaginary origin: they thus 'negotiate new inscriptions in different discourses so as to make them all end up at the same desired destination'.[113] Indeed, '*all* Wordsworth's journeyings are excursions or tours which loop back to 'home at Grasmere'.[114]

Given this, Hanley is particularly interested in the relation of Wordsworth's journeys (literal and imaginary) to the symbolic geography of eighteenth-century travel narratives, and in particular the emergence in this period of the 'Grand Tour' as the rite of passage through which sons confirmed their independence, their 'attainment of political authority' and self-inscription into the patriarchal order. Journeying to the centre of a cultural tradition, '[t]he symbol for completed self-inscription was the arrival at Rome'.[115] How does the Wordsworthian journey – figuratively, always returning to an Imaginary Grasmere – relate to the discourse of paternal cultural authority in which all paths to linguistic manhood lead to a symbolic 'Rome'?

With great ambivalence, is Hanley's answer. Crucial here – as so often – is the 1805 *Prelude*'s recounting of the poet's 'Crossing of the Alps' in 1790. Here, the failure of the actual Alps to live up to the standards of the imagined Alps emerges as a potential site of conflict between the Imaginary and Symbolic 'reality'. This forces Wordsworth to confront the fact 'that his original imaginary relation with natural objects must (and can be satisfactorily) transferred to one with language'.[116] What he does next, while revising *The Prelude* in 1804, is overcome the disappointment of forced entry into the (paternal) Symbolic Order by rewriting it as if it were merely the rearticulation of the (maternal) Imaginary:

■ In the act of rewriting his Alpine experience in March 1804, it suddenly comes to Wordsworth that the imaginary signified may be re-articulated in an alternative discourse. The subject-formation had been confirmed within the Symbolic order, emerging without Oedipal struggle because always already there, and the mist that appeared to be withholding power simply dissipates itself as it becomes transformed into the figure of his own 'unfathered' endowments:

> Imagination! – lifting up itself
> Before the eye and progress of my song
> Like an unfathered vapour, here that power,
> In all the might of its endowments, came
> Athwart me. I was lost as in a cloud,
> Halted without a struggle to break through,
> And now, recovering, to my soul I say
> 'I recognize thy glory.' □

[1805, VI, 525–532]

Imagination, the 'unfathered' vapour, emerges as the hidden power behind the Symbolic all along: there is no need for alienation or psychic trauma in Wordsworth's landscape, then: the route across the Alps towards Symbolic Rome *also* leads to Imaginary Grasmere, enabling Wordsworth to be a poet of the world without, in a sense, ever leaving the womb.

Hanley's reading owes much to a tradition of psychoanalytic criticism on *The Prelude* that stretches back to Herbert Read and F.W. Bateson. However, its simultaneous engagement with questions of cultural and political history highlights one of the hallmarks of Wordsworth commentary over the past decade or so: a resistance to the theoretical tribalism of the 1980s and early 1990s. Thus, the emergence of neoformalism indicates an increasing willingness among critics to entertain non-reductive considerations of the aesthetic, while the rise of ecocriticism demonstrates a readiness in some quarters to prioritize ethical considerations over those of methodology. Each of these developments, to a greater or lesser extent, prizes the creation of new concepts, the forging of new critical connections and pathways over the preservation of political coherence or theoretical hygiene. In doing so, they testify to the continuing hold exercised over modern thought by *The Prelude*'s ambivalent commitment to truthfulness and imagination.

Conclusion: *The Prelude* Revisited

In concluding, I would like to return to Jonathan Bishop's claim, originally cited in Chapter 2, that '*The Prelude* is at the center of our experience of Wordsworth; at the center of our experience of *The Prelude* are those "spots of time" where Wordsworth is endeavouring to express key moments in the history of his imagination'. These 'spots' he lists as the events surrounding

■ the famous Stolen Boat episode, the Dedication to poetry, the Discharged Soldier, the Dream of the Arab-Quixote, the memory of the Winander Boy, the Drowned Man, Entering London, the father and the Child and the Blind Beggar, Simplon Pass, The Night in Paris, Robespierre's Death, and Snowdon.[1] □

If Bishop is right, and those hallowed, renovating 'spots of time' in *The Prelude* have indeed become the centre of our experience and appreciation of Wordsworth the poet, then what this *Guide* has revealed, I hope, is that they have also become a fertile ground for the interpretation and re-interpretation of his work. This volume has already documented how, for example, Bishop's own Freudian reading of the 'Stolen Boat' episode (Chapter 2) is indirectly answered and revised by Nigel Wood's more specifically Oedipal interpretation (Chapter 4). In a similar way, David Ellis's psychoanalysis of the 'Drowned Man' (Chapter 4) is countered by Richard Bourke's reading of the same passage as an exercise in the politics of Wordsworth's 'domesticated' sublime (Chapter 6). The 'Snowdon' passage, already troublesome textually (Chapter 1), is famously glossed by M.H. Abrams in Hegelian terms as the scene where the mind confronts nature only to find there the reflection of its own powers (Chapter 3). Wood, however, reads the episode as a displaced eruption of the unconscious (Chapter 4).

Other 'spots' have been revisited more often in this volume. Thus, the 'Blind Beggar' episode is cited by Frances Ferguson as an instance of how *The Prelude* betrays the way in which identity and meaning depend not upon an act of consciousness, but upon a wholly linguistic 'otherness' (Chapter 4). This reading is in turn partially supported by the argument behind Toby Benis's claim that the revisions Wordsworth carried out on the passage between 1799 and 1805 demonstrate the poet's increasing desire to integrate his own 'vagrant' poetic persona into the mainstream of society (Chapter 6). Against this, however, we encountered Nicholas Roe's insistence that a later set of revisions to the same lines reveal the enduring radicalism of Wordsworth's 'introspective Jacobinism' (Chapter 5).

More contested still, predictably, is perhaps the timeliest spot of them all: 'Simplon Pass', a passage that Newton Stallknecht cites in support of his claim that the intellectual roots of *The Prelude* lie in the theology of the seventeenth-century theologian Jakob Boehme (Chapter 2). William Empson, on the other hand, finds that the treatment in this section of a single word, 'sense', reveals a great deal about Wordsworth's ambivalence towards sensory perception (Chapter 3), an uneasiness also detected by Geoffrey Hartman, for whom the hymn to Imagination in Simplon Pass displays *The Prelude*'s 'via naturaliter negativa', a dialectical process whereby the poet's mind learns from nature that the condition of its own growth and development must be a *blindness* to (i.e., a negation of) nature itself (Chapter 3). Hartman's experiential, phenomenological interpretation is later countered by (among others) Susan Wolfson's reading of the passage as an exploration of imagination's dependence upon form as a *process* (Chapter 6), while for Michael Wiley, drawing upon the work of Lefebvre, the episode is an example of a Wordsworthian 'blank', one of the strategies whereby *The Prelude* constructs alternative political orders by imagining new utopian spaces (Chapter 6). Finally, following Lacan, Keith Hanley sees 'Simplon Pass' as the culmination of a 'travel' narrative in which Wordsworth tries to have his Oedipal cake and eat it by figuring the power of poetic imagination as an 'unfathered vapour' (VI, 527) (Chapter 6).

Surveying the many varieties of Wordsworth criticism in this way, it is easy to empathize with the poet at Tintern Abbey, continually revisiting the scene of a previous revelation and finding its significance not so much erased, exactly, as transformed or written over. Just as Wordsworth found no single answer to the meaning of the scene laid out before him in the Wye Valley, so we scrutinize the palimpsest of *Prelude* criticism in vain for conclusive answers to our obstinate questioning of the poem's final significance. As I suggested at the end of Chapter 6, however, the most recent commentary has tended to celebrate rather than lament such indeterminacy. A good example of this growing tendency is an essay recently written for the *Romantic Circles* website by Ron Broglio. Broglio is influenced by the French post-structuralist philosopher Gilles Deleuze (1925–95). At the centre of Deleuze's thought is the idea of the contingency, materiality, and vitality of human life. He denigrates notions of unity, stability, and contemplation, and emphasizes the importance of difference, becoming, and the creation of new concepts.

Broglio agrees with this view, and argues that, once we dispense with the categories of philosophy, phenomenology, and psychoanalysis, we find 'new couplings and assemblages' in Wordsworth that 'are *not* subsumed within the Oedipal, within the Imaginary and Symbolic'.[2] *The Prelude*, Broglio maintains, produces figures of radical contingency and materiality, such as the Drowned Man in Book V, the Discharged Soldier in Book IV, and the Blind Beggar in Book VII, but struggles to contain them. Here, like Langan and Harrison, Broglio registers the disturbingly singular power of the 'vagrant' – the figure of the individual wandering without purpose, endlessly making unpredictable connections – to unsettle the 'language of religion and moral law' that the poet seeks to affirm:

■ Each of these characters disturbs by his literalness and physicality. Their nomadism, their wanderings, are contained by a language of religion and moral law as well as by turning the encounters into a reflection on the poet's own interiority, identity, and imagination which coopts and shuts down the radical potential of these vagrants.[3] □

Broglio's commentary suggests one possible future direction for the critical reception of *The Prelude*. It may be, indeed, that *The Prelude* is itself a 'nomadic' text with no essence, forging contingent connections with other texts and concepts. Perhaps this is one reason why, after over 150 years of criticism, it has never been successfully 'coopted', but continues, like the vagrants in its own margins, to generate meanings for readers in surprising and unpredictable ways.

Notes

Introduction: The 'Huge and Mighty Forms' of *The Prelude*

1 See Ian Reid, *Wordsworth and the Formation of English Studies* (Ashgate, 2004).

1 In The Cathedral Ruins: *The Prelude* from Conception to Criticism

1 See Nicholas Roe, 'William Wordsworth', *Literature of the Romantic Period: A Bibliographical Guide*, ed. Michael O'Neill (Oxford: Clarendon Press, 1998), pp. 45–64. Roe gives a valuable synopsis of the ongoing debate over which version of *The Prelude* should be considered 'authoritative'.

2 William Wordsworth, *The Prelude 1799, 1805, 1850*, eds, Jonathan Wordsworth, M.H. Abrams, and Stephen Gill (W.W. Norton & Co., 1979).

3 See, for example, Mark L. Reed, 'Introduction', *The Thirteen-Book Prelude*, vol. 1 (Cornell University Press, 1991). Reed argues that in addition to what scholars know as the 'AB-Stage *Prelude*' (1805), there exists a distinct 'C-Stage' text dating from 1818–20.

4 For the relationship between *The Prelude* and *The Recluse*, see Kenneth R. Johnston, *Wordsworth and 'The Recluse'* (New Haven: Yale University Press, 1984).

5 Samuel Taylor Coleridge, 'To Wordsworth, 12 October 1799', Wordsworth (1979), p. 529.

6 William Wordsworth, 'To Richard Sharp, 29 April 1804', *Wordsworth*: The Prelude. *A Casebook*, eds, W.J. Harvey and Richard Gravil (Macmillan, 1972), p. 42.

7 Dorothy Wordsworth, 'To Catherine Clarkson, 13 February 1804', Wordsworth (1979), p. 531.

8 'Wordsworth to Thomas De Quincey, 6 March, 1804', Harvey and Gravil (1972), p. 39–40.

9 William Wordsworth, *The Five-Book Prelude*, ed. Duncan Wu (Blackwell, 1997).

10 In the 1850 version, Books X–XIV appear with the following titles: X. 'Residence in France – Continued'; XI. 'France – Continued'; XII. 'Imagination and Taste, How Impaired and Restored'; XIII. 'Imagination, How Impaired and Restored – Concluded'; XIV. 'Conclusion'.

11 'Wordsworth to Sir George Beaumont, 3 June 1805', Harvey and Gravil (1972), p. 42.

12 William Wordsworth, 'Preface to *The Excursion*, 1814', Wordsworth (1979), p. 535.

13 Stephen Gill, *Wordsworth: A Life* (Oxford: Clarendon Press, 1989), pp. 303–4.

14 William Hazlitt, 'From a Review of *The Excursion*, *Examiner* 21, 28 August, 2 October 1814', *William Wordsworth: A Critical Anthology*, ed. Graham McMaster (Penguin Books, 1972), p. 116.

15 Francis Jeffrey, 'From a Review of *The Excursion*, *Edinburgh Review* November 1814', MacMaster (1972), pp. 122–3.

16 Quoted in Gill (1989), p. 390.

17 Isabella Fenwick, 'To Henry Taylor, 28 March, 1839', Wordsworth (1979), p. 537.

18 Christopher Wordsworth, Jr., 'To Joshua Watson, 14 June 1850', Wordsworth (1979), p. 539.

19 Thomas De Quincey, 'William Wordsworth', *Tait's Edinburgh Magazine* VI (1839), Wordsworth (1979), p. 546.

20 'The Prelude', *Eclectic Review* XXVIII (1850), Wordsworth (1979), pp. 547–50.

21 'The Prelude,' *Tait's Edinburgh Magazine*, XVII (1850), Wordsworth (1979), p. 551.

22 'Wordsworth's Autobiographical Poem', *Gentleman's Magazine* XXXIV (1850), Wordsworth (1979), pp. 552–3.

23 'The Prelude', *Graham's Magazine* XXXVII (1850), Wordsworth (1979), pp. 554.

24 'The Prelude', *British Quarterly Review* xii (1850), Wordsworth (1979), pp. 555–6.

25 'The New Poem by Wordsworth', *Dublin University Magazine* XXXVI (1850), Wordsworth (1979), p. 557.

26 'The Prelude', *Examiner*, No. 2217 (1850), Wordsworth (1979), pp. 558–9.

27 John Stuart Mill, quoted in Gill (1989), p. 480, n. 43.

28 F.W. Bateson, *Wordsworth: A Re-Interpretation*, 2nd ed. (London: Longmans, 1956), p. 197.

29 Richard Holt Hutton, 'The Genius of Wordsworth', *Literary Essays* (1871), Harvey and Gravil, (1972), pp. 58–61.

30 Walter Pater, 'Wordsworth', Harvey and Gravil (1972), p. 66–70.

31 Leslie Stephen, 'Wordsworth's Ethics', McMaster (1972), pp. 199–200, 203.

32 Matthew Arnold, 'From the Introduction to *Poems of Wordsworth*', McMaster (1972), p. 221.

33 McMaster (1972), pp. 222–3.

34 McMaster (1972), pp. 226–31.

2   Revaluations: The Early Twentieth Century

1 A.C. Bradley, 'From *Oxford Lectures on Poetry* (1909)', *William Wordsworth: A Critical Anthology*, ed. Graham McMaster (Penguin Books, 1972), pp. 243–4.

2 McMaster (1972), p. 245.

3 McMaster (1972), p. 245.

4 McMaster (1972), p. 245.

5 McMaster (1972), p. 246–7.

6 Helen Darbishire, 'Wordsworth's *Prelude*', *Wordsworth*: The Prelude. *A Casebook*, eds, W.J. Harvey and Richard Gravil (Macmillan, 1972), p. 82.

7 Harvey and Gravil (1972), pp. 83–4.

8 Herbert Read, *Wordsworth* (Faber and Faber Ltd., 1930), pp. 20–1.

9 Read (1930), p. 33.

10 Read (1930), p. 49.

11 Read (1930), p. 117.

12 Read (1930), p. 145.

13 Read (1930), p. 142.

14 F.W. Bateson, *Wordsworth: A Re-Interpretation*, 2nd ed. (London: Longmans, 1956), p. vii.

15 Bateson (1956), p. ix.

16 Bateson (1956), pp. 55–6.

17 Bateson (1956), pp. 202–3.

18 Jonathan Bishop, 'Wordsworth and the Spots of Time', Harvey and Gravil (1972), pp. 134–5.

19 Harvey and Gravil (1972), p. 149.

20 Bateson (1956), pp. v–vi.

21 F.R. Leavis, *Revaluation: Tradition & Development in English Poetry* (London: Chatto & Windus, 1936), p. 8.

22 Leavis (1936), p. 169.

23 Leavis (1936), p. 174.

24 Leavis, (1936), pp. 155–6.

25 Leavis, (1936), pp. 162–3.

26 A.N. Whitehead, 'From *Science and the Modern World*,' *William Wordsworth: A Critical Anthology*, McMaster (1972), p. 292.

27 McMaster (1972), pp. 293–4.
28 McMaster (1972), pp. 324–5.
29 Arthur Beatty, *William Wordsworth: His Doctrine and Art in their Historical Relations*, 2nd ed. University of Wisconsin Studies in Language and Literature 24 (Madison, 1927), p. 5.
30 Beatty (1927), pp. 108.
31 Beatty (1927), pp. 115–16.
32 Beatty (1927), p. 288.
33 Newton P. Stallknecht, *Strange Seas of Thought: Studies in William Wordsworth's Philosophy of Man and Nature* (Durham: Duke University Press, 1945), p. 10.
34 Stallknecht (1945), p. 66.
35 Stallknecht (1945), pp. 110–11.
36 Stallknecht (1945), p. 235.
37 Stallknecht (1945), p. 245.
38 McMaster (1972), p. 395.
39 McMaster (1972), p. 398.
40 David Ferry, *The Limits of Mortality: An Essay on Wordsworth's Major Poems* (Wesleyan University Press, 1959), p. ix.
41 Ferry (1959), p. 3.
42 Ferry (1959), p. 4.
43 Ferry (1959), p. 157.
44 Ferry (1959), p. 157–8.

3   Style, Philosophy, and Phenomenology

1 William Empson, 'Sense in *The Prelude*', Wordsworth (1979), p. 625.
2 Wordsworth (1979), p. 639.
3 Wordsworth (1979), p. 631.
4 Wordsworth (1979), p. 636.
5 Wordsworth (1979), p. 637.
6 Wordsworth (1979), p. 640.
7 Wordsworth (1979), p. 641.
8 Herbert Lindenberger, *On Wordsworth's* Prelude (Princeton University Press, 1963), p. vii.
9 Lindenberger (1963), p. xiii.
10 Lindenberger (1963), p. 5.
11 Lindenberger (1963), pp. 6–7.
12 Lindenberger (1963), pp. 9–10.
13 Lindenberger (1963), pp. 44–5.
14 Christopher Ricks, 'Wordsworth: "A Pure Organic Pleasure from the Lines"', *William Wordsworth: A Critical Anthology*, ed. Graham McMaster (Penguin Books, 1972), p. 505.
15 McMaster (1972), p. 507.
16 McMaster (1972), p. 510.
17 McMaster (1972), pp. 511–12.
18 McMaster (1972), p. 512.
19 Morse Peckham, 'A Post-Enlightenment Imagination', *Wordsworth*: The Prelude. *A Casebook*, eds, W.J. Harvey and Richard Gravil (Macmillan, 1972), p. 212.
20 Harvey and Gravil (1972), p. 214.
21 Harvey and Gravil (1972), pp. 215–16.
22 Harvey and Gravil (1972), p. 216.
23 Robert Langbaum, 'The Evolution of Soul in Wordsworth's Poetry,' Harvey and Gravil (1972), p. 218.
24 Harvey and Gravil (1972), p. 219.
25 Harvey and Gravil (1972), pp. 219–20.

26 Harvey and Gravil (1972), p. 225.
27 M.H. Abrams, *Natural Supernaturalism: Tradition and Revolution in Romantic Literature* (W.W. Norton & Company, Inc., 1971), pp. 12–13.
28 Abrams (1971), p. 65.
29 Abrams (1971), p. 68.
30 Abrams (1971), p. 75.
31 Abrams (1971), p. 77.
32 Abrams (1971), p. 79.
33 Abrams (1971), pp. 286–8.
34 Geoffrey Hartman, 'The Via Naturaliter Negativa', *William Wordsworth's* The Prelude: *A Casebook*, ed. Stephen Gill (Oxford University Press, 2006), pp. 181–2.
35 Gill (2006), pp. 183–4.
36 Gill (2006), p. 186.
37 Gill (2006), pp. 186–7.
38 Gill (2006), p. 188.
39 Gill (2006), p. 189.
40 Gill (2006), p. 195.
41 Gill (2006), p. 199.
42 Harold Bloom, *The Ringers in the Tower: Studies in the Romantic Tradition* (The University of Chicago Press, 1971), p. 13.
43 Bloom (1971), p. 13.
44 Bloom (1971), p. 14.
45 Bloom (1971), p. 15.
46 Bloom (1971), p. 23.
47 Bloom (1971), p. 23.
48 Bloom (1971), p. 19.
49 Bloom (1971), p. 31.

4 Writing the Self: Deconstruction, Feminism, and Psychoanalysis

1 Nigel Wood, 'Introduction', *The Prelude*, ed. Nigel Wood. Theory and Practice Series (Buckingham: Open University Press, 1993), p. 4.
2 Wood (1993), p. 6.
3 Paul de Man, 'Autobiography as De-Facement', *The Rhetoric of Romanticism* (Columbia University Press, 1984), p. 70.
4 De Man (1984), p. 70.
5 De Man (1984), pp. 70–1.
6 De Man (1984), p. 71.
7 Paul de Man, 'Wordsworth and the Victorians', *The Rhetoric of Romanticism* (1984), p. 85.
8 De Man (1984), p. 86.
9 De Man (1984), p. 87.
10 De Man (1984), p. 92.
11 Paul de Man, 'Time and History in Wordsworth', *Romanticism*, ed. Cynthia Chase (Longman, 1993), pp. 60–61. This essay was originally the fourth in a series of six lectures on *Contemporary Criticism and the Problem of Romanticism* delivered by de Man as the Christian Gauss Seminar in Criticism at Princeton University between April and May 1967. It was published in *Diacritics* 17.4 (1987): pp. 4–17.
12 Chase (1993), pp. 72–3.
13 Frances Ferguson, *Wordsworth: Language as Counter-Spirit* (Yale University Press, 1977), p. xi.
14 Ferguson (1977), p. xii.
15 Ferguson (1977), p. xiii.

16 Ferguson (1977), p. xvi.

17 Ferguson (1977), p. 126.

18 Ferguson (1977), pp. 127–8.

19 Ferguson (1977), pp. 129–30.

20 Ferguson (1977), pp. 143–4.

21 Ferguson (1977), pp. 144–5.

22 Ferguson (1977), p. 154.

23 Mary Jacobus, 'Genre, Gender, and Autobiography: Vaudracour and Julia', *Wordsworth*, New Casebooks, ed. John Williams (Macmillian, 1993), p. 192.

24 Williams (1993), p. 190.

25 Williams (1993), p. 193.

26 Williams (1993), p. 196.

27 Williams (1993), p. 203.

28 Marlon B. Ross, 'Naturalizing Gender: Woman's Place in Wordsworth's Ideological Landscape', *English Literary History* 53.2 (1986): p. 391.

29 Ross (1986), p. 391.

30 Ross (1986), p. 392.

31 Margaret Homans, *Bearing the Word: Language and Female Experience in Nineteenth-Century Woman's Writing* (University of Chicago Press, 1986), p. 1.

32 Homans (1986), p. 2.

33 Homans (1986), p. 6.

34 Homans (1986), p. 7.

35 Homans (1986), p. 4.

36 Homans (1986), p. 6.

37 Homans (1986), p. 5.

38 Homans (1986), pp. 41–2.

39 Homans (1986), p. 42.

40 Homans (1986), p. 43.

41 Homans (1986), pp. 43–4.

42 Gayatri Chakravorty Spivak, 'Sex and History in *The Prelude* (1805): Books IX to XIII', Williams (1993), p. 173.

43 Williams (1993), p. 173.

44 Williams (1993), p. 174.

45 Williams (1993), p. 175.

46 Williams (1993), p. 177.

47 Williams (1993), p. 181.

48 Williams (1993), p. 184.

49 Anne Mellor, 'Writing the Self/Self Writing', Gill (2006), p. 294.

50 Gill (2006), p. 295.

51 Gill (2006), p. 296.

52 Gill (2006), p. 298.

53 Gill (2006), p. 299.

54 Wood (1993), p. 20.

55 Wood (1993), p. 22.

56 Wood (1993), p. 22.

57 Wood (1993), p. 23.

58 Richard J. Onorato, *The Character of the Poet: Wordsworth in* The Prelude (Princeton University Press, 1971), p. viii.

59 Onorato (1971), p. 17.

60 Onorato (1971), pp. 63–4.

61 Onorato (1971), p. 368.

62 Onorato (1971), p. 384.

63 David Ellis, *Wordsworth, Freud and the Spots of Time: Interpretation in* The Prelude (Cambridge University Press, 1985), p. 2.
64 Ellis (1985), pp. 5–6.
65 Ellis (1985), p. 95.
66 Ellis (1985), p. 94.
67 Ellis (1985), p. 99.
68 Ellis (1985), pp. 94–5.
69 Ellis (1985), p. 162.
70 Ellis (1985), p. 163.

5 Spots of Time: The New Historicism

1 Nigel Wood, 'Introduction', *The Prelude*, ed. Nigel Wood. Theory and Practice Series (Buckingham: Open University Press, 1993), pp. 23–4.
2 Wood (1993), p. 25.
3 Wood (1993), p. 24.
4 Marilyn Butler, *Romantics, Rebels and Reactionaries* (Oxford University Press, 1981), p. 67.
5 Howard Erskine-Hill, 'Wordsworth and the Conception of *The Prelude*', *William Wordsworth's* The Prelude*: A Casebook*, ed. Stephen Gill (Oxford University Press, 2006), p. 305.
6 Gill (2006), p. 306.
7 Gill (2006), pp. 310–11.
8 Gill (2006), p. 311.
9 Gill (2006), p. 312.
10 Nicholas Roe, 'Revising the Revolution: History and Imagination in *The Prelude*, 1799, 1805, 1850', *Romantic Revisions*, eds, Robert Brinkley and Keith Hanley (Cambridge University Press, 1992), p. 88.
11 Brinkley and Hanley (1992), p. 91.
12 Brinkley and Hanley (1992), p. 92.
13 Brinkley and Hanley (1992), p. 92.
14 Brinkley and Hanley (1992), p. 101.
15 Roger Sales, 'William Wordsworth and the Real Estate', *Wordsworth*, New Casebooks, ed. John Williams (Macmillian, 1993), p. 92.
16 Williams (1993), p. 93.
17 Williams (1993), p. 110.
18 Williams (1993), pp. 106–7.
19 Williams (1993), p. 107.
20 Williams (1993), p. 108.
21 Jerome McGann, *The Romantic Ideology: A Critical Investigation* (University of Chicago Press, 1983), p. 81.
22 McGann (1983), p. 82.
23 McGann (1983), p. 85.
24 McGann (1983), p. 90.
25 McGann (1983), p. 91.
26 McGann (1983), p. 91.
27 James Chandler, *Wordsworth's Second Nature: A Study of the Poetry and Politics* (University of Chicago Press, 1984), pp. 31-2.
28 Chandler (1984), p. 55.
29 Chandler (1984), p. 67.
30 Chandler (1984), p. 67.
31 Chandler (1984), p. 72.
32 Chandler (1984), p. 74.
33 Chandler (1984), p. 75.

34 Chandler (1984), p. 75.
35 David Simpson, *Wordsworth's Historical Imagination: The Poetry of Displacement* (Methuen, 1987), p. 1.
36 Simpson (1987), p. 2.
37 Simpson (1987), p. 3.
38 Simpson (1987), p. 109.
39 Simpson (1987), p. 122.
40 Simpson (1987), p. 123.
41 Simpson (1987), pp. 123–4.
42 Simpson (1987), p. 139.
43 Marjorie Levinson, *Wordsworth's Great Period Poems: Four Essays* (Cambridge University Press, 1986), p. 1.
44 Levinson (1986), p. 13.
45 Levinson (1986), p. 2.
46 Levinson (1986), p. 5.
47 Levinson (1986), pp. 5–6.
48 Levinson (1986), p. 3.
49 Levinson (1986), p. 121.
50 Levinson (1986), pp. 121–2.
51 Levinson (1986), p. 123.
52 Levinson (1986), p. 122.
53 Levinson (1986), p. 123.
54 Levinson (1986), p. 123.
55 Wood (1993), p. 98.
56 Clifford Siskin, 'Working *The Prelude*: Foucault and the New History', Wood (1993), p. 105.
57 Wood (1993), p. 101.
58 Wood (1993), pp. 101–2.
59 Wood (1993), p. 102.
60 Wood (1993), p. 103.
61 Wood (1993), p. 105.
62 Wood (1993), p. 109.
63 Wood (1993), p. 111.
64 Wood (1993), p. 115.
65 Wood (1993), p. 116.
66 Wood (1993), p. 121.
67 Alan Liu, *Wordsworth: The Sense of History* (Chicago University Press, 1989), p. 39.
68 Liu (1989), p. 37.
69 Liu (1989), p. 40.
70 Liu (1989), p. 39.
71 Liu (1989), p. 46.
72 Liu (1989), p. 41.
73 Liu (1989), p. 40.
74 Liu (1989), p. 39.
75 Liu (1989), p. 38.
76 Liu (1989), p. 31.
77 Liu (1989), p. 38.
78 Liu (1989), p. 363.
79 Liu (1989), p. 365.
80 Liu (1989), p. 380.
81 Liu (1989), pp. 380–1.
82 Liu (1989), p. 382.
83 Liu (1989), pp. 382–3.

174 NOTES

84 Liu (1989), p. 384.
85 Liu (1989), p. 31.

6 *The Prelude* and The Present

1 Susan Wolfson, *Formal Charges: The Shaping of Poetry in British Romanticism* (Stanford: Stanford University Press, 1997), p. 1.
2 Wolfson (1997), p. 10.
3 Wolfson (1997), p. 230.
4 Wolfson (1997), p. 231.
5 Wolfson (1997), p. 4.
6 Wolfson (1997), p. 14.
7 Wolfson (1997), p. 23.
8 Wolfson (1997), p. 30.
9 Wolfson (1997), p. 101.
10 Wolfson (1997), pp. 108–9.
11 Wolfson (1997), p. 104.
12 Wolfson (1997), p. 27.
13 Wolfson (1997), p. 104.
14 Wolfson (1997), pp. 129–31.
15 Wolfson (1997), p. 132.
16 Thomas Pfau, *Wordsworth's Profession: Form, Class, and the Logic of Early Romantic Cultural Production* (Stanford University Press, 1997), pp. 5–6.
17 Pfau (1997), p. 263.
18 Pfau (1997), p. 240.
19 Pfau (1997), p. 7.
20 Pfau (1997), p. 12.
21 Pfau (1997), p. 7.
22 Pfau (1997), p. 16.
23 Pfau (1997), p. 10.
24 Pfau (1997), p. 14.
25 Pfau (1997), p. 264.
26 Pfau (1997), p. 264.
27 Pfau (1997), p. 265.
28 Pfau (1997), p. 267.
29 Pfau (1997), p. 312.
30 Pfau (1997), p. 313.
31 Pfau (1997), p. 382.
32 Geraldine Friedman, *The Insistence of History: Revolution in Burke, Wordsworth, Keats, and Baudelaire* (Stanford University Press, 1996), p. 5.
33 Friedman (1996), p. 2.
34 Friedman (1996), p. 3.
35 Friedman (1996), p. 4.
36 Friedman (1996), p. 6.
37 Friedman (1996), p. 8.
38 Friedman (1996), p. 66.
39 Friedman (1996), p. 69.
40 Friedman (1996), pp. 71–2.
41 Friedman (1996), p. 72.
42 Friedman (1996), p. 78.
43 Friedman (1996), p. 90.
44 Richard Bourke, *Romantic Discourse and Political Modernity: Wordsworth, the Intellectual and Cultural Critique* (Harvester Wheatsheaf, 1993), p. ix.
45 Bourke (1993), p. x.

46 Bourke (1993), p. 5.
47 Bourke (1993), p. xi.
48 Bourke (1993), p. 2.
49 Bourke (1993), pp. 240–1.
50 Bourke (1993), p. 246.
51 Bourke (1993), p. 245.
52 Bourke (1993), p. 255.
53 Jonathan Bate, 'A Language that is Ever Green', *William Wordsworth's* The Prelude: *A Casebook*, ed. Stephen Gill (Oxford University Press, 2006), p. 381.
54 Gill (2006), p. 384.
55 Gill (2006), p. 388.
56 Gill (2006), p. 395.
57 Gill (2006), p. 398.
58 Karl Kroeber, *Ecological Literary Criticism: Romantic Imagining and the Biology of Mind* (Columbia University Press, 1994), pp. 1–2.
59 Kroeber (1994), p. 3.
60 Kroeber (1994), p. 2.
61 Kroeber (1994), p. 5.
62 Kroeber (1994), p. 19.
63 Kroeber (1994), p. 70.
64 Kroeber (1994), pp. 80–1.
65 James McKusick, Introduction, 'Romanticism and Ecology,' *Romantic Circles: Praxis Series* 1 Nov 2001, 1 Feb 2008 <http://www.rc.umd.edu/praxis/ecology/mckusick/mckusick_intro.html> p. 2.
66 McKusick (2001), p. 4.
67 McKusick (2001), p. 11.
68 McKusick (2001), p. 12.
69 Gary Harrison, *Wordsworth's Vagrant Muse: Poetry, Poverty and Power* (Wayne State University Press, 1994), p. 16.
70 Harrison (1994), p. 17.
71 Harrison (1994), p. 18.
72 Harrison (1994), p. 21.
73 Harrison (1994), p. 23.
74 Harrison (1994), p. 24.
75 Harrison (1994), p. 73.
76 Harrison (1994), p. 74.
77 Harrison (1994), p. 75.
78 Celeste Langan, *Romantic Vagrancy: Wordsworth and the Simulation of Freedom* (Cambridge University Press, 1995), p. 15.
79 Langan (1995), p. 7.
80 Langan (1995), p. 12.
81 Langan (1995), p. 17.
82 Langan (1995), p. 21.
83 Langan (1995), p. 19.
84 Langan (1995), p. 25.
85 Langan (1995), p. 28.
86 Langan (1995), p. 29.
87 Langan (1995), p. 140.
88 Langan (1995), p. 141.
89 Langan (1995), p. 142.
90 Langan (1995), p. 142.
91 Toby Benis, *Romanticism on the Road: The Marginal Gains of Wordsworth's Homeless* (Macmillan, 2000), p. 1.
92 Benis (2000), p. 2.

93 Benis (2000), p. 3.
94 Benis (2000), p. 4.
95 Benis (2000), p. 19.
96 Benis (2000), p. 168.
97 Benis (2000), p. 190.
98 Benis (2000), p. 20.
99 Benis (2000), pp. 203–4.
100 Benis (2000), p. 206.
101 Benis (2000), p. 208.
102 Benis (2000), p. 216.
103 Amanda Gilroy, 'Introduction', *Romantic Geographies: Discourses of Travel 1775–1844*, ed. Amanda Gilroy (Manchester University Press, 2000), p. 3.
104 John Wyatt, *Wordsworth and the Geologists* (Cambridge University Press, 1995), pp. 160–1.
105 Michael Wiley, *Romantic Geography: Wordsworth and Anglo-European Spaces* (Macmillan, 1998), p. 3.
106 Wiley (1998), p. 3.
107 Wiley (1998), p. 7.
108 Wiley (1998), p. 13.
109 Wiley (1998), p. 15.
110 Wiley (1998), pp. 15–16.
111 Wiley (1998), p. 16.
112 Keith Hanley, 'Wordsworth's Grand Tour', Gilroy (2000), p. 71.
113 Gilroy (2000), p. 73.
114 Gilroy (2000), p. 72.
115 Gilroy (2000), p. 74.
116 Gilroy (2000), p. 78.

Conclusion: *The Prelude* Revisited

1 Jonathan Bishop, 'Wordsworth and the Spots of Time', *Wordsworth*: The Prelude. *A Casebook*, eds, W.J. Harvey and Richard Gravil (Macmillan, 1972), p. 134.
2 Ron Broglio, 'Wandering the Landscape with Wordsworth and Deleuze', 'Romanticism and the New Deleuze', *Romantic Circles: Praxis Series* 1 Jan 2008, 1 Feb 2008 <http://www.rc.umd.edu/praxis/deleuze/broglio/broglio.html> p. 8.
3 Broglio (2008), p. 9.

Bibliography

I. WORKS CITED

A) WORKS CITED THROUGHOUT

Harvey, W.J. and Richard Gravil, eds. *Wordsworth*: The Prelude. Casebook Ser. Macmillan, 1972.

Gill, Stephen, ed. *William Wordsworth's* The Prelude: *A Casebook*. Oxford University Press, 2006.

McMaster, Graham, ed. *William Wordsworth: A Critical Anthology*. Penguin Books, 1972.

Williams, John, ed. *Wordsworth*. New Casebooks Ser. Macmillian, 1993.

Wood, Nigel, ed. *The Prelude*. Theory and Practice Series. Open University Press, 1993.

Wordsworth, William. *The Prelude 1799, 1805, 1850*, eds., Jonathan Wordsworth, M.H. Abrams, and Stephen Gill. W.W. Norton & Co., 1979.

B) WORKS CITED BY CHAPTER

Introduction: The 'huge and mighty forms' of The Prelude

Reid, Ian. *Wordsworth and the Formation of English Studies*. Ashgate, 2004.

1 In the cathedral ruins: The Prelude *from conception to criticism*

Arnold, Matthew. 'From the Introduction to *The Poems of Wordsworth'*. [Excerpt in McMaster (1992), pp. 221–35].

De Quincey, Thomas. '"William Wordsworth", *Tait's Edinburgh Magazine* VI (1839)'. [Excerpt in Wordsworth (1979), pp. 545–7].

Hazlitt, William. 'Review of *The Excursion, Examiner* 21, 28 August, 2 October 1814'. [Excerpt in McMaster (1972), pp. 114–20].

Hutton, Richard Holt. '"The Genius of Wordsworth", *Literary Essays* (1871)'. [Excerpt in Harvey and Gravil (1972), pp. 58–65].

Jeffrey, Francis. 'Review of *The Excursion, Edinburgh Review* November 1814'. [Excerpt in McMaster (1972), pp. 122–6].

'"The New Poem by Wordsworth", *Dublin University Magazine* XXXVI (1850)'. [Excerpt in Wordsworth (1979), p. 557].

Pater, Walter. '"Wordsworth", *Appreciations* (1874)'. [Excerpt in Harvey and Gravil (1972), pp. 66–72].

'"The Prelude", *British Quarterly Review* xii (1850)'. [Excerpt in Wordsworth (1979), pp. 555–6].

'"The Prelude", From *Eclectic Review* XXVIII (1850)'. [Excerpt in Wordsworth (1979), pp. 547–50].

'"The Prelude", *Examiner*, No. 2217 (1850)'. [Excerpt in Wordsworth (1979), pp. 558–9].

'"The Prelude", *Graham's Magazine* XXXVII (1850)'. [Excerpt in Wordsworth (1979), pp. 553–4].

'"The Prelude", From *Tait's Edinburgh Magazine*, XVII (1850)'. [Excerpt in Wordsworth (1979), pp. 550–2].

Stephen, Leslie. '"Wordsworth's Ethics", *Hours in a Library*, Third Series (1879)'. [Excerpt in McMaster (1972), pp. 199–221].

' "Wordsworth's Autobiographical Poem", *Gentleman's Magazine* XXXIV (1850)'. [Excerpt in Wordsworth (1979), pp. 552–3].

2   *Revaluations: The early twentieth century*

Bradley, A.C. *Oxford Lectures on Poetry*. London, 1909. [Excerpt in McMaster (1972), pp. 243–60].

Bateson, F.W. *Wordsworth: A Re-Interpretation*. 2nd ed. Longmans, 1956.

Beatty, Arthur. *William Wordsworth: His Doctrine and Art in their Historical Relations*. 2nd ed. University of Wisconsin Studies in Language and Literature 24. Madison, 1927.

Bishop, Jonathan. 'Wordsworth and the Spots of Time'. *English Literary History* 26 (1959): pp. 45–65. [Excerpt in Harvey and Gravil (1972), pp. 134–54].

Darbishire, Helen. 'Wordsworth's *Prelude*'. *The Nineteenth Century* 99 (1926): pp. 718–31. [Excerpt in Harvey and Gravil (1972), pp. 81–98].

Ferry, David. *The Limits of Mortality: An Essay on Wordsworth's Major Poems*. Wesleyan University Press, 1959.

James, D.G. *Poetry and Scepticism*. George Allen and Unwin Ltd., 1937. [Excerpt in McMaster (1972), pp. 301–27].

Jones, John. *The Egotistical Sublime: A History of Wordsworth's Imagination*. Chatto & Windus, 1954. [Excerpt in McMaster (1972), pp. 391–401].

Leavis, F.R. *Revaluation: Tradition & Development in English Poetry*. London: Chatto & Windus, 1936.

Read, Herbert. *Wordsworth*. Faber and Faber Ltd., 1930.

Stallknecht, Newton P. *Strange Seas of Thought: Studies in William Wordsworth's Philosophy of Man and Nature*. Duke University Press, 1945.

Whitehead, A.N. *Science and the Modern World*. Cambridge University Press, 1926. [Excerpt in McMaster (1972), pp. 287–301].

3   *Style, philosophy, and phenomenology*

Abrams, M.H. *Natural Supernaturalism: Tradition and Revolution in Romantic Literature*. W.W. Norton & Company, Inc., 1971.

Bloom, Harold. *The Ringers in the Tower: Studies in the Romantic Tradition*. The University of Chicago Press, 1971.

Empson, William. *The Structure of Complex Words*. Chatto & Windus, 1951. [Excerpt in Wordsworth (1979), pp. 625–42].

Hartman, Geoffrey. *Wordsworth's Poetry 1787–1814*. Yale University Press, 1971. [Excerpt in Gill (2006), pp. 181–208].

Langbaum, Robert. 'The Evolution of Soul in Wordsworth's Poetry'. *PMLA* 82 (1967): pp. 265–72. [Excerpt in Harvey and Gravil (1972), pp. 218–36].

Lindenberger, Herbert. *On Wordsworth's* Prelude. Princeton University Press, 1963.

Peckham, Morse. *Beyond the Tragic Vision: The Quest for Identity in the Nineteenth Century*. George Braziller, 1962.

Ricks, Christopher. *The Force of Poetry*. Oxford University Press, 1987. [Excerpt in Gill (2006), pp. 43–72].

4   *Writing the self: Deconstruction, feminism, and psychoanalysis*

Ellis, David. *Wordsworth, Freud and the Spots of Time: Interpretation in* The Prelude. Cambridge University Press, 1985.

Ferguson, Frances. *Wordsworth: Language as Counter-Spirit*. Yale University Press, 1977.

Homans, Margaret. *Bearing the Word: Language and Female Experience in Nineteenth-Century Woman's Writing*. University of Chicago Press, 1986.

Jacobus, Mary. *Romanticism, Writing, and Sexual Difference: Essays on* The Prelude. Oxford University Press, 1989. [Excerpt in Williams (1993), pp. 188–207].

Man, Paul de. *The Rhetoric of Romanticism*. Columbia University Press, 1984.

——. 'Time and History in Wordsworth'. *Romanticism*. Ed. Cynthia Chase. Longman, 1993. pp. 55–77.

Mellor, Anne. *Romanticism and Gender* (Routledge, 1993). [Excerpt in Gill (2006), pp. 293–304].

Onorato, Richard J. *The Character of the Poet: Wordsworth in* The Prelude. Princeton University Press, 1971.

Ross, Marlon B. 'Naturalizing Gender: Woman's Place in Wordsworth's Ideological Landscape'. *English Literary History* 53.2 (1986): pp. 391–409.

Spivak, Gayatri Chakravorty. 'Sex and History in *The Prelude* (1805): Books IX to XIII'. [Excerpt in Williams (1993), pp. 172–87].

5   *Spots of time: The New Historicism*

Butler, Marilyn. *Romantics, Rebels and Reactionaries*. Oxford University Press, 1981.

Chandler, James. *Wordsworth's Second Nature: A Study of the Poetry and Politics*. University of Chicago Press, 1984.

Erskine-Hill, Howard. *Poetry of Opposition and Revolution: Dryden to Wordsworth*. Oxford University Press, 1996. [Excerpt in Gill (2006), pp. 305–20].

Levinson, Marjorie. *Wordsworth's Great Period Poems: Four Essays*. Cambridge University Press, 1986.

Liu, Alan. *Wordsworth: The Sense of History*. Chicago University Press, 1989.

McGann, Jerome. *The Romantic Ideology: A Critical Investigation*. University of Chicago Press, 1983.

Roe, Nicholas. 'Revising the Revolution: History and Imagination in *The Prelude*, 1799, 1805, 1850'. *Romantic Revisions*. Eds Robert Brinkley and Keith Hanley. Cambridge University Press, 1992. pp. 103–35.

Sales, Roger. *English Literature in History 1780–1830: Pastoral and Politics*. Hutchinson, 1983. [Excerpt in Williams (1993), pp. 92–111].

Simpson, David. *Wordsworth's Historical Imagination: The Poetry of Displacement*. Methuen, 1987.

Siskin, Clifford. 'Working *The Prelude*: Foucault and the New History'. [Excerpt in Wood (1993), pp. 98–124].

6   The Prelude *and the present*

Bate, Jonathan. *Romantic Ecology: Wordsworth and the Environmental Tradition*. Routledge, 1991. [Excerpt in Gill (2006), pp. 377–402].

Benis, Toby. *Romanticism on the Road: The Marginal Gains of Wordsworth's Homeless*. Macmillan, 2000.

Bourke, Richard. *Romantic Discourse and Political Modernity: Wordsworth, the Intellectual and Cultural Critique*. Harvester Wheatsheaf, 1993.

Friedman, Geraldine. *The Insistence of History: Revolution in Burke, Wordsworth, Keats, and Baudelaire*. Stanford University Press, 1996.

Gilroy, Amanda, ed. *Romantic Geographies: Discourses of Travel 1775–1844*. Manchester University Press, 2000.

Hanley, Keith. 'Wordsworth's Grand Tour'. Gilroy (2000), pp. 71–92.

Harrison, Gary. *Wordsworth's Vagrant Muse: Poetry, Poverty and Power*. Wayne State University Press, 1994.

Kroeber, Karl. *Ecological Literary Criticism: Romantic Imagining and the Biology of Mind*. Columbia University Press, 1994.

Langan, Celeste. *Romantic Vagrancy: Wordsworth and the Simulation of Freedom*. Cambridge University Press, 1995.

McKusick, James. Introduction. 'Romanticism and Ecology'. *Romantic Circles: Praxis Series*. 1 Nov 2001, 1 Feb 2008 <http://www.rc.umd.edu/praxis/ecology/mckusick/mckusick_intro.html>.

Pfau, Thomas. *Wordsworth's Profession: Form, Class, and the Logic of Early Romantic Cultural Production*. Stanford University Press, 1997.

Wiley, Michael. *Romantic Geography: Wordsworth and Anglo-European Spaces*. Macmillan, 1998.

Wyatt, John. *Wordsworth and the Geologists*. Cambridge University Press, 1995.

Wolfson, Susan. *Formal Charges: The Shaping of Poetry in British Romanticism*. Stanford: Stanford University Press, 1997.

Conclusion

Broglio, Ron. 'Wandering the Landscape with Wordsworth and Deleuze'. 'Romanticism and the New Deleuze'. *Romantic Circles: Praxis Series* 1 Jan 2008, 1 Feb 2008 <http://www.rc.umd.edu/praxis/deleuze/broglio/broglio.html>.

II. FURTHER READING

A) TEXTS OF *THE PRELUDE*

Wordsworth, William. *The Five-Book Prelude*. Ed. Duncan Wu. (Blackwell, 1997).

——. *The Fourteen-Book Prelude*. Ed. W.J.B. Owen. Cornell Wordsworth Ser. Cornell University Press, 1985.

——. *The Prelude, 1798–9, by William Wordsworth*. Ed. Stephen Parrish. Cornell Wordsworth Ser. (Cornell University Press, 1977).

——. *The Prelude, 1799, 1805, 1850*. Eds. Jonathan Wordsworth, M.H. Abrams, and Stephen Gill (Norton, 1979).

——. *The Prelude, or Growth of a Poet's Mind by William Wordsworth*. Ed. Ernest de Selincourt (Oxford, 1926).

——. *The Thirteen Book Prelude*. Ed. Mark Reed. Cornell Wordsworth Ser. Cornell University Press, 1991.

B) BIBLIOGRAPHIES

Hanley, Keith. *An Annotated Bibliography of William Wordsworth*. Harvester Wheatsheaf, 1995.

——. 'Textual Issues and a Guide to Further Reading'. Gill (2003), pp. 246–64.

Roe, Nicholas. 'William Wordsworth'. *Literature of the Romantic Period: A Bibliographical Guide*. Ed. Michael O'Neill. Oxford: Clarendon Press, 1998. pp. 45–64.

C) BIOGRAPHIES

Gill, Stephen. *Wordsworth: A Life*. Oxford University Press, 1989.

Moorman, Mary. *William Wordsworth: A Biography*. 2 vols. Oxford University Press, 1957–65.

Barker, Juliet. *Wordsworth: A Life*. Viking, 2000.

Johnston, Kenneth R. *The Hidden Wordsworth,* Norton, 1998.

Wu, Duncan. *Wordsworth: An Inner Life*. Blackwell, 2002.

D) BOOKS ON OR WITH CHAPTERS ON *THE PRELUDE*

Chase, Cynthia. *Decomposing Figures: Rhetorical Readings in the Romantic Tradition*. Johns Hopkins University Press, 1986.

Clancey, Richard W. *Wordsworth's Classical Undersong: Education, Rhetoric and Poetic Truth.* Macmillan, 2000.

Gaskell, Ronald. *Wordsworth's Poem of the Mind: An Essay on* The Prelude. Edinburgh University Press, 1991.

Gill, Stephen, ed. *The Cambridge Companion to Wordsworth.* Cambridge University Press, 2003.

——. *William Wordsworth: The Prelude.* Landmarks of World Literature Ser. Cambridge University Press, 1991.

Havens, Raymond Dexter. *The Mind of a Poet: A Study of Wordsworth's Thought with Particular Reference to* The Prelude. Johns Hopkins University Press, 1941.

Johnston, Kenneth R. *Wordsworth and* The Recluse. Yale University Press, 1984.

Kneale, J. Douglas. *Monumental Writing: Aspects of Rhetoric in Wordsworth's Poetry.* University of Nebraska Press, 1988.

McConnell, Frank D. *The Confessional Imagination: A Reading of Wordsworth's* Prelude. Johns Hopkins University Press, 1974.

Nichols, Ashton. *The Revolutionary 'I': Wordsworth and the Politcs of Self-Presentation.* Macmillan, 1998.

Wolfson, Susan. *The Questioning Presence: Wordsworth, Keats, and the Interrogative Mode in Romantic Poetry.* Cornell University Press, 1986.

E) GENERAL WORDSWORTH STUDIES

Averill, James H. *Wordsworth and the Poetry of Human Suffering.* Cornell University Press, 1980.

Barth, J. Robert. *Romanticism and Transcendence: Wordsworth, Coleridge and the Religious Imagination.* University of Missouri Press, 2003.

Beer, John. *Wordsworth and the Human Heart.* Macmillan, 1978.

Bewell, Alan. *Wordsworth and the Enlightenment: Nature, Man, and Society in the Experimental Poetry.* Yale University Press, 1989.

Bialostosky, Don H. *Wordsworth, Dialogics and the Practice of Criticism.* Cambridge University Press, 1992.

Blank, Kim. *Wordsworth and Feeling: The Poetry of an Adult Child.* Fairleigh Dickinson University Press, 1995.

Bromwich, David. *Disowned by Memory: Wordsworth's Poetry of the 1790s.* University of Chicago Press, 1998.

Cowell, Raymond, ed. *Critics on Wordsworth.* Readings in Literary Criticism Ser. George Allen and Unwin Ltd, 1973.

Darbishire, Helen. *Wordsworth.* Longmans, 1953.

Easthope, Antony. *Wordsworth Now and Then: Romanticism and Contemporary Culture.* Open University Press, 1993.

Friedman, Michael. *The Making of a Tory Humanist: William Wordsworth and the Idea of Community.* Columbia University Press, 1979.

Fulford, Tim. *Romanticism and Masculinity: Gender, Politics and Poetics in the Writings of Burke, Coleridge, Cobbett, Wordsworth, De Quincey and Hazlitt.* Macmillan, 1999.

Gill, Stephen. *Wordsworth and the Victorians.* Oxford University Press, 1998.

Gravil, Richard. *Wordsworth's Bardic Vocation 1787–1842.* Palgrave, 2003.

Hanley, David P. *Wordsworth and the Hermeneutics of Incarnation.* Pennsylvania State University Press, 1993.

Hamilton, Paul. *Wordsworth.* Harvester, 1986.

Hartman, Geoffrey. *The Unremarkable Wordsworth.* Methuen, 1987.

Kelley, Theresa M. *Wordsworth's Revisionary Aesthetics.* Cambridge University Press, 1988.

McFarland, Thomas. *Romanticism and the Forms of Ruin: Wordsworth, Coleridge and Modalities of Fragmentation.* Princeton University Press, 1981.

——. *Wordsworth: Intensity and Achievement.* Oxford University Press, 1992.

Magnuson, Paul. *Coleridge and Wordsworth: A Lyrical Dialogue.* Princeton University Press, 1988.

Miller, J. Hillis. *The Linguistic Moment: From Wordsworth to Stevens.* Princeton University Press, 1985.

Newlyn, Lucy. *Coleridge, Wordsworth and the Language of Allusion.* Oxford University Press, 1986.

Nichols, Ashton. *The Revolutionary 'I': Wordsworth and the Politics of Self-Presentation.* St Martin's Press, 1998.

Pace, Joel and Matthew Scott, eds. *Wordsworth in American Literary Culture.* Macmillan, 2005.

Perkins, David. *Wordsworth and the Poetry of Sincerity.* Harvard University Press, 1964.

Prickett, Stephen. *Coleridge and Wordsworth: The Poetry of Growth.* Cambridge University Press, 1970.

Purkis, John. *A Preface to Wordsworth.* Longman, 2000.

Quinney, Laura. *The Poetics of Disappointment: Wordsworth to Ashbery.* University Press of Virginia, 1999.

Roe, Nicholas. *The Politics of Nature: Wordsworth and Some Contemporaries.* Macmillan, 1992.

——. *Wordsworth and Coleridge: The Radical Years.* Oxford University Press, 1988.

Rzepka, Charles J. *The Self as Mind: Vision and Identity in Wordsworth, Coleridge and Keats.* Harvard University Press, 1986.

Simpson, David. *Wordsworth and the Figurings of the Real.* Macmillan, 1982.

Sperry, Willard. *Wordsworth's Anti-Climax.* Harvard University Press, 1935.

Ulmer, William A. *The Christian Wordsworth 1798–1805.* State University of New York Press, 2001.

Woof, Robert, ed. *William Wordsworth: The Critical Heritage.* Routledge, 2001.

Wordsworth, Jonathan. *William Wordsworth: The Borders of Vision.* Oxford University Press, 1982.

Wu, Duncan. *Wordsworth's Reading 1800–1815.* Cambridge University Press, 1995.

——. *Wordsworth's Reading 1770–1799.* Cambridge University Press, 1993.

Index